# GMAT®
# Math Workbook

## Tenth Edition

**ACKNOWLEDGMENTS**

**Lead Editor:** Craig Harman

**Contributing Editor:** Paula L. Fleming, MA, MBA

**Special thanks to our faculty authors and reviewers**

Harry Broome; Christopher Cosci; Jack Hayes, MBA; Gordon Spector; Chris Sun; and Ethan Weber

**Additional special thanks to** Nomi Beesen, Rebecca Berthiaume, Kim Bowers, Robin Garmise, Rita Garthaffner, Joanna Graham, Laurel Haines, Mandy Luk, Jennifer Moore, Camellia Mukherjee, Monica Ostolaza, Carly Schnur, Jay Thomas, Oscar Velazquez, Michael Wolff, Amy Zarkos, and the countless others who made this project possible



Published by Kaplan Publishing, a division of Kaplan, Inc.
750 Third Avenue
New York, NY 10017



ISBN: 978-1-50626-352-6
10 9 8 7 6 5 4 3 2 1

Kaplan Publishing print books are available at special quantity discounts to use for sales promotions, employee premiums, or educational purposes. For more information or to purchase books, please call the Simon & Schuster special sales department at 866-506-1949.

# TABLE OF CONTENTS

**Other Kaplan Books for GMAT Prep**

*Kaplan GMAT Prep Plus*

*Kaplan GMAT Verbal Workbook*

*Kaplan GMAT Complete* (all three books)

## kaptest.com/publishing

The material in this book is up-to-date at the time of publication. However, the Graduate Management Admission Council may have instituted changes in the test or test registration process after this book was published. Be sure to carefully read the materials you receive when you register for the test.

If there are any important late-breaking developments—or changes or corrections to this book—we will post that information online at **kaptest.com/publishing**.

# How to Use This Book

## WELCOME TO KAPLAN'S *GMAT MATH WORKBOOK*

Congratulations on your decision to pursue an MBA or other graduate management degree and thank you for choosing Kaplan for your GMAT preparation. You've made the right decision in acquiring this book—Kaplan has prepared students to take standardized tests for over 80 years, and our researchers and editors know more about preparing for the GMAT than anyone else.

This book is designed to benefit anyone who is looking to score higher on the GMAT. Within these pages, you'll find concrete advice that will help you perform better on the Quantitative Reasoning section of the test. And, because this is a workbook, you'll also find practice questions—lots and lots of practice questions.

If you are looking for a book that provides even more extensive advice and covers the entire GMAT (including the Verbal Reasoning section), we recommend purchasing our comprehensive compendium of GMAT test knowledge, Kaplan's *GMAT Prep Plus*. If, on the other hand, you are looking for a book that provides GMAT verbal strategies and lots of verbal practice, pick up a copy of Kaplan's *GMAT Verbal Workbook*.

## YOUR BOOK AND YOUR ONLINE RESOURCES

There are two components of your *GMAT Math Workbook* study package: your book, which includes instruction and practice, and your online resources, which include more practice sets and a full-length, computer-adaptive practice test. We here at Kaplan strongly encourage you to use these online resources. Since the GMAT is taken on a computer, getting comfortable tackling questions in that format is a valuable way to prepare for what you will encounter on Test Day. To register your online resources, have this book handy and follow these simple steps:

GO ONLINE

*kaptest.com/login*

1. Go to **kaptest.com/moreonline**.
2. Follow the onscreen instructions.

Each part of your *GMAT Math Workbook* serves a purpose in helping you improve your performance. Following are brief descriptions of the different sections of this book.

## Part One: Getting Started

The first step to a higher score is to know exactly what you can expect to find on the Quantitative Reasoning section of the GMAT. In Chapter 1, Introduction to GMAT Math, we'll list the core math concepts that you'll need to know, describe how the Quantitative Reasoning section is scored on the GMAT, and introduce you to the two types of math questions (Problem Solving and Data Sufficiency). We'll also explain how the computer-adaptive test (CAT) format differs from traditional paper-and-pencil tests in the way it determines your score, and we'll tell you how you can use this format to your advantage.

Next, you'll learn the ins and outs of the two types of questions in the Quantitative Reasoning section of the GMAT: Problem Solving and Data Sufficiency. In Chapters 2 and 3, you will learn proven Kaplan methods and strategies to help you handle each of these question types with confidence. Of course, since this is a workbook, you'll also get to apply these methods and strategies on lots of practice test questions.

## Part Two: Math Content Practice and Review

Once you have the big picture and strategies from Part One, the next step is to dive in and start testing your knowledge of GMAT math. Part Two of this book gives you a complete tour of the major math content areas that you will see on Test Day. Chapter 4 focuses on Arithmetic and Number Properties; Chapter 5 on Algebra; Chapter 6 on Formulas, Statistics, and Data Analysis; and Chapter 7 on Geometry. Since each chapter builds on the material in earlier chapters, many students benefit from working through them in order.

In each chapter, you'll first find drills that test your understanding of the core concepts, followed by test-like practice questions. After you complete the drills and check your performance, assess your ability level. If you found the drills difficult or the concepts unfamiliar, use the Math Reference in the back of the book to brush up on key concepts before jumping into the practice questions. If, on the other hand, you did well on the drills, jump straight to the practice questions and use the Math Reference as needed.

Answers and explanations for the test questions are at the end of each chapter. We highly recommend that you read the explanations for all of the questions—even those you got right. Often the explanations discuss strategies that could have gotten you the correct answer more quickly and efficiently. That can make a big difference in your score on the Quantitative Reasoning section.

## Part Three: Putting It All Together

With a handle on the big picture, a detailed review of the major content areas, and practice with the Kaplan methods and strategies, it's time to show your stuff. Part Three of this book contains our best effort to replicate (on paper) the experience of taking an actual GMAT Quantitative Reasoning Section, mixing the math question types in the same manner that an actual GMAT would. Here's your chance to bring together all your newly acquired strategies and get a sense of what the GMAT Quantitative Reasoning section feels like.

Chapter 8 actually contains two different practice sections. We highly recommend that you take one practice section at a time, timing yourself to make sure that you are completing questions at a realistic pace. Then review your results and read through the explanations for all of the questions in the set before attempting the second practice section. You can learn just as much from the explanations of the questions you got right as from the explanations of the questions you got wrong. You'll pick up tips and learn to be more efficient, saving you time that you can then apply to harder questions.

## Part Four: Math Reference

As you continue to study and increase your score, you'll want a convenient way to look up math concepts for a quick review. Chapter 9, Math Reference, is designed for exactly this purpose.

If, after working through this book, you would like to explore more Kaplan practice resources, check out the variety of options available at **kaptest.com/gmat**.

Thanks for choosing Kaplan. We wish you the best of luck on your journey to business school and beyond.

PART ONE

# Getting Started

CHAPTER 1

# Introduction to GMAT Math

*Been there, done that.* If you're considering applying to business school, then you've already seen all the math you need for the GMAT. You would have covered the relevant math content before you finished high school. In fact, the math that appears on the GMAT is almost identical to the math tested on the SAT or ACT. You don't need to know trigonometry. You don't need to know calculus. No surprises—it's all material you've seen before. The problem is, you may not have seen it lately. When was the last time you had to add a bunch of fractions without a calculator?

No matter how much your memories of junior high algebra classes have dimmed, don't panic. The GMAT tests a limited number of core math concepts in predictable ways. Certain topics come up in every test, and, chances are, these topics will be expressed in much the same way; even some of the words and phrases appearing in the questions are predictable. Since the test is so formulaic, we can show you the math you're bound to encounter. Some practice on test-like questions, such as those in the following chapters, will prepare you for the questions you will see on the actual test.

## How Math Is Scored on the GMAT

The GMAT will give you a scaled quantitative score from 0 to 60. (The average score is approximately 40.) This score reflects your performance on the math portion of the test compared to all other GMAT test takers.

You will also receive an overall score that reflects your performance on both the Quantitative and the Verbal portions of the test. This is a scaled score from 200 to 800.

The GMAT also gives you separate scores for the Integrated Reasoning and the Analytical Writing Assessment sections. These scores are not factored into your Quantitative or Verbal scores or into your overall 200–800 score.

## Test Overview

The GMAT is a computer-adaptive test, or CAT. You take this test on a computer at a testing center. Here's a quick overview of the Quantitative section.

There are 31 questions to be done in 62 minutes. Of these, about 17 or 18 will be Problem Solving, with the remainder being Data Sufficiency. However, due to the adaptive nature of the test, this breakdown may vary.

Some of the questions in the GMAT Quantitative section will be experimental questions. These are questions that are being tested for future use in the GMAT question pool and are not being scored at this time. Since there is no way to tell the experimental questions from the scored questions, you should treat all questions as if they are scored.

### Problem Solving Questions

In Problem Solving questions, you are given a question and asked to choose the correct answer from a list of five choices. Here's a sample Problem Solving question.

**Example:**

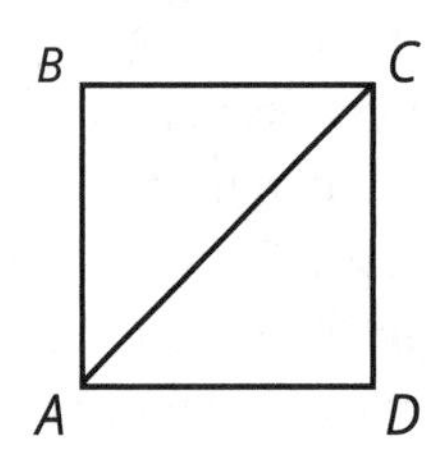


If the perimeter of the square above is 8, what is the area of triangle *ACD*?

- O 1
- O 2
- O 4
- O 6
- O 8

**Answer:** Because the figure is a square, it has four equal sides. Therefore, since the perimeter of the square is 8, each side must be $8 \div 4 = 2$. The area of the square is then the height and width multiplied together, or $2 \times 2 = 4$. The area of the triangle is half of this, or **2**.

## Data Sufficiency Questions

In Data Sufficiency, a question is followed by two statements containing certain information. Your task is to determine whether the information provided by the statements is sufficient to answer the question. All Data Sufficiency questions have the same five answer choices.

Here's a sample Data Sufficiency question.

**Example:** Is $x$ even?

(1) $x$ is a multiple of 6.

(2) $x$ is a multiple of 5.

- O Statement (1) ALONE is sufficient to answer the question, but Statement (2) is not sufficient.
- O Statement (2) ALONE is sufficient to answer the question, but Statement (1) is not sufficient.
- O BOTH statements TOGETHER are sufficient to answer the question, but NEITHER statement ALONE is sufficient.
- O EACH statement ALONE is sufficient to answer the question.
- O Statements (1) and (2) TOGETHER are NOT SUFFICIENT to answer the question.

**Answer:** To answer this Yes/No question, you could use your knowledge of number properties, or you could pick some numbers. If you use the picking numbers strategy, evaluate Statement (1) by listing some multiples of 6: 6, 12, 18, 24, 30, . . . All are even. Evaluate Statement (2) by listing some multiples of 5: 5, 10, . . . Stop there, since it's clear you can have even and odd values for $x$. Since all multiples of 6 are even, but multiples of 5 may or may not be even, Statement (1) ALONE, but not Statement (2), is sufficient to answer the question definitively. Thus, the **first choice** is correct.

# Math Content

The range of math topics tested is fairly limited. The GMAT covers only the math that US students usually see during or before their first two years of high school. No trigonometry, no advanced algebra, no calculus. The topics that are tested include algebra, arithmetic, number properties, proportions, basic statistics, certain specific math formulas, and geometry. Algebra and arithmetic are the most commonly tested topics—they are tested either directly or indirectly on a majority of questions. Geometry generally shows up in less than one-sixth of all GMAT math questions, but these questions can often be among the most challenging for test takers, so you may benefit from a thorough review of these concepts.

One thing that makes the GMAT Quantitative section so challenging is how the different areas of math are combined to make questions more difficult. For instance, a question that asks you about triangles could also require you to solve a formula algebraically and apply your understanding of ratios to find the correct answer.

## Reasoning Skills

While mastering fundamental skills is an essential part of your success on the GMAT, high-level thinking and reasoning abilities are perhaps more important. The GMAT uses math as a platform to build questions that test your critical thinking and problem-solving abilities.

In GMAT terms, a critical thinker is a creative problem solver who engages in critical inquiry. One of the traits of successful test takers is their skill at asking the right questions. GMAT critical thinkers first consider what they're being asked to do, then study the given information and ask the right questions, especially "How can I get the answer in the most direct way?" and "How can I use the question format to my advantage?"

For instance, the answer choices in a GMAT Problem Solving question often give clues to the solution. Use them. You might even discover opportunities to find the answer to a difficult question by plugging the answer choices into the information in the question—a strategy we call "backsolving."

Likewise, as you examine a Data Sufficiency question, you'll learn to ask: "What information will I need to answer this question?" or "How can I determine whether more than one solution is possible?"

Almost every question on the Quantitative section of the GMAT could be solved using more than one approach. The time constraints on the GMAT are designed to reward those test takers who, through critical thinking and practice, have honed their ability to identify and execute the most efficient approach to every problem they might see on Test Day.

Another important skill is pattern recognition. Most people fail to appreciate the level of constraint that standardization places on test makers. Because the test makers must give reliable, valid, and comparable scores to many thousands of students each year, they're forced to reward the same skills on every test. They do so by repeating the same kinds of questions with the same traps and pitfalls, which are susceptible to the same strategic solutions. Inexperienced test takers treat every problem as if it were a brand-new task, whereas the GMAT rewards those who spot the patterns and use them to their advantage. As you practice with more and more GMAT questions, stay attuned to patterns you see; certain math concepts appear regularly enough on the GMAT to warrant memorization.

Paraphrasing will be an essential skill as well; the GMAT rewards those who can reduce difficult, abstract, or polysyllabic prose to simple terms. You will often be asked to paraphrase English as "math" to solve word problems or to simplify complicated equations using arithmetic or algebra. Rather than become intimidated by the complicated wording of a question, a smart test taker will ask, "How might I rephrase this question more simply?" Putting GMAT prose into your own words helps you get a handle on the situation being described and know what to do next.

Details present a dilemma: missing them can cost you points. But if you try to absorb every fact in a complicated word problem all at once, you may find yourself overwhelmed, slowed down, and still unable to determine the best approach because you haven't sorted through the information to determine what's most important. The GMAT test makers reward test takers for paying attention to "the right details"—the ones that make the difference between right and wrong answers. One of the most important details to pay attention to is what the question is asking you to solve for. Identifying up front what you need to solve for is important on the GMAT because the answer choices will often include options that represent "the right answer to the wrong question": the value you might come up with if you did all the math correctly but solved accidentally for a different unknown in the problem.

## Computer-Adaptive Testing

The GMAT is a type of computer-based test known as a computer-adaptive test. In this kind of test, your performance on previous questions affects the question you will see next. In other words, the test adapts to your ability level. This means that as you answer more questions correctly, you will see more difficult questions. On the other hand, if you answer a series of questions incorrectly, you will begin to see questions that are less difficult.

### How a CAT Finds Your Score

Because of the adaptive nature of the test, your score is not calculated by the raw number of questions you answer correctly. Instead, your score is determined by the difficulty level of the questions you answer at the end of the section. Here's how it works.

When you start a section, the computer:

- Assumes you have an average score.
- Gives you a handful of questions that are mostly medium difficulty.

After the first few questions, the GMAT begins to adapt to your performance.

In general, if you answer questions correctly:

- Your score goes up.
- You are given harder questions.

And if you answer questions incorrectly:

- Your score goes down.
- You are given easier questions.

After a while, you will reach a level where most of the questions will seem difficult to you. At this point, you'll get roughly as many questions right as you get wrong. This is your scoring level. The computer uses your scoring level in calculating your scaled score.

Another consequence of the test's adaptive nature is that for the bulk of the test, you'll be getting questions at the limit of your ability. While every question is equally important to your final score, harder questions generate higher scores and easier questions lower scores. Thus, it's important to perform well from the very beginning of the test, since you want to begin scoring in the high band as quickly as possible. But it's also important to have enough time to answer those tough questions correctly, since you will be penalized for any questions you leave unanswered. Therefore, while it's important to do well at the beginning of the test, it's not advisable to spend so much time on the first few questions that you fall behind; your "reward" will be hard questions without enough time to answer them. Work at a steady pace of about 1 question every 2 minutes, or 10 questions every 20 minutes. Your goal is to hit the last question with 2 or 3 minutes on the clock.

Here are a few other implications of the adaptive nature of the test.

- There is no preset order of difficulty; the difficulty level of the questions you're getting is dependent on how well you have done on the preceding questions. The harder the questions are, the better you are doing. So, if you seem to be getting only hard questions, don't panic: it's a good sign! However, it's hard to tell the difficulty of a question during the test. A hard question might seem easy to you because it happens to be in one of your strong areas, or an easier question may seem harder under the stress of Test Day. So, don't waste any time or energy trying to figure out where on the difficulty curve you are; focus on answering the question in front of you as efficiently as possible.
- Once you leave a question, you cannot return to it. That's it. Kiss it goodbye. This is one reason why you should never rush on the CAT. Make sure that you have indicated the right answer before you confirm it, then move on. The CAT rewards meticulous test takers.
- On a CAT, you must answer a question to move on to the next one. If you can't solve it, you'll have to guess in order to move on. Consequently, intelligent guessing can make the difference between a mediocre score and a great one. Guess intelligently and strategically—eliminate any answer choices that you determine are wrong and guess among those remaining. The explanations to the questions in this book will demonstrate techniques for eliminating answer choices strategically.
- One final, important point. There is a penalty for unanswered questions on the CAT. Every question you leave unanswered will decrease your score by a greater amount than a question that you answered incorrectly! This means that you should answer all the questions on the test, even if you have to guess randomly to finish a section.

CHAPTER 2

# Problem Solving Questions

**LEARNING OBJECTIVES**

After studying this chapter, you will be able to:

- Describe the format of a Problem Solving question
- State the steps of the Kaplan Method for Problem Solving questions
- Explain how the picking numbers and backsolving strategies can be applied to Problem Solving questions

There are two types of questions that comprise the Quantitative section of the GMAT: Problem Solving and Data Sufficiency. Problem Solving questions are a bit more common, making up roughly one-half to two-thirds of questions in this section. These types of questions measure your ability to use logic and analysis, and they can test any of the math concepts presented on the GMAT.

The directions for Problem Solving questions are similar to the following:

> **Directions:** Solve the problems and choose the best answer.
>
> **Note:** Unless otherwise indicated, the figures accompanying the questions have been drawn as accurately as possible and may be used as sources of information for answering the questions.
>
> All figures lie in a plane except where noted.
>
> All numbers used are real numbers.

Problem Solving questions present a question stem that contains enough information to solve the problem followed by five answer choices. In every case, just one answer choice will be correct.

Here's an example of a Problem Solving question. You'll solve this question later in this chapter.

A corporation matches contributions to its employees' retirement accounts according to the following rules: in any year, the corporation matches 80 percent of the first $2,500 of each employee's contributions and 60 percent of each employee's contributions above $2,500. If the corporation contributed $2,780 to an employee's retirement account over a year, how much did the employee contribute?

- O $3,000
- O $3,200
- O $3,500
- O $3,600
- O $3,800

## Kaplan Method for Problem Solving Questions

**LEARNING OBJECTIVES**

After this lesson, you will be able to:

- List the steps of the Kaplan Method for Problem Solving
- Explain the purpose of each step of the Kaplan Method for Problem Solving
- Perform the steps of the Kaplan Method to answer Problem Solving questions

It's important to use a systematic approach to every question on the GMAT. Having a systematic approach will help you work efficiently and keep your focus on the critical thinking the GMAT rewards. Get in the habit of following the four-step Kaplan Method described below. Internalize these steps as you practice so that they're automatic on Test Day.

**THE KAPLAN METHOD FOR PROBLEM SOLVING**

1. Analyze the question
2. State the task
3. Approach strategically
4. Confirm your answer

### Step 1: Analyze the Question

Read through the entire question first, without pausing for details, to get a sense of the overall problem. Determine what concepts the question is testing and notice what information the question provides. Finally, be sure to look at the answer choices: they might trigger an important insight.

### Step 2: State the Task

Make sure you know what you're solving for. The right answer to the wrong question is a wrong answer. The GMAT doesn't care how sincerely you tried or how well you did the math if you didn't answer the question correctly.

### Step 3: Approach Strategically

Review the information provided to find the simplest approach that allows you to make sense of the problem and get to the answer. There is rarely a single "right approach"; choose the easiest for you given the specific problem. If there are variables, name them in a way that makes it easy to remember what they stand for. For example, call the unknown quantity "Bill's age" $B$ and the unknown quantity "Jenny's age" $J$. You might be able to solve for what you need without calculating the value of every variable involved in the problem. If a question seems to require enormous amounts of complex calculations, there's likely to be a shorter way to get to the answer. Look for shortcuts that require less work.

### Step 4: Confirm Your Answer

You can't go back to check your work after completing the section, so build that step into your work on each problem by rereading the question after you think you've finished. If possible, check that your answer makes sense. For example, if you're solving for the price of a coat when it's on sale, your answer should be less than the regular price. Also check your arithmetic or algebra—note that this is easier to do if you've written out your work on your notepad. If you notice a wrinkle to the problem that you missed earlier, do any additional work needed (if you have time) and change your answer. Finally, confirm that you did indeed solve for the right thing, which you identified in step 2.

## Problem Solving Strategies

**LEARNING OBJECTIVES**

After this lesson, you will be able to:

- Describe how the picking numbers and backsolving strategies work
- Identify situations in which it may be helpful to pick numbers or backsolve
- Apply the picking numbers and backsolving strategies to appropriate Problem Solving questions

To answer Problem Solving questions, there are two important strategies you can often rely on. The first is picking numbers, and the second is backsolving. Knowing these two methods on Test Day may allow you to get to the correct answers much more quickly and efficiently. On other questions, however, traditional algebra may be more efficient, so practice the strategies now in order to learn how to recognize which questions are best solved with a given approach.

### Picking Numbers

Picking numbers is often an efficient way to tackle questions that involve unknowns or multiple variables. It's also a quick way to solve ratio or percent word problems and can be a useful strategy for algebra questions when you can't solve using more traditional techniques.

Simply put, picking numbers means plugging in concrete values for unknowns in a problem. Pick numbers that fit the specifics of the question and are easy to work with. For example, if a problem presents an algebraic expression involving multiple variables, it might make sense to pick small, simple numbers like 2, 3, and 4. In a ratio problem, pick a number that is divisible by all the denominators in the given fractions. In percent problems, it is almost always best to pick 100, since calculating percentages of 100 is straightforward.

Here's an example of a problem in which picking numbers works well:

> At a certain manufacturing company, payroll costs rose by 25 percent from year 1 to year 2 and rose 10 percent from year 2 to year 3. What was the percent increase in payroll costs over the entire two-year period?
>
> O 30%
>
> O 35%
>
> O 37.5%
>
> O 40%
>
> O 42.5%

Let the year 1 payroll cost be \$100. (Your number doesn't have to be realistic or believable, just easy to work with.) Payroll costs in year 2 rise 25%. Since 25% of 100 is 25, year 2's payroll costs are \$125.

In year 3, payroll costs rise another 10%. Here's an important point: that's 10% of year 2's payroll, not year 1's. Since 10% of \$125 is \$12.50, year 3's payroll is now \$125 + \$12.50 = \$137.50. Therefore, payroll costs rose \$37.50 from year 1 to year 3. Since you started with \$100, the percent change over the entire period is **37.5%**.

Here's another example:

Marlon has a total of $x$ cookies in packages that hold $y$ cookies each. If Marlon eats $z$ of these packages of cookies, what is the number of packages that remain?

- O $yz - x$
- O $x - \frac{z}{y}$
- O $x - yz$
- O $\frac{x}{y} - z$
- O $\frac{z}{x} - y$

Say that there are 20 cookies, so $x = 20$. For simplicity, make the number of cookies per package 2, so $y = 2$. Say Marlon eats 4 of the packages of cookies, so $z = 4$.

The question asks for the number of packages that remain. First, figure out how many total packages Marlon started with. Since there are 20 cookies and 2 cookies per package, he started with 10 packages of cookies. If he eats 4 packages, there will be 6 remaining. Therefore, you need to find the answer choice that yields 6 when you plug in the values you picked for each of the variables. More than one choice may give you the right value with the numbers you happened to pick, so be sure to test each answer. If more than one results in 6, you'll have to pick another set of numbers to see which one is actually correct.

- O $2 \times 4 - 20 = -12$. Eliminate.
- O $20 - \frac{4}{2} = 18$. Eliminate.
- O $20 - 2 \times 4 = 12$. Eliminate.
- O $\frac{20}{2} - 4 = 6$. This is what you wanted. Keep it for now and check (E).
- O $\frac{4}{20} - 2 = -1\frac{4}{5}$. That's not right. Thus, **(D)**, $\frac{x}{y} - z$, is the correct answer.

## Backsolving

As the name implies, backsolving means putting the answer choices back into the question to see which answer works. Backsolving is especially handy when inserting answer choices into the question stem seems quicker than setting up equations and solving. When you see integers (whole numbers that are easy to work with), backsolving is often a good strategy.

It's time to revisit the question from the beginning of the chapter, and this time you'll use backsolving to answer it. Note that this question has integers in the answer choices, and they are arranged in order from least to greatest. Every GMAT question with numeric answer choices will arrange them either from least to greatest or vice versa.

Here is an example:

A corporation matches contributions to its employees' retirement accounts according to the following rules: in any year, the corporation matches 80 percent of the first $2,500 of each employee's contributions and 60 percent of each employee's contributions above $2,500. If the corporation contributed $2,780 to an employee's retirement account over a year, how much did the employee contribute?

- $3,000
- $3,200
- $3,500
- $3,600
- $3,800

Since each answer choice represents a possible amount of the employee's contribution, you can pick an answer choice, assume that this was the amount of the contribution, and apply the corporation's rules to that choice. The answer choice that results in a corporate contribution of $2,780 is correct.

Start with (B). If it's correct, then the employee contributed $3,200. The corporation pays 80% of the first $2,500, so that's $2,000. It also pays 60% of anything above $2,500, so that's 60% of ($3,200 – $2,500) = 60% of $700 = $420. Thus, if the employee contributed $3,200, the corporation contributed $2,000 + $420 = $2,420. However, that's not enough; the question stem says that the corporation actually contributed $2,780. Therefore, (B) is too small. And, since (A) is smaller than (B), it has to be too small as well.

So that means that (A) and (B) are both wrong and you can eliminate them. Next, try (D). If it's too large, (C) must be the correct answer. If it's too small, (E) must be the correct answer.

According to (D), $3,600, the corporation again contributes 80% of $2,500, which is $2,000, plus 60% of the remaining $1,100, which is $660, for a total contribution of $2,660. That's still too small, so you can eliminate both (C) and (D). **(E)** must be the correct answer. No need to check it!

In most cases, backsolving allows you to find the correct answer by checking no more than two possibilities. It's an especially powerful tool when you can determine whether the choice you tried was too high or too low, as you could here. It's an even more powerful tool when you can eliminate one or more choices up front. For instance, if one of the choices for this question was $2,780, you could have eliminated that immediately; because the corporation's match amount was $2,780 and it matches only part of the employee's contribution, the employee's contribution has to be greater than that.

## Word Problems

Many Problem Solving questions are presented in the form of word problems. The key to solving word problems is to isolate the words and phrases that relate to a particular mathematical operation. In the next section is a table that shows the most common key words and phrases and their mathematical translation.

Many people dislike word problems, and not unreasonably, since you must go to the trouble of translating the problem before you can start working on it. But in some ways, this actually makes the problem easier. Once you've translated the problem, you will generally find that the concepts and processes involved are rather straightforward. The test makers figure that they've made the problem difficult enough by adding the extra step of translating from English to math. So, once you have passed this step, you stand an excellent chance of being able to solve the problem.

## Translating English into Algebra

The translation table lists some common English words and phrases and the corresponding arithmetic operations.

| Translation Table | |
|---|---|
| Equals, is, was, will be, has, costs, adds up to, is the same as | $=$ |
| Times, of, multiplied by, product of, twice, double, triple | $\times$ |
| Divided by, per, out of, each, ratio of __ to __ | $\div$ |
| Plus, added to, sum, combined, and, more than, total | $+$ |
| Minus, subtracted from, less than, decreased by, difference between | $-$ |
| What, how much, how many, a number | $x$, $n$, etc. |

Here is an example:

Steve is now five times as old as Craig was 5 years ago. If the sum of Craig's and Steve's ages is 35, in how many years will Steve be twice as old as Craig?

- O 2
- O 5
- O 10
- O 15
- O 25

Let $c$ = Craig's current age and $s$ = Steve's current age. Translate the first sentence to get the first equation:

| $s$ | $=$ | $5(c-5)$ |
|---|---|---|
| Steve's current age | is | Five times Craig's age 5 years ago |

Translate the first part of the second sentence to get the second equation:

| $c+s$ | $=$ | 35 |
|---|---|---|
| The sum of Craig's and Steve's ages | is | 35 |

Now you're ready to solve for the two unknowns. Solve for $c$ in terms of $s$ in the second equation:

$$c + s = 35$$
$$c = 35 - s$$

Now plug this expression for $c$ into the first equation and solve for $s$:

$$s = 5(c - 5)$$
$$s = 5(35 - s - 5)$$
$$s = 5(30 - s)$$
$$s = 150 - 5s$$
$$6s = 150$$
$$s = 25$$

Plug this value for $s$ into either equation to solve for $c$:

$$c = 35 - s$$
$$c = 35 - 25$$
$$c = 10$$

So Steve is currently 25 and Craig is currently 10. This isn't what the question asked for, though. At this point, either set up an equation to find the number of years after which Steve will be twice as old as Craig or backsolve.

Here's how to set up the equation. Let $x$ be the number of years from now in which Steve will be twice as old as Craig.

| $25 + x$ | $=$ | $2(10 + x)$ |
|---|---|---|
| Steve's age in $x$ years | is | Twice Craig's age in $x$ years |

Solve this equation for $x$:

$$25 + x = 20 + 2x$$
$$5 = x$$

So Steve will be twice as old as Craig in 5 years. **(B)** is correct.

Alternatively, you could backsolve. Knowing that Steve is currently 25 and Craig is currently 10, start by trying (B), 5. When you age each person by 5 years, you find that Steve is now 30 and Craig is now 15. Steve is now twice Craig's age, as stipulated in the question, so **(B)** is correct.

### TAKEAWAYS

- Every Problem Solving question has only one correct answer choice.
- On some questions, straightforward math may be the best approach; however, picking numbers, backsolving, and finding logical shortcuts are often better ways to attack problems.
- Picking numbers is often the best approach when a question presents multiple variables or percents/ratios with unknown values.
- Backsolving is often an efficient approach when the answers are simple numerical values.
- When a question seems to require daunting amounts of tedious calculations, a shortcut is likely available as a reward for the test taker who can find it.

## Problem Solving Practice Set

Try the following questions. Use the four-step Kaplan Method for Problem Solving and look for opportunities to pick numbers and backsolve. Answers and explanations are at the end of this chapter.

$\frac{5}{9}, \frac{5}{12}, \frac{23}{48}, \frac{11}{24}, \frac{3}{7}$

1. What is the positive difference between the largest and smallest of the fractions listed above?

- O $\frac{1}{12}$
- O $\frac{5}{36}$
- O $\frac{1}{4}$
- O $\frac{1}{3}$
- O $\frac{7}{18}$

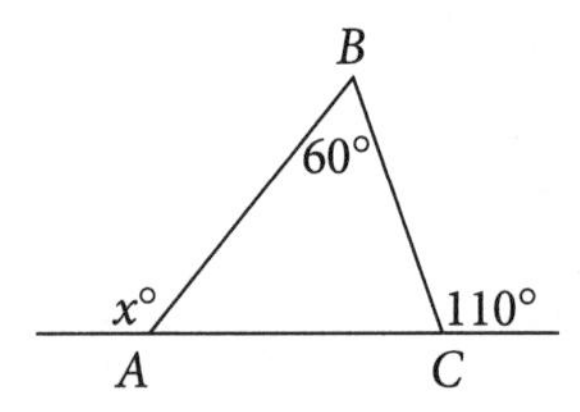


2. In the figure shown above, what is the value of $x$?

- O 70
- O 110
- O 130
- O 150
- O 170

3. The temperature readings at noon for three consecutive days are 9°, −6°, and 8°. What is the reading at noon on the fourth day, if the average (arithmetic mean) noon temperature of all four days is 4°?

- O −11°
- O −7°
- O 2°
- O 4°
- O 5°

4. If $x = 2$, then $3^x + (x^3)^2 =$

- O 18
- O 42
- O 45
- O 70
- O 73

5. If a store had sold a stereo for \$600, the store would have made a 20 percent profit. Instead, the store sold the stereo for a 40 percent loss. At what price was the stereo sold?

- O \$300
- O \$315
- O \$372
- O \$400
- O \$440

6. Which of the following describes all values of $x$ that are solutions to the inequality $|x + 2| > 6$?

   - O $x > 4$
   - O $x > 8$
   - O $x < -8$ or $x > 4$
   - O $x < 4$ or $x > 8$
   - O $-8 < x < 4$

7. The base of a ladder rests on the ground 24 feet from a building, and the top of the ladder touches the wall of the building 18 feet above the ground. If the wall is vertical and the ground is level, how long is the ladder?

   - O 26
   - O 28
   - O 29
   - O 30
   - O 32

8. A 1-inch-wide frame is placed around a 9-inch by 5-inch rectangular photograph. What is the area of the frame, in square inches?

   - O 15
   - O 32
   - O 45
   - O 60
   - O 77

9. Bucky leaves Amity for Truro, which is 8 miles away, at the same time that Robin leaves Truro for Amity on the same road. If neither traveler stops along the way and they meet 2 miles from Amity, what is the ratio of Bucky's average speed to Robin's average speed?

   - O $\frac{1}{4}$
   - O $\frac{1}{3}$
   - O $\frac{1}{1}$
   - O $\frac{3}{1}$
   - O $\frac{4}{1}$

10. If $b \neq -2$ and $\frac{a+3}{b+2} = \frac{3}{5}$, what is $b$ in terms of $a$?

   - O $\frac{5}{3}a + 1$
   - O $\frac{3}{5}a + 3$
   - O $\frac{5}{3}a + 3$
   - O $\frac{3}{5}a - 1$
   - O $\frac{5}{3}a - 3$

11. If the diameter of a circle increases by 50 percent, by what percent will the area of the circle increase?

   - O 25%
   - O 50%
   - O 100%
   - O 125%
   - O 225%

12. If four people working at the same rate can do $\frac{2}{3}$ of a job in 40 minutes, how many minutes would it take one person working at this rate to do $\frac{2}{5}$ of the job?

- O 80
- O 88
- O 92
- O 96
- O 112

13. Cement, gravel, and sand are to be mixed in the ratio 3:5:7, respectively. If 5 tons of cement are available, and there is enough gravel and sand available to use all the cement, how many tons of the mixture can be made?

- O 15
- O 20
- O 25
- O 30
- O 75

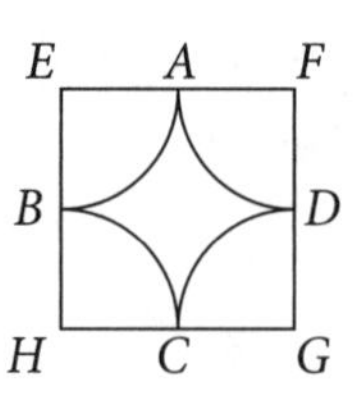


14. In the figure shown, if *EFGH* is a square and the arcs are all quarter-circles of length $\pi$, what is the perimeter of *EFGH*?

- O 1
- O 2
- O 4
- O 8
- O 16

15. A certain book costs $12 more in hardcover than in softcover. If the softcover price is $\frac{2}{3}$ the hardcover price, how much does the book cost in hardcover?

- O $8
- O $15
- O $18
- O $20
- O $36

Answers follow on the next page. ▶ ▶ ▶

## Answer Key

1. B
2. C
3. E
4. E
5. A
6. C
7. D
8. B
9. B
10. C
11. D
12. D
13. C
14. E
15. E

## Answers and Explanations

**1. B**

You're given a list of fractions with different numerators and denominators. To find the difference between the largest and smallest fractions, first determine which is the largest and which is the smallest.

Because $\frac{5}{9} > \frac{1}{2}$, and because all the other fractions are less than $\frac{1}{2}$, that means $\frac{5}{9}$ is the greatest. The other four are close together, but you can efficiently find a common denominator for $\frac{5}{12}, \frac{11}{24}$, and $\frac{23}{48}$. Convert everything to 48ths: $\frac{5}{12} = \frac{20}{48}$ and $\frac{11}{24} = \frac{22}{48}$, so $\frac{5}{12} < \frac{11}{24} < \frac{23}{48}$. Is $\frac{5}{12} < \frac{3}{7}$? Using the cross-multiplication method, $7 \times 5 = 35$ and $12 \times 3 = 36$, so $\frac{5}{12} < \frac{3}{7}$. That means that $\frac{5}{12}$ is the smallest fraction.

Now, subtract $\frac{5}{12}$ from $\frac{5}{9}$ to find the difference between the largest and smallest fractions. To subtract one fraction from another, give them the same denominator. Here, the least common denominator of the two fractions is 36.

$$\frac{5}{9} \times \frac{4}{4} = \frac{20}{36} \text{ and } \frac{5}{12} \times \frac{3}{3} = \frac{15}{36}$$

$$\frac{20}{36} - \frac{15}{36} = \frac{5}{36}$$

This question tests your knowledge of fractions and fraction operations (Chapter 4: Arithmetic and Number Properties) and how to find the range between two numbers (Chapter 6: Formulas, Statistics, and Data Analysis).

**2. C**

Because the angle with measure $x°$ is an exterior angle of triangle $ABC$, its measure must equal the sum of the measures of the two remote interior angles of the triangle: $\angle ABC$ and $\angle BCA$. The measure of $\angle ABC$ is given. Since $\angle BCA$ and 110° form a straight line, $\angle BCA = 180° - 110° = 70°$.

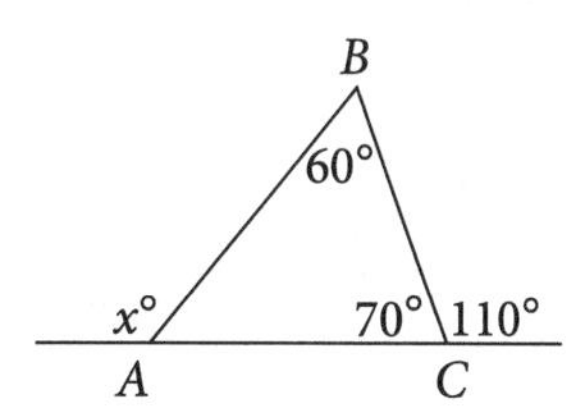


Therefore, $x = 60 + 70$, or 130.

This question tests your knowledge of lines/angles and triangles (Chapter 7: Geometry).

**3. E**

The formula for average is Average $= \frac{\text{Total of values}}{\text{Number of values}}$. If the average temperature over four days is 4°, the sum of the daily noon temperatures must be $4 \times (4°) = 16°$. Over the first three days, the sum is $(9°) + (-6°) + (8°) = 11°$. On the fourth day, the temperature at noon must be 5° to bring the sum up to 16° and the average up to 4°.

You could also have used backsolving. Given the temperatures already recorded, since the final average temperature is positive, a temperature well below zero is unlikely. Start with (D), 4°. The average temperature would be $\frac{9° + (-6°) + 8° + 4°}{4} = \frac{15°}{4} < 4°$. The fourth day must have a temperature greater than 4°, so the correct answer must be **(E)**, 5°.

This question tests your knowledge of averages (Chapter 6: Formulas, Statistics, and Data Analysis).

**4. E**

Substitute 2 for $x$ and do the arithmetic:

$$\begin{aligned} 3^x + \left(x^3\right)^2 &= 3^2 + \left(2^3\right)^2 \\ &= 3^2 + 8^2 \\ &= 9 + 64 \\ &= 73 \end{aligned}$$

This question tests your knowledge of exponents (Chapter 4: Arithmetic and Number Properties).

**5. A**

First, find the cost of the stereo to the store, then subtract 40% of this to find the price at which the stereo was sold. The selling price equals the store's cost plus the profit. The store would have made a 20% profit if it had sold the stereo for \$600, so \$600 must be 120% of the store's cost: $600 = 1.2x$. For ease of calculation, convert 1.2 to $\frac{6}{5}$:

$$\begin{aligned} 600 &= \frac{6}{5}x \\ x &= \frac{5}{6} \times 600 = 500 \end{aligned}$$

So the stereo cost the store \$500. However, the dealer actually sold the stereo at a loss of 40%. Since 40% of 500 is $0.4 \times 500 = 200$, the dealer sold the stereo for \$500 − \$200 = \$300.

This question tests your knowledge of percents (Chapter 4: Arithmetic and Number Properties).

**6. C**

Rewrite an equation or inequality involving absolute value as two equations or inequalities. Here, either $x + 2 > 6$ or $x + 2 < -6$. Simplify the first inequality by subtracting 2 from both sides to get $x > 4$. Likewise, simplify the second inequality by subtracting 2 from both sides to get $x < -8$.

This question tests your knowledge of inequalities (Chapter 5: Algebra) and absolute value (Chapter 4: Arithmetic and Number Properties).

**7. D**

Drawing a diagram makes visualizing the situation much easier.

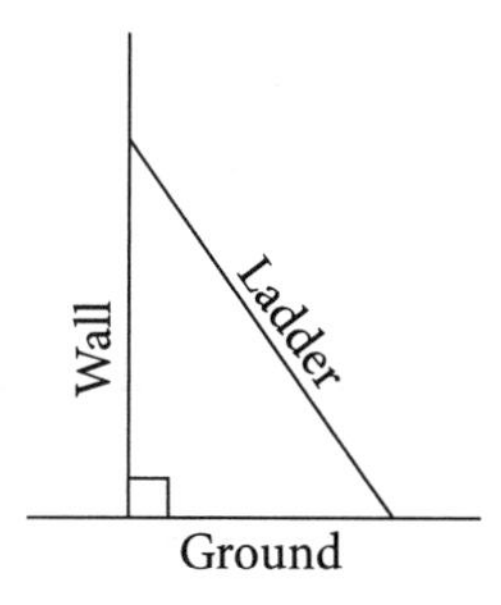


This forms a right triangle, and the length of the ladder is the hypotenuse of the triangle. Add the known dimensions:

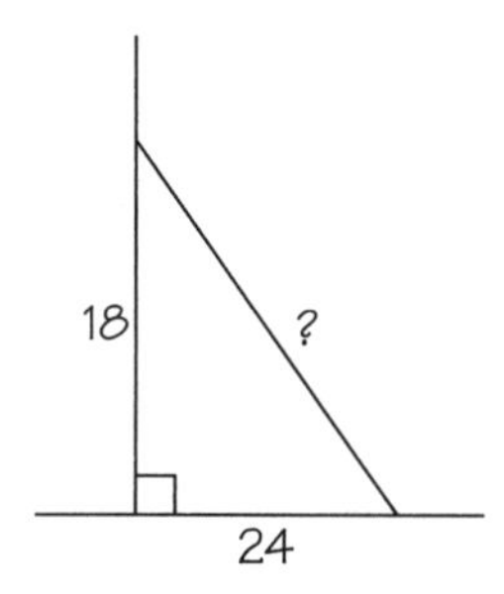


Notice that 18 is $3 \times 6$ and 24 is $4 \times 6$, so this is the Pythagorean triple 3:4:5 triangle multiplied by 6. Thus, the hypotenuse is $5 \times 6 = 30$.

This question tests your knowledge of triangles (Chapter 7: Geometry).

**8. B**

The area of the frame is the area of the framed photograph minus the area of just the photograph. The photograph is $9 \times 5 = 45$ square inches. A frame adds 1 inch to *each* side of the photograph, so the total dimensions of the photograph and the frame are 11 by 7. (A common error is to add 1 inch to the photograph's height and width and think the frame is only 10 by 6. Drawing a quick sketch will help you avoid this mistake.)

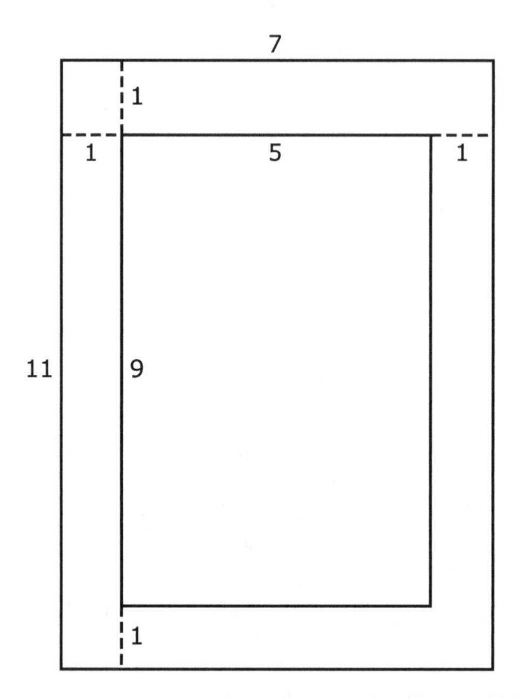


The total area of the framed photograph is $11 \times 7 = 77$ square inches. Subtract the area of the photo from this total to get an area of $77 - 45 = 32$ square inches for the frame itself.

This question tests your knowledge of the area of quadrilaterals (Chapter 7: Geometry).

**9. B**

Drawing a diagram will help you calculate the distances. Bucky and Robin meet 2 miles from Amity; since Amity is 8 miles from Truro, they must be $8 - 2 = 6$ miles from Truro.

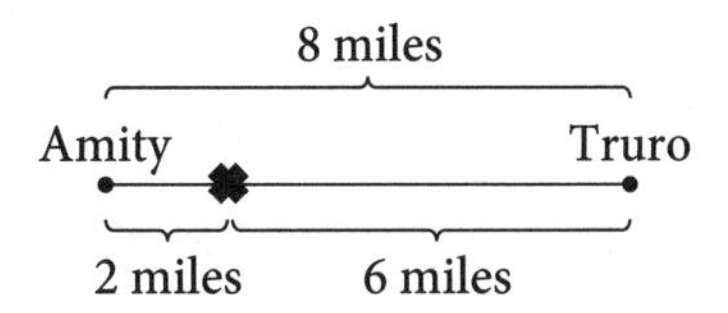


They left at the same time, so Bucky traveled 2 miles in the same time it took Robin to travel 6 miles. Because they traveled for the same time, the ratio of their average speeds will be the same as the ratio of their distances. (There's no need to actually calculate each person's speed, which can't be done with the information given.)

$$\frac{\text{Bucky's average speed}}{\text{Robin's average speed}} = \frac{\text{Bucky's distance}}{\text{Robin's distance}}$$
$$= \frac{2}{6}$$
$$= \frac{1}{3}$$

This question tests your knowledge of ratios (Chapter 4: Arithmetic and Number Properties).

**10. C**

To find $b$ in terms of $a$, manipulate the equation so that $b$ is by itself on one side. Clear the fractions and then solve for $b$:

$$5\left(\cancel{b+2}\right)\frac{a+3}{\cancel{b+2}} = \cancel{5}(b+2)\frac{3}{\cancel{5}}$$
$$5a + 15 = 3b + 6$$
$$5a + 9 = 3b$$
$$\frac{5a+9}{3} = b$$
$$\frac{5a}{3} + 3 = b$$

Alternately, you could pick numbers for $a$ and $b$. Make sure to choose numbers that are valid in the equation in the question stem. If you pick $a = 3$, then the numerator $a + 3 = 6$. For the fraction to reduce to $\frac{3}{5}$, $b + 2$ must equal 10, so $b = 8$. Now plug in 3 for $a$ in each answer choice and find which equal(s) 8. Only **(C)** works: $\frac{5}{3}a + 3 = \frac{5}{3}(3) + 3 = 5 + 3 = 8$.

This question tests your knowledge of algebraic operations (Chapter 5: Algebra).

**11. D**

An efficient method to answer this question is to pick a value for the diameter of the circle, such as 4. Thus, the radius is 2, which means that the area is $\pi(2)^2$, or $4\pi$. With the 50% increase, the new radius is $1.5 \times 2 = 3$, which means that the area of the circle becomes $\pi(3)^2$, or $9\pi$. The percent increase is the amount of change divided by the base amount times 100%, or $\frac{9\pi - 4\pi}{4\pi}(100\%) = \frac{5\pi}{4\pi}(100\%) = 125\%$.

This question tests your knowledge of circles (Chapter 7: Geometry) and percents (Chapter 4: Arithmetic and Number Properties).

**12. D**

If four people can do $\frac{2}{3}$ of the job in 40 minutes, then multiply by $\frac{3}{2}$ to find that in $\frac{3}{2} \times 40$ min $= 60$ min, the four people could do $\frac{3}{2} \times \frac{2}{3} = 1$ job. If it takes 4 people 60 minutes to complete the job, it would take 1 person 4 times that long, or 240 minutes, to do the work. The question asks how long it would take 1 person to do $\frac{2}{5}$ of the job: $\frac{2}{5} \times 240 = 96$ minutes.

This question tests your knowledge of rates (Chapter 6: Formulas, Statistics, and Data Analysis).

**13. C**

Since the ratio of cement to gravel to sand is 3:5:7, every 3 portions of cement yields $3 + 5 + 7 = 15$ portions of the mixture. Therefore, the weight of the total mixture is $\frac{15}{3} = 5$ times as much as the weight of cement. There are 5 tons of cement available, so $5 \times 5$ tons $= 25$ tons of the mixture can be made.

This question tests your knowledge of ratios (Chapter 4: Arithmetic and Number Properties).

**14. E**

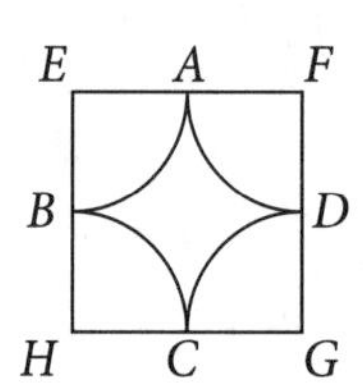


The perimeter of a square is the sum of the lengths of the four sides or, since all sides are equal, 4 times the side length. Each side of square *EFGH* consists of two radii of the quarter-circles. If you were to combine these four quarter-circles, you'd have a circle with a circumference of $4\pi$. Use the circumference formula to solve for the radius:

$$\text{Circumference} = 2\pi r = 4\pi$$
$$r = 2$$

So, each side of square *EFGH* has length $2 + 2$, or 4. Therefore, the perimeter of the square is 4(4), or 16.

This question tests your knowledge of circles and quadrilaterals (Chapter 7: Geometry).

**15. E**

Call the softcover price $S$ and the hardcover price $H$. Then convert the words into two equations:

$$H = S + 12$$
$$S = \frac{2}{3}H$$

Now since you're solving for $H$, substitute $\frac{2}{3}H$ from the second equation for $S$ in the first equation:

$$H = \frac{2}{3}H + 12$$
$$\frac{1}{3}H = 12$$
$$H = 36$$

The hardcover price is \$36.

You could also have used critical thinking to eliminate some choices and then backsolved this question. Since the softcover price is $\frac{2}{3}$ the hardcover price, the hardcover's price must be divisible by 3. Eliminate (A) and (D). Now try (C). If the hardcover costs \$18 and the softcover is \$12 less, the softcover must be \$6; however, this is $\frac{1}{3}$, not $\frac{2}{3}$, the hardcover price. The hardcover must cost more so that subtracting \$12 doesn't result in such a small fraction of its price. Eliminate (B) and (C). The correct choice is **(E)**.

This question tests your knowledge of algebra operations (Chapter 5: Algebra).

CHAPTER 3

# Data Sufficiency Questions

**LEARNING OBJECTIVES**

After studying this chapter, you will be able to:

- Describe the format of a Data Sufficiency question
- State the steps of the Kaplan Method for Data Sufficiency questions
- Explain how to solve a Data Sufficiency question strategically by doing as little calculation as possible

Data Sufficiency (DS) questions on the GMAT are formatted differently than Problem Solving questions, and they may well be different from any questions you have ever encountered on a standardized test before. Because of this, you will be able to recognize a Data Sufficiency question the instant you see it and adopt the proper mindset to approach it strategically.

Here's an example of a Data Sufficiency question. You'll solve this question later in this chapter.

Is the product of $x$, $y$, and $z$ equal to 1?

(1) $x + y + z = 3$

(2) $x$, $y$, and $z$ are each greater than 0.

- O Statement (1) ALONE is sufficient, but Statement (2) is not sufficient.
- O Statement (2) ALONE is sufficient, but Statement (1) is not sufficient.
- O BOTH statements TOGETHER are sufficient, but NEITHER statement ALONE is sufficient.
- O EACH statement ALONE is sufficient.
- O Statements (1) and (2) TOGETHER are NOT sufficient.

At the top, the question stem states the question. It may or may not provide additional information, but there is never enough information in the stem to answer the question. Below the question stem are two numbered statements with more information. Your task is to evaluate these statements and decide whether they provide enough information to answer the question posed. You do *not* need to perform the calculations that would be necessary to answer the math question. All that is required to correctly answer a Data Sufficiency question is to determine whether there is enough information that you *could* answer the math question. Actually doing the calculations is a waste of your valuable time.

The answer choices are always exactly the same for Data Sufficiency questions. Don't read these every time you encounter a DS question. Instead, memorize the wording and order of the choices. A helpful way to do this is to use the mnemonic "12TEN."

**1**—short for "Statement **(1)** ALONE is sufficient, but Statement (2) is not sufficient."

**2**—short for "Statement **(2)** ALONE is sufficient, but Statement (1) is not sufficient."

**T**—short for "Together," as in "BOTH statements **T**OGETHER are sufficient, but NEITHER statement ALONE is sufficient."

**E**—short for "Either" or "Each," as in "**E**ACH statement ALONE is sufficient."

**N**—short for "Neither" or "Not," as in "Statements (1) and (2) TOGETHER are **N**OT sufficient."

Just by looking at this sample question, you may have already surmised that Data Sufficiency questions should be approached differently than other types of questions. The Kaplan Method for Data Sufficiency outlines that approach.

## Kaplan Method for Data Sufficiency Questions

**LEARNING OBJECTIVES**

After this lesson, you will be able to:

- State the steps of the Kaplan Method for Data Sufficiency questions
- Explain the purpose of each step of the Kaplan Method for Data Sufficiency
- Perform the steps of the Method to answer Data Sufficiency questions

This method is the essential systematic approach to mastering Data Sufficiency. Use this approach for every Data Sufficiency question. It will allow you to eliminate wrong answer choices efficiently and will guarantee that you avoid the common Data Sufficiency mistake of subconsciously combining the statements instead of considering them separately at first.

**THE KAPLAN METHOD FOR DATA SUFFICIENCY**

1. Analyze the question stem
    - Determine Value or Yes/No
    - Simplify
    - Identify what is needed to answer the question
2. Evaluate the statements using 12TEN

### Step 1: Analyze the Question Stem

Step 1 consists of three parts: (1) determine whether you're looking at a Value question or a Yes/No question, (2) simplify any information you're given, and (3) determine what sort of information would allow you to answer the question.

#### Value or Yes/No?

There are two types of DS questions, Value and Yes/No. How you approach the question will vary depending upon the type.

A Value question asks whether there is sufficient information to come up with a single value in response to the question. Information that permits more than one value as an answer is insufficient.

To correctly answer a Yes/No question, you need to be able to determine whether the answer is always yes or always no. Information that allows the answer to be sometimes yes and sometimes no is insufficient. A mental hurdle that many students must overcome is the tendency to equate *no* with *wrong*. For Data Sufficiency questions, being able to answer the question "definitely no" is, in fact, sufficient. The question is not asking whether there is sufficient information to say yes; it asks whether there is sufficient information to say yes *or* no with absolute certainty.

Here's an example of how your approach to the two types of DS questions will differ.

**Value question:** What is the value of $x$?

**Yes/No question:** Is $x \leq -1$?

(1) $x = -1, 0,$ or $1$

(2) $x = 0$ or $1$

For the Value question, neither statement is sufficient by itself since there are three possible values in Statement (1) and two possible values in Statement (2). Furthermore, even when both statements are considered together, the value could still be either 0 or 1, since those values are included in both statements. Therefore, the correct choice using 12TEN is N, "Neither," which is the fifth choice, or **(E)**.

Now consider the Yes/No question. Sufficiency does not require being able to determine a single, exact value, just that you can say for certain whether $x$ is less than or equal to $-1$. If a statement provides enough information to answer the question with a definite yes or a definite no, it's sufficient. In Statement (1), if $x = -1$, then $x$ is less than or equal to $-1$. However, if $x = 0$ or 1, then $x$ is not less than or equal to $-1$. So, Statement (1) is insufficient. For Statement (2), in both cases $x$ is not less than or equal to $-1$. Thus, the answer is "definitely no," and Statement (2) is sufficient. The correct choice in 12TEN is "2," which is the second choice, or **(B)**, among the answers.

So, the same information in the statements can yield different answers, depending on the question asked.

### Simplify

When information helpful to solving is provided in the question stem, you will probably need to simplify it or, at least, consider its implications. An example would be a quadratic equation that can be factored to more easily identify the possible values of a variable. Or, if there is wording in the stem that can be converted to arithmetic or algebra, this is the time to do that.

### Determine What Is Needed to Answer the Question

This third part of step 1 is vital but too often omitted. It is much easier to evaluate the statements if you know what sort of information would make a statement sufficient.

### Step 1: An Example

Here's an example of how to approach step 1:

If $w \neq x$, $w \neq z$, and $x \neq y$, is $\dfrac{(x-y)^3(w-z)^3}{(w-z)^2(x-y)(w-x)^2} > 0$?

(1) $x > y$

(2) $w > z$

This is a Yes/No question that asks whether or not a fraction containing multiple variable expressions is positive. A fraction is positive when the numerator and denominator are either both positive or both negative. If the numerator and denominator are of opposite signs, the fraction is negative. So this question boils down to whether you have enough information to determine whether the top and bottom of the fraction are the same sign or have different signs. If a statement provides that information, it is sufficient.

At first glance, this may look scary. But take a closer look at that fraction. There are a lot of shared terms in the numerator and the denominator. Using the laws of exponents, you can cancel some of the terms:

$$\frac{(x-y)^{\cancel{3}\,2}(w-z)^{\cancel{3}\,1}}{\cancel{(w-z)^2}\,\cancel{(x-y)}\,(w-x)^2} > 0$$

Doing this simplifies the question to "Is $\frac{(x-y)^2(w-z)}{(w-x)^2} > 0$ ?" This is looking better already.

You don't know anything about the values of $w$, $x$, $y$, and $z$, but what *do* you know? For one thing, a squared term is never negative. So, there's no way that $(x-y)^2$ or $(w-x)^2$ is negative. In fact, since $w \neq x$ and $x \neq y$, they can't be zero, either. The only thing that matters is the sign of $(w-z)$. This question is really asking: "Is $w - z > 0$?" Through simplification, you have identified the simple fact that is needed to answer the question.

## Step 2: Evaluate the Statements Using 12TEN

Start by considering each statement separately, but keep in mind that any information that is in the stem applies to both statements. Write 12TEN on your notepad and cross off the choices as you eliminate them.

- If Statement (1) is sufficient, you are left with 1 and E as the eligible choices.
  - If Statement (2) is also sufficient, then E is correct.
  - If Statement (2) is insufficient, then 1 is correct.
- If Statement (1) is insufficient, then 2, T, and N are the remaining options.
  - If Statement (2) is sufficient, then 2 is the correct choice.
  - If Statement (2) is insufficient, then cross out 2, leaving T or N as possibilities.
- *Only* if neither statement is sufficient on its own will you consider the statements together.
  - If the two statements together are sufficient, cross out N, leaving T.
  - If the two statements combined are still not sufficient, cross out T, leaving N.

Be aware that the two statements in DS questions will always be true, and they will never contradict each other. Many students get caught up in trying to determine whether a *statement* is true. It is! Keep your focus on whether the statement allows you to answer the *question*.

### Step 2: The Example Continues

Keep going with the question for which you've already executed step 1. Evaluate each statement one at a time.

Statement (1), $x > y$, provides no information about $w - z$, so it is insufficient. Cross out 1 and E.

You must now develop temporary amnesia and forget everything about Statement (1) as you move on to Statement (2). This may trip you up at first, but as you work more practice questions, it will become easier!

Statement (2) says that $w > z$, so $w - z > 0$. That answers the question with a definite yes, so Statement (2) is sufficient and the correct choice is the "2" in 12TEN, or **(B)**.

Because one of the statements worked, your job is done; you won't combine statements for this question. If both statements were insufficient by themselves, you could now recover from your temporary amnesia and use the information from the stem and both statements to decide whether there was now sufficient information to answer the question. There's more to know about combining statements, which you'll learn after a practice question.

## Practice

Apply the steps of the Kaplan Method to answer this question:

If $x^3 < x$, is $x > x^2$?

(1) $x > -5$

(2) $x < -2$

### Step 1: Analyze the Question Stem

This is a Yes/No question, so you don't need to know the exact value of $x$. If the given information allows you to determine that $x$ is definitely greater than $x^2$ or definitely not greater than $x^2$, you have sufficiency.

The question stem has already given you some information about $x$. Think about what values of $x$ could result in $x^3 < x$. For positive values greater than 1, $x^3$ is greater than $x$. For positive fractions, however, $x^3$ is less than $x$. For example, $\left(\frac{1}{2}\right)^3 = \frac{1}{8}$. But, if $x$ is a negative fraction, the opposite is true. For example, $\left(-\frac{1}{2}\right)^3 = -\frac{1}{8}$. However, if $x$ is less than $-1$, then $x^3 < x$. As an example, $(-2)^3 = -8$. For 0 or 1, $x^3$ is equal to $x$.

Therefore, the information that $x^3 < x$ means that $x$ is either a positive fraction or less than $-1$. Now consider these two possibilities: If $x$ is a positive fraction, then $x > x^2$. But, if $x$ is a negative number, squaring it will produce a positive result and $x < x^2$. If a statement limits $x$ to one or the other of these categories, then that statement is sufficient.

### Step 2: Evaluate the Statements Using 12TEN

Statement (1) limits $x$ to values greater than $-5$. This includes values from both categories, $x$ less than $-1$ and $x$ being a positive fraction. Therefore, Statement (1) is insufficient. Eliminate 1 and E.

Statement (2) limits the value of $x$ to numbers less than $-2$. This excludes positive fractions, so $x^2$ must be greater than $x$. Statement (2) alone is sufficient. This is the "2" in 12TEN. Select the second choice, **(B)**, and move on.

## Combining Statements

The only circumstance that will require combining statements is when neither statement, by itself, is sufficient, leaving T or N as the only possible correct choices. Combining the statements means treating them as one long statement. If this sentence, containing the information from both statements, provides enough information to answer the question, then the correct choice is T (the third choice). If not, then N (the fifth choice) is correct.

Here is a relatively straightforward example.

What is the value of $x$?

(1) $x + y = 3$

(2) $x - y = 1$

For this Value question, there is nothing to simplify in step 1, nor do you know what information is required. You just know you need enough information to calculate a single value for $x$.

Move on to step 2. Each equation in the statements is a single linear equation with two variables. Each statement, by itself, is insufficient to solve for $x$, so proceed to combine the statements. Now there are two distinct linear equations and two variables, and when you have as many distinct linear equations as you have variables, you can solve for each of the variables. Don't actually solve for $x$! Just knowing you could is enough. Since there is sufficient information to determine a distinct value for $x$ when the statements are combined, the correct choice is that, together, the statements are sufficient. Pick "T," the third choice, or **(C)**.

Sometimes evaluating each of the two statements for a Value question will identify more than one possible value. Consider this example:

> What is the value of $x$?
>
> (1) $x^2 = 2$
>
> (2) $x^2 - x - 2 = 0$

As with the previous example, there is nothing to simplify in step 1, nor do you know what information is required. Solving the equation in Statement (1) results in $x = 2$ or $-2$. That's two values, so Statement (1) is insufficient. Solving the equation in Statement (2) results in $x = -1$ or 2. Thus, each statement by itself is insufficient. When you combine these statements, because of the exponent, you don't have two *linear* equations, so you can't apply that rule as you did in the previous question. However, you don't need to use algebra. Since the value $x = 2$ is the only value that satisfies the equations in both statements, together the statements are sufficient to determine a unique value for $x$. Pick T, or **(C)**.

## Data Sufficiency Strategies

**LEARNING OBJECTIVES**

After this lesson, you will be able to:

- Identify Data Sufficiency questions for which the picking numbers strategy is helpful and apply picking numbers efficiently
- Describe types of Data Sufficiency questions for which little or no calculation may be required
- Use strategic guessing when appropriate to manage your pacing on Data Sufficiency questions

### Picking Numbers

When using picking numbers for Problem Solving questions, you usually attempt to select numbers that will make one of the choices correct. When using picking numbers for Data Sufficiency questions, however, the goal is to try to prove the statements insufficient by picking numbers that will produce different results. In order to do this, you will have to pick at least two sets of numbers. If they produce contradictory answers, then the statement is insufficient. Proving sufficiency is more difficult. If you keep plugging in different numbers and getting the same result, look for a pattern that will show that no matter what allowable numbers you use, the result will be the same. You can use this strategy for many Data Sufficiency questions that contain variables, unknown quantities, or percents of an unknown whole.

Answer this question by picking numbers:

> What is the units digit of positive integer $n$?
>
> (1) Dividing $n$ by 12 yields a remainder of 4.
>
> (2) Dividing $n$ by 10 yields a remainder of 4.

**Explanation:** There is nothing to simplify in step 1 of this Value question, so proceed to step 2. Pick numbers to attempt to prove Statement (1) insufficient. Start with $n = 16$, which is $12 \times 1 + 4$. This leaves a remainder of 4 when divided by 12. The units digit in this case is 6. Now try $12 \times 2 + 4 = 28$. This also leaves a remainder of 4 when divided by 12, but the units digit is 8. Therefore, Statement (1) is insufficient. Eliminate 1 and E.

For Statement (2), possible numbers include 14, 24, 34, etc. So, there is a pattern because 10 times any integer has a units digit of 0. Statement (2) alone is sufficient. **(B)** is correct.

Here is the question from the beginning of this chapter. See if you can solve it before reading the explanation that follows.

> Is the product of $x$, $y$, and $z$ equal to 1?
>
> (1) $x + y + z = 3$
>
> (2) $x$, $y$, and $z$ are each greater than 0.

**Explanation:** This is a Yes/No question. Information that lets you conclude that $xyz = 1$ or $xyz \neq 1$ will be sufficient. There's nothing to simplify here, but brainstorm a bit about the values for these variables that would make their product either equal 1 or not equal 1. If $x$, $y$, and $z$ all equal 1, then the answer is yes. If two variables are reciprocals of each other and the third variable is 1, then the answer is also yes. If any variable is equal to zero, the product will be zero and the answer is no. If either one or all three variables are negative (and none equals zero), the product will be negative and the answer is also no.

Statement (1) says the sum of the variables is 3 but doesn't provide any information about what the variables are. You could pick $x = 1$, $y = 1$, and $z = 1$, and that would answer the question with a yes. But you could also pick $x = 0$, $y = 2$, and $z = 1$, and that would answer the question with a no. This statement is insufficient. Eliminate 1 and E.

Statement (2) tells you all the values are positive, but again, they could all equal 1, making the answer yes. Or they could all equal 100, making the answer no. Eliminate 2.

Together, the statements say that $x$, $y$, and $z$ are three positive values whose sum is 3. They could all equal 1, or two could be reciprocals of each other and the third could equal 1. However, they could also be $\frac{1}{2}$, $\frac{1}{2}$, and 2, which would multiply to $\frac{1}{2}$. You still can't rule in or out the possibility that their product is 1, so eliminate T and choose N, or **(E)**.

## Questions That May Not Require Any Calculation

As you saw in the first example in "Combining Statements," the "$N$-variable, $N$-equations" rule can be used to determine sufficiency. The rule states that to determine the values of $N$ different variables, you need at least $N$ distinct linear equations. If the question asks for the value of $x$ and the statements are two equations such as $x + y = 7$ and $2x + y = 12$, you could tell at a glance that the statements are insufficient individually but, when combined, are sufficient because they are two distinct linear equations that together could be solved for $x$. Be careful rushing to judgment, however, because there are a couple of twists that you might encounter. Consider this example:

What is the value of $x$?

(1) $2y = 6 - x$

(2) $3x + 6y = 18$

This is a Value question, and there is nothing to simplify in step 1. Each of the two statements has one linear equation with two variables, so, individually, they are insufficient. At first glance, it might seem that the statements are sufficient when taken together because there are two linear equations with two variables. However, the *N*-equations rule depends upon *distinct* equations. When the equation in Statement (1) is rearranged, it becomes $x + 2y = 6$. This is the same as the other equation if it were simplified by having all its terms divided by 3. The equations are not distinct, so, even taken together, the statements are insufficient. Eliminate T and choose N, or **(E)**.

Here's another twist:

What is the value of $y + \frac{1}{2}x$?

(1) $2y = 6 - x$

(2) $3x + 6y = 18$

This question asks for the value of an expression that combines the two variables. In this case, you may or may not need two distinct linear equations. As shown in the example above, the two equations are equivalent. It's easier to see the relationship to the expression in the stem by looking at the equation in Statement (2). If you divide all the terms in this equation by 6, the result is $y + \frac{1}{2}x = 3$. (Rearranging the equation in Statement (1) to $2y + x = 6$ and dividing by 2 produces the same result.) Thus, either statement is sufficient to determine a unique value for the expression. Eliminate N and choose T, or **(C)**.

## Strategic Guessing

When you encounter a very complex question or one that involves a concept that you don't understand, the best strategy can be strategic guessing. You may even skip one of the statements completely. Knowing the sufficiency of one statement but not the other improves your odds of a correct guess. If you know that Statement (1) is insufficient, then your choices are limited to 2, T, and N; you now have a one in three chance of guessing the correct choice rather than the one in five chance with which you started. (The same holds true for Statement (2)'s being insufficient—the remaining choices are 1, T, and N.) Furthermore, if you ascertain that one of the statements is sufficient, you have only two remaining choices, making your chances of guessing correctly even better.

Apply the strategic guessing strategy to this question:

What is the value of $x$?

(1) $x^2 - 3x = -2$

(2) $x^3 + 6 = 7x$

There is nothing to simplify in step 1 of this Value question. Statement (1) is a quadratic equation. You could rearrange the equation so that one side is equal to zero, then factor to get the possible values of $x$. However, unless the quadratic is a perfect square, there will be two possible values of $x$. Assume, for now, that Statement (1) is insufficient and look at Statement (2).

This is even more formidable than Statement (1) because it has an $x^3$ term, which means that the equation could have as many as three solutions. (You might have been able to see that one of the solutions is $x = 1$ just by "eyeballing" the equation.) Assume that Statement (2) is also insufficient.

Now, you have two choices: T or N. You can either grind through the math to find the possible values of $x$ for the equations in either statement, or you can make a strategic guess. Given that there may be two possible values for $x$ in Statement (1) and up to three for Statement (2), the only way that the statements would be sufficient when taken together would be if there were only a single common solution. Thus, guessing that even taken together the statements are insufficient would be a good guess.

If you are curious, the possible values of $x$ based on Statement (1) are 1 and 2, and the possible values based on Statement (2) are 1, 2, and $-3$. Taken together, $x$ could still be either 1 or 2. Out of 12TEN, the answer is N. Choose **(E)**.

## TAKEAWAYS

As you practice mastering Data Sufficiency questions, remember the following:

- Memorize and use 12TEN so that you never have to read the choices.
- Value questions require being able to determine a unique value for sufficiency; you can correctly solve an equation, but if the result is more than one value, that is insufficient.
- In Yes/No questions, the statements may result in ranges or multiple values, but they can still be sufficient if they answer the question with a definitive yes or no.
- When a statement in a Yes/No question leads to an answer of "always no," that is sufficient.
- Taking the time to do the up-front analysis to identify what information is needed to determine sufficiency will pay off when evaluating the statements.
- When evaluating Statement (2), disregard Statement (1), and vice versa.
- Do not take the time to do unnecessary calculations; think about sufficiency rather than solving.
- Never combine statements unless each statement is insufficient by itself.
- Use strategic guessing when you are faced with complex questions and are concerned about time.

## Data Sufficiency Practice Set

Try the following questions. Use the two-step Kaplan Method for Data Sufficiency and look for opportunities to pick numbers, solve without algebra, and guess strategically. Answers and explanations are at the end of this chapter.

*Note:* Because the Data Sufficiency answer choices are always the same and should be memorized, we have omitted them here. If you need a refresher on the choices or the 12TEN mnemonic, review the section at the beginning of this chapter.

1. Is $x > y$?

   (1) $x - y > 0$

   (2) $x + y > 0$

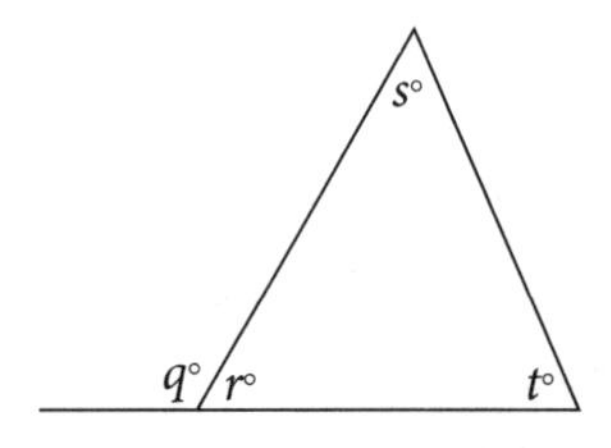


2. What is the value of $q$ if $s = 50$?

   (1) $q > r$

   (2) $t = 80$

3. What is the average score of the bowlers in a bowling tournament?

   (1) Seventy percent of the bowlers average 120, and the other 30 percent average 140.

   (2) Each of the 300 bowlers in the tournament bowled 3 games.

4. Every student graduating from College A is either a 4-year student or a transfer student. If the college is graduating an equal number of 4-year students and transfer students, what fraction of the students who graduate with honors are transfer students?

   (1) Of the 700 transfer students graduating, 300 are graduating with honors.

   (2) Fifty percent more transfer students than 4-year students are graduating with honors.

5. What is greater, $x$ or $\frac{1}{x}$?

   (1) $4x^2 = 1$

   (2) $\left(x - \frac{1}{2}\right)(x + 2) = 0$

6. Is $|x| > 3$?

   (1) $2x = 15 - x^2$

   (2) $\frac{x}{4} - \frac{3}{4} = 0$

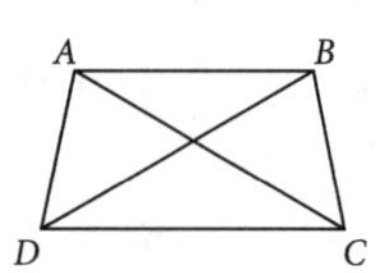


7. Is the quadrilateral shown above a rectangle?

   (1) The area of $\Delta ABD$ is one-half the area of $ABCD$.

   (2) The area of $\Delta ABC$ is one-half the area of $ABCD$.

8. If $y$ equals 75 percent of $x$, what is the value of $y$?

   (1) $x > 150$

   (2) $x - y = 74$

9. A train traveled the first 120 miles of its journey at an average speed of 60 miles per hour, the next 120 miles at an average speed of $y$ miles per hour, and the final 120 miles of its journey at an average speed of 160 miles per hour. What is the value of $y$?

   (1) The first 120 miles took 1 hour longer to travel than did the second 120 miles.

   (2) The average speed for the total journey was 96 miles per hour.

10. What is the sum of an arithmetic sequence of integers for which the least value is 2?

    (1) The greatest number is 62.

    (2) There are 31 individual values in the sequence.

11. Points $A$, $B$, and $C$ in the $xy$-coordinate plane are connected to form a triangle. If the coordinates of $A$, $B$, and $C$ are, respectively, (2,2), (2,5), and $(x,2)$, what is the area of triangle $ABC$?

    (1) $x^2 = 4x + 12$

    (2) $|x| = 6$

12. The profits of Company C increased by 10 percent from year 1 to year 2 and by another 10 percent from year 2 to year 3. Did the profits of Company C exceed $1,000,000 in year 3?

    (1) Company C's profits in year 1 were greater than $825,000.

    (2) Company C's profits in the year prior to year 1 were greater than $1,000,000.

13. What is the value of the positive integer $x$?

    (1) $\frac{1}{7}+\frac{1}{4}+\frac{x}{3}<\frac{13}{12}$

    (2) $0.25 < 0.15x < 0.50$

14. What is the value of $\frac{a}{b}$?

    (1) $\frac{x^a}{x^b} = x^2$

    (2) $16^{\frac{a}{b}} = 4$

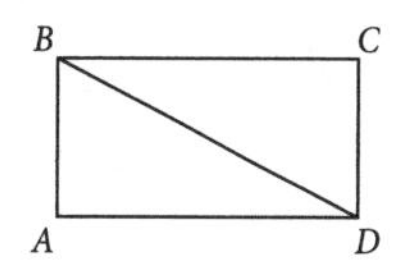


15. What is the perimeter of the rectangle shown above?

    (1) Diagonal $BD$ has length 10.

    (2) $\angle BDA$ has measure 30°.

## Answer Key

1. A
2. B
3. A
4. B
5. B
6. B
7. E
8. B
9. D
10. C
11. A
12. E
13. C
14. B
15. C

## Answers and Explanations

**1. A**

This is a Yes/No question that asks whether one variable is greater than another. There is no information to simplify.

Statement (1): $x - y > 0$ can be simplified by adding $y$ to both sides to get $x > y$. This statement is sufficient, so in terms of 12TEN, eliminate 2, T, and N.

Statement (2) shows that the sum of $x$ and $y$ is positive but provides no information about the relative values of $x$ and $y$. Statement (2) is thus insufficient, so eliminate E. **(A)** is correct.

This question tests your knowledge of number properties (Chapter 4: Arithmetic and Number Properties) and inequalities (Chapter 5: Algebra).

**2. B**

This Value question asks for the measure of an external angle, $q$, of a triangle. If you can determine the value of $r$, you can calculate $q$ since the two angles form a straight line and thus total 180°. Because the stem gives the value of $s$, and because the interior angles of a triangle sum to 180°, knowing the value of $t$ would also enable you to find $r$ and thus $q$.

Statement (1) states that $q$ is greater than $r$. This is not sufficient to yield a specific value for $q$, so Statement (1) is insufficient. In terms of 12TEN, eliminate 1 and E.

Statement (2) gives the value of $t$, which is sufficient. **(B)** is correct.

This question tests your knowledge of angles and triangles (Chapter 7: Geometry).

**3. A**

This is a Value question. You'll need to be able to find the average score of all the bowlers.

Statement (1) gives the average scores of two groups and what fraction of the whole each part represents. You could use a weighted average to find the average of the whole group. Statement (1) is sufficient. In terms of 12TEN, eliminate 2, T, and N.

Statement (2) tells how many games each bowler bowled but gives no information about their scores. Statement (2) is insufficient. **(A)** is correct.

This question tests your knowledge of averages (Chapter 6: Formulas, Statistics, and Data Analysis).

**4. B**

This is a Value question. In order to get the fraction of the students who graduate with honors that are transfer students, you need enough information to figure out the relationship between the total number of honors graduates and the number of transfer students graduating with honors.

Statement (1) provides the number of transfer students graduating with honors. However, no information is given about how many 4-year students are graduating with honors, so you can't determine what fraction of all honors students the transfer students are. Statement (1) is insufficient. In terms of 12TEN, eliminate 1 and E.

The information that 50% more transfer students than 4-year students graduate with honors, per Statement (2), enables you to determine the relative numbers of the two categories as a part-to-part ratio. You could use this to set up a part-to-whole ratio that answers the question. **(B)** is correct.

This question tests your knowledge of ratios (Chapter 4: Arithmetic and Number Properties).

**5. B**

This is a Yes/No question that requires you to determine whether a variable is greater than its reciprocal. A number is greater than its reciprocal if the number is greater than 1 or if it is between 0 and –1. (Never forget negative numbers!) If it is between 0 and 1 or less than –1, then the reciprocal is greater than the number. For instance, the reciprocal of $\frac{1}{2}$ is 2, and $2 > \frac{1}{2}$. Information that allows an answer of "definitely yes" or "definitely no" will be sufficient.

Statement (1) provides an equation for $x$. Divide both sides by 4 to get $x^2 = \frac{1}{4}$. There are two possible values for $x$: $\frac{1}{2}$ and $-\frac{1}{2}$. If $x$ is $\frac{1}{2}$, then $\frac{1}{x}$ will be greater than $x$; if $x$ is $-\frac{1}{2}$, then $x$ will be greater than $\frac{1}{x}$. Statement (1) is insufficient. In terms of 12TEN, eliminate 1 and E.

Statement (2) says that the product of two binomials is zero; therefore, one of the factors is zero. Either $x - \frac{1}{2} = 0$, in which case $x = \frac{1}{2}$, or $x + 2 = 0$, in which case $x = -2$. In either case, the reciprocal of $x$ will be greater than $x$ itself. If $x = \frac{1}{2}$, then $\frac{1}{x} = 2$; if $x = -2$, then $\frac{1}{x} = -\frac{1}{2}$. Statement (2) is sufficient. **(B)** is correct.

This question tests your knowledge of number properties (Chapter 4: Arithmetic and Number Properties) and quadratic equations (Chapter 5: Algebra).

**6. B**

To answer this Yes/No question, you'll need to know the possible values of $x$. If $x > 3$ or $x < -3$, the answer is yes. If $-3 \leq x \leq 3$, the answer is no. Solve the equation in each statement for $x$.

The equation in Statement (1) is a quadratic that can be rearranged as $x^2 + 2x - 15 = 0$. This factors to $(x + 5)(x - 3) = 0$, so $x$ can be either $-5$ or 3. If $x$ is $-5$, then $|x| = 5$, which is greater than 3. However, if $x = 3$, then $|x| = 3$, which is not greater than 3. Therefore, Statement (1) is insufficient. In terms of 12TEN, eliminate 1 and E.

To simplify the equation in Statement (2), multiply the terms by 4 to get $x - 3 = 0$, which means that $x = 3$. This is not greater than 3, making the answer to the question a definite no. Statement (2) is sufficient. **(B)** is correct.

This question tests your knowledge of quadratic equations (Chapter 5: Algebra) and absolute values (Chapter 4: Arithmetic and Number Properties).

**7. E**

This Yes/No question asks whether the given figure is a rectangle. A rectangle is a quadrilateral with four right angles with diagonals of equal length. Information that allows you to determine that *ABCD* definitely is or is not a rectangle would be sufficient.

Statement (1) states that $\Delta ABD$ is one-half the area of the whole quadrilateral; this implies that $\Delta ABD$ and $\Delta BCD$ have the same area. This does not tell you anything about *ABCD*, however. It could be a rectangle, but it could also be a parallelogram or symmetrical trapezoid. In terms of 12TEN, eliminate 1 and E.

Statement (2) just uses the other diagonal to divide the figure, so it is insufficient for the same reason as Statement (1). Eliminate 2 and evaluate the statements together.

Each statement says essentially the same thing: that the diagonals divide the quadrilateral into two equal-area triangles. Thus, even taken together, the statements are insufficient. **(E)** is correct.

This question tests your knowledge of quadrilaterals (Chapter 7: Geometry).

**8. B**

This Value question gives the percent relationship of $x$ and $y$ and asks for the value of $y$. Knowing $x$ would enable you to determine the value of $y$.

Statement (1) tells you that $x$ is greater than 150; this is not sufficient to pin down a specific value of $y$, only a minimum value. Statement (1) is insufficient. In terms of 12TEN, eliminate 1 and E.

Statement (2) gives a linear equation involving $x$ and $y$. The question stem provides another linear equation with these variables: $y = 0.75x$. Thus, you can now solve for each variable, and Statement (2) is sufficient. **(B)** is correct.

This question tests your knowledge of percents (Chapter 4: Arithmetic and Number Properties).

**9. D**

This Value question asks for the average speed during one of the three legs of the trip. Set up a table to organize the information:

| Leg | Time | Speed | Distance |
|---|---|---|---|
| 1 | | 60 | 120 |
| 2 | | $y$ | 120 |
| 3 | | 160 | 120 |
| Total | | | 360 |

Fill in the times by dividing distance by speed:

| Leg | Time | Speed | Distance |
|---|---|---|---|
| 1 | 2 | 60 | 120 |
| 2 | $\frac{120}{y}$ | $y$ | 120 |
| 3 | $\frac{3}{4}$ | 160 | 120 |
| Total | $2\frac{3}{4} + \frac{120}{y}$ | | 360 |

So, either the average speed or the total actual time of the journey would be sufficient to calculate the value of $y$.

The information in Statement (1) can be used to set up the equation $2 = \frac{120}{y} + 1$, which can be solved for $y$, so it is sufficient. In terms of 12TEN, eliminate 2, T, and N.

Use the overall average speed in Statement (2) to set up an equation for the total journey:
$360 = 96\left(2\frac{3}{4} + \frac{120}{y}\right)$. This equation can be solved for $y$, so Statement (2) is sufficient. **(D)** is correct.

This question tests your knowledge of multi-stage rate problems (Chapter 6: Formulas, Statistics, and Data Analysis).

**10. C**

This Value question asks for the sum of an arithmetic sequence of numbers. In an arithmetic sequence, the values are evenly spaced. The sum of the values of an arithmetic sequence can be calculated if you know the spacing between the values, the number of values, and a specific value along with its position in the sequence.

Statement (1) states that the greatest number in the sequence is 62. However, you are still lacking the spacing of the values. For instance, if the sequence is consecutive integers, there would be 61 values, but if the sequence is even numbers, there would be 31 values. Statement (1) is insufficient. In terms of 12TEN, eliminate 1 and E.

Statement (2) provides the number of values but not the greatest value or the spacing, so Statement (2) is also insufficient. Eliminate 2 and evaluate the statements together.

Combining the statements, there are 31 evenly spaced values from 2 to 62. Thus, together, the statements are sufficient to calculate the sum of the numbers in this arithmetic sequence. **(C)** is correct.

This question tests your knowledge of sequences (Chapter 5: Algebra).

**11. A**

This Value question gives the coordinates of two vertices of a triangle in the $xy$-plane and the $y$-coordinate of the third vertex and asks for the area of the triangle. Because the $x$-coordinates of points $A$ and $B$ are the same, $AB$ is a vertical line with length $5 - 2 = 3$. Similarly, having the same $y$-coordinates means that $AC$ is a horizontal line, with length $|x - 2|$. Thus, triangle $ABC$ is a right triangle, and knowing the lengths of $AB$ and $AC$ will be sufficient to calculate the area of triangle $ABC$. Determining the value of $x$ will enable you to get the length of $AC$.

Statement (1) is a quadratic, so you may be tempted to say that having two solutions means that it is insufficient. However, you should evaluate $x$ to be certain. The rearranged equation $x^2 - 4x - 12 = 0$ factors to $(x - 6)(x + 2) = 0$, so $x$ can be either 6 or $-2$. Since the $x$-coordinate of $A$ is 2, either value means that the length of $AC$ is 4. Statement (1) is sufficient. In terms of 12TEN, eliminate 2, T, and N.

Statement (2) states that $|x| = 6$. Thus, $x$ could be either 6 or $-6$. These values result in different lengths for $AC$, so Statement (2) is insufficient. **(A)** is correct.

This question tests your knowledge of coordinate geometry and quadratic equations (Chapter 5: Algebra).

**12. E**

This Yes/No question asks whether the profits of a company were greater than $1 million dollars in a certain year. Since the question stem provides only percent increases from year to year, you'll need a baseline number to find the answer to the question.

From Statement (1), calculate that the profits in year 2 were greater than 1.1 times $825,000, which is $907,500. A further 10% increase in year 3 means that profits that year were greater than $907,500 + $90,750 = $998,250. Thus, the profits in year 3 may or may not have been greater than $1,000,000. Statement (1) is insufficient. In terms of 12TEN, eliminate 1 and E.

Statement (2) tells you the "year 0" profit, but not the change from that year to year 1. So, Statement (2) is also insufficient. Eliminate 2 and proceed to evaluate the statements together.

Combining the statements, the information in Statement (2) adds nothing meaningful to the calculations derived from Statement (1). Even taken together, the statements are insufficient. **(E)** is correct.

This question tests your knowledge of percents (Chapter 4: Arithmetic and Number Properties).

**13. C**

This Value question offers nothing to analyze or simplify.

Clear the fractions in Statement (1) by using a common denominator:

$\frac{4\times3\times1}{4\times3\times7}+\frac{7\times3\times1}{7\times3\times4}+\frac{7\times4\times x}{7\times4\times3}<\frac{7\times13}{7\times12}$. This simplifies to $\frac{12}{84}+\frac{21}{84}+\frac{28x}{84}=\frac{33+28x}{84}<\frac{91}{84}$.
So, $33 + 28x < 91$, or $28x < 58$. Since $x$ is a positive integer, $x$ can be either 1 or 2. Statement (1) is insufficient. In terms of 12TEN, eliminate 1 and E.

From Statement (2), deduce that $x$ must be at least 2 so that $0.15x$ is greater than 0.25. However, the maximum value of $x$ is 3, since $0.15(3) = 0.45$, but $0.15(4) = 0.52$, which is greater than 0.50. Since both 2 and 3 are permissible values for $x$, Statement (2) is also insufficient. Eliminate 2 and evaluate the statements together.

Combining the statements, the only permissible value of $x$ that is a solution for both statements is 2. Therefore, taken together, the statements are sufficient. **(C)** is correct.

This question tests your knowledge of isolating a variable (Chapter 5: Algebra) and working with fractions (Chapter 4: Arithmetic and Number Properties).

**14. B**

There is nothing to simplify in the stem of this Value question. Use the rules of exponents to evaluate the statements.

Statement (1) simplifies to $x^{a-b} = x^2$, which means that $a - b = 2$. There are a lot of values of $a$ and $b$ that satisfy this equation, so this isn't sufficient to tell you what $\frac{a}{b}$ equals. In terms of 12TEN, eliminate 1 and E.

For Statement (2), remember the rules of fractional exponents: $16^{\frac{a}{b}} = \sqrt[b]{16^a}$. The statement tells you that this equals 4. Since 4 is the square root of 16, then $\frac{a}{b}$ must be equal to $\frac{1}{2}$. Thus, Statement (2) is sufficient. **(B)** is correct.

This question tests your knowledge of exponents (Chapter 4: Arithmetic and Number Properties).

**15. C**

This Value question asks for the perimeter of a rectangle. To find that, you need the length and the width. Statement (1) provides neither, only the length of a diagonal. If *ABCD* were a square, that would be sufficient, but you need more information for a rectangle. Statement (1) is insufficient. In terms of 12TEN, eliminate 1 and E.

Statement (2) gives the measure of $\angle BDA$. This is also insufficient, since it tells you nothing about the lengths of the rectangle's sides. Eliminate 2 and evaluate the statements together.

Putting both statements together, knowing the length of one side of a 30-60-90 triangle enables you to calculate the lengths of all the sides, because the sides are in the ratio $x{:}x\sqrt{3}{:}2x$. Thus, when combined, the statements are sufficient. **(C)** is correct.

This question tests your knowledge of triangles and quadrilaterals (Chapter 7: Geometry).

PART TWO

# Math Content Practice and Review

CHAPTER 4

# Arithmetic and Number Properties

**LEARNING OBJECTIVES**

After studying this chapter, you will be able to:

- Describe which topics in arithmetic and number properties are tested on the GMAT
- Identify questions that involve arithmetic and number properties concepts
- Apply the Kaplan Methods for Problem Solving and Data Sufficiency to questions testing a variety of arithmetic and number properties concepts

Many of the Quantitative questions you will see on the GMAT involve arithmetic and number properties. These are the building blocks of the math you will need to know in order to perform well on Test Day. Specifically, the GMAT will test your understanding of:

- Arithmetic terms and standard math symbols
- Order of operations
- Properties of addition, subtraction, multiplication, and division
- Properties of even and odd numbers
- Properties of positive and negative numbers
- Absolute value
- Factors, multiples, and remainders
- Exponents and roots
- Fractions, decimals, and percents
- Ratios

In this chapter, you will first see a set of drills that covers the concepts listed above. Work through the drills and then check your performance. Review the explanation of each question to see the steps taken to arrive at the correct answer.

As you review, assess your current ability. If you find that you struggled with certain drills and would like to refresh your understanding of the concepts tested, check out the Arithmetic and Number Properties section of Chapter 9: Math Reference before tackling the practice set at the end of this chapter.

If you instead feel comfortable with your performance on the drills and confident in your abilities, then proceed directly to the practice set of GMAT-style questions. You will see both Problem Solving and Data Sufficiency questions. Apply your knowledge of arithmetic and number properties to these questions and tackle them strategically, using the step-by-step approach outlined in the Kaplan Methods.

When you finish the practice set, fully review every question by reading through its explanation—even for the questions that you answered correctly. In any question where the explanation discusses concepts unfamiliar to you, use the Math Reference chapter to further your understanding.

## Arithmetic and Number Properties Drills

Try these drills to test your proficiency with arithmetic and number properties. Use the answer key and explanations at the end of the chapter to check your work.

1. $7+5\times\left(\frac{1}{4}\right)^2-6\div(2-3)=$

2. Is the following expression even or odd: $42 \times 21 \times 69$?

3. $(-3)\times 4\times\left(-\frac{1}{6}\right)\times\left(-\frac{1}{12}\right)\times 16=$

4. What are the first five prime numbers greater than 50?

5. $|6+(-3)|-|3+(-6)|=$

6. $\left|-\left(\frac{1}{4}\right)^2\right|=$

7. What is the prime factorization of 162?

8. What is the smallest positive integer divisible by both 18 and 7?

9. What is the greatest number less than 153 that is divisible by 3 and 7?

10. $(2^2)^4=$

11. $(2^5)\left(\frac{1}{2^6}\right)=$

12. $\sqrt{5}+\sqrt{125}=$

13. Restate the following expression as an integer: $\sqrt{2}\sqrt{50}$.

14. $\frac{1}{2}\left(\frac{1}{3}+\frac{1}{4}\right)=$

15. $1.69\times 0.002=$

16. Simplify $\frac{3}{5}\times\frac{3}{8}\times\frac{2}{3}$.

17. Simplify the complex fraction $\dfrac{\frac{4}{5}+\frac{1}{3}}{\frac{5}{6}-\frac{2}{5}}$.

18. 75% of 16 =

19. What percent of 40 is 22?

20. Of 25 students in a class, 15 have completed their assignments. What percent of students in the class have not completed their assignments?

21. The price of a car accessory that originally cost $80 was discounted by 25%. What is the discounted price of the car accessory?

22. If the ratio of the number of public health experts to the number of business leaders on a committee of 25 members is 2:3, and no committee member is both a public health expert and a business leader, how many members of the committee are business leaders?

23. At a certain school, every student takes either violin lessons or flute lessons but not both. If the ratio of violinists to flutists in a class is 4:3 and there are 24 violinists, how many flutists are in the class?

24. A punch recipe calls for 3 pints of ginger ale for every 2 quarts of juice. How many pints of ginger ale will be needed to mix with 10 quarts of juice?

25. The ratio of Anna's age to Emma's age is 3:5, and the ratio of Emma's age to Nicholas's age is 3:5. What is the ratio of Anna's age to Nicholas's age?

Once you've completed these drills, check your performance by reviewing the answers and explanations at the end of this chapter. If you feel confident in your skill with arithmetic and number properties, try the GMAT-style questions in the next practice set. If you want a refresher, check out the Arithmetic and Number Properties section in the Math Reference chapter at the end of the book.

# Arithmetic and Number Properties Practice Set

Try the following questions, using the Kaplan Method for Problem Solving and looking for opportunities to use picking numbers and backsolving. Answers and explanations are at the end of this chapter.

1. What is the value of $\left(3\sqrt{3}\right)\left(\sqrt{15}\right)+\sqrt{5}$?

   - O $10\sqrt{5}$
   - O $5\sqrt{23}$
   - O $9\sqrt{10}$
   - O $10\sqrt{10}$
   - O 45

2. $\dfrac{(0.02)(0.0003)}{0.002}=$

   - O 0.3
   - O 0.03
   - O 0.003
   - O 0.0003
   - O 0.00003

3. $\dfrac{\frac{1}{6}+\frac{1}{3}+2}{\frac{3}{4}+\frac{5}{4}+3}=$

   - O $\frac{1}{3}$
   - O $\frac{1}{2}$
   - O $\frac{5}{8}$
   - O $\frac{2}{3}$
   - O 1

4. How many odd integers are between $\frac{10}{3}$ and $\frac{62}{3}$?

   - O 19
   - O 18
   - O 10
   - O 9
   - O 8

5. If $n$ is an odd number, which of the following must be even?

   - O $\frac{n-1}{2}$
   - O $\frac{n+1}{2}$
   - O $n^2+2n$
   - O $2n+2$
   - O $3n^2-2n$

6. For how many positive integers $x$ is $\frac{130}{x}$ an integer?

   - O Eight
   - O Seven
   - O Six
   - O Five
   - O Three

7. The sum of three consecutive integers is 312. What is the sum of the next three consecutive integers?

- 315
- 321
- 330
- 415
- 424

8. On a certain street map, $\frac{3}{4}$ inch represents 1 mile. What distance, in miles, is represented by $1\frac{3}{4}$ inches?

- $1\frac{1}{2}$
- $1\frac{3}{4}$
- $2\frac{1}{3}$
- $2\frac{1}{2}$
- $5\frac{1}{4}$

9. An alloy of tin and copper uses 6 pounds of copper for every 2 pounds of tin. If 200 pounds of this alloy are made, how many pounds of tin are required?

- 25
- 50
- 100
- 125
- 150

10. During October, a store had sales of $30,000. If this was a 20 percent increase over the September sales, what were the September sales?

- $22,500
- $24,000
- $25,000
- $27,000
- $28,000

11. The population of a certain town increases by 50 percent every 50 years. If the population in 1950 was 810, in what year was the population 160?

- 1650
- 1700
- 1750
- 1800
- 1850

12. $\frac{4^3 - 4^2}{2^2} =$

- 1
- 2
- 4
- 12
- 16

13. If $27^n = 9^4$, then $n =$

- $\frac{4}{3}$
- 2
- $\frac{8}{3}$
- 3
- 8

14. At a certain high school, $\frac{2}{3}$ of the students play on sports teams. Of the students who play sports, $\frac{1}{4}$ play on the football team. If there are a total of 240 students in the high school, how many students play on the football team?

- O 180
- O 160
- O 80
- O 60
- O 40

15. A class of 40 students is to be divided into smaller groups. If each group is to contain 3, 4, or 5 people, what is the largest number of groups possible?

- O 8
- O 10
- O 12
- O 13
- O 14

16. If an item costs $800 after a 20 percent discount, what was the amount of the discount?

- O $200
- O $160
- O $120
- O $80
- O $20

17. On a scaled map, a distance of 10 centimeters represents 5 kilometers. If a street is 750 meters long, what is its length on the map, in centimeters? (1 kilometer = 1,000 meters)

- O 0.015
- O 0.15
- O 1.5
- O 15
- O 150

Try the following questions, using the Kaplan Method for Data Sufficiency and looking for opportunities to pick numbers, solve without algebra, and guess strategically. Answers and explanations are at the end of this chapter.

*Note:* Because the Data Sufficiency answer choices are always the same and should be memorized, we have omitted them here. If you need a refresher on the choices or the 12TEN mnemonic, review Chapter 3 on Data Sufficiency.

18. What is the selling price of a radio after its original price is reduced by 20 percent?

(1) The price before the reduction was $120.

(2) The price after the reduction is $24 less than the price before the reduction.

19. Is 6 a factor of $n + 3$?

(1) $n$ is even and divisible by 3.

(2) $n$ is divisible by 6.

20. If 60 percent of the employees at Company X are in sales, does Company X have more than 100 sales employees?

(1) Company X has more than 150 employees.

(2) Company X has 74 more sales employees than non-sales employees.

21. Five years ago at Laboratory B, the ratio of doctorate to nondoctorate researchers was 2:3. If no researchers have resigned or earned their doctorates, what is the current ratio?

    (1) In the last 5 years, 50 percent more nondoctorates than doctorates have been hired.

    (2) Fifty doctorates were hired during the last 5 years.

22. Is the sum of five consecutive integers odd?

    (1) The first number is odd.

    (2) The average (arithmetic mean) of the five numbers is odd.

23. If $x$ and $y$ are positive integers, is $xy$ evenly divisible by 4?

    (1) $y + 2$ is divisible by 4.

    (2) $x - 2$ is divisible by 4.

24. A certain bread recipe calls for whole wheat flour, white flour, and oat flour in the ratio of 3:2:1, respectively. How many cups of oat flour are needed to make a loaf of bread?

    (1) A total of 30 cups of whole wheat and white flour are needed to make 3 loaves of bread.

    (2) Two more cups of whole wheat flour than white flour are needed for every loaf.

25. If Company Y's profits decreased $1.5 million from last year to this year, what was the percent decrease in profits?

    (1) If the profits had decreased by $2 million, there would have been a 40 percent decrease.

    (2) This year's profits were $3.5 million.

## Answer Key

### Arithmetic and Number Properties Drills

1. $13\frac{5}{16}$
2. Even
3. $-\frac{8}{3}$
4. 53, 59, 61, 67, 71
5. 0
6. $\frac{1}{16}$
7. $2 \times 3 \times 3 \times 3 \times 3$
8. 126
9. 147
10. $2^8$
11. $\frac{1}{2}$
12. $6\sqrt{5}$
13. 10
14. $\frac{7}{24}$
15. 0.00338
16. $\frac{3}{20}$
17. $\frac{34}{13}$
18. 12
19. 55%
20. 40%
21. $60
22. 15
23. 18
24. 15
25. 9:25

### Arithmetic and Number Properties Practice Set

1. A
2. C
3. B
4. E
5. D
6. A
7. B
8. C
9. B
10. C
11. C
12. D
13. C
14. E
15. D
16. A
17. C
18. D
19. D
20. B
21. A
22. D
23. C
24. D
25. D

# Answers and Explanations

## Arithmetic and Number Properties Drills

**1.** Parentheses $7+5\times\left(\frac{1}{4}\right)^2-6\div(-1)=$

Exponents $7+5\left(\frac{1}{16}\right)-6\div(-1)=$

Multiply/Divide $7+\frac{5}{16}-(-6)=$

Add/Subtract $7+\frac{5}{16}+6=\mathbf{13\frac{5}{16}}$

**2.** The product of an even number and either an even or odd number is an even number. Since 42 is even, the product of the three numbers is **even**.

**3.** First, simplify by cancellation: $\cancel{(-3)\times(4)}^{-1}\times\left(-\frac{1}{\cancel{6}^{3}}\right)\times\left(-\frac{1}{\cancel{12}^{1}}\right)\times\cancel{16}^{8}$

Multiply all the terms. The result will be negative because an odd number (3) of the terms are negative: $-1\times\left(-\frac{1}{3}\right)\times(-1)\times 8=-\mathbf{\frac{8}{3}}$.

**4.** You don't need to check even numbers greater than 2, so start with 51 and check the increasing odd numbers for factors:

| Number | Result |
|---|---|
| 51, 57, 63, 69 | Sum of digits divisible by 3, so divisible by 3 |
| 55, 65 | End in 5, so divisible by 5 |
| **53, 59, 61, 67, 71** | Not divisible by 7, 11, or 13—prime |

**5.** $|6+(-3)|-|3+(-6)|=|3|-|-3|=3-3=\mathbf{0}$

**6.** $\left|-\left(\frac{1}{4}\right)^2\right|=\left|-\left(\frac{1}{4}\right)\left(\frac{1}{4}\right)\right|=\left|-\frac{1}{16}\right|=\mathbf{\frac{1}{16}}$

**7.** 162 = 81 × 2 and 81 = 3 × 3 × 3 × 3. Therefore, the prime factorization of 162 is **2 × 3 × 3 × 3 × 3**.

**8.** 18 = 2 × 3 × 3. This has no common factors with 7, so the smallest positive integer divisible by both 7 and 18 is 7 × 18 = **126**.

**9.** A number that is divisible by both 3 and 7 is divisible by 3 × 7 = 21. If you divide 153 by 21, you get 7 with a remainder. Therefore, the largest multiple of 21 that is less than 153 is 21 × 7 = **147**.

**10.** $\left(2^2\right)^4 = 2^{2\times 4} = \mathbf{2^8}$

**11.** $\left(2^5\right)\left(\frac{1}{2^6}\right) = \frac{2^5}{2^6} = 2^{5-6} = 2^{-1} = \mathbf{\frac{1}{2}}$

**12.** $\sqrt{5} + \sqrt{125} = \sqrt{5} + \sqrt{25\times 5} = \sqrt{5} + \sqrt{25}\sqrt{5} = \sqrt{5} + 5\sqrt{5} = \mathbf{6\sqrt{5}}$

**13.** $\sqrt{2}\sqrt{50} = \sqrt{2\times 50} = \sqrt{100} = \mathbf{10}$

**14.**

$$\frac{1}{2}\left(\frac{1}{3} + \frac{1}{4}\right) =$$

$$\frac{1}{2}\left(\frac{4}{4}\left(\frac{1}{3}\right) + \frac{3}{3}\left(\frac{1}{4}\right)\right) =$$

$$\frac{1}{2}\left(\frac{4}{12} + \frac{3}{12}\right) =$$

$$\frac{1}{2}\left(\frac{7}{12}\right) = \mathbf{\frac{7}{24}}$$

**15.** $1.69\times 0.002 = 1.69\times\left(2\times 10^{-3}\right) = 3.38\times 10^{-3} = \mathbf{0.00338}$

**16.** $\frac{3}{5}\times\frac{{}^{1}\cancel{3}}{{}_{4}\cancel{8}}\times\frac{\cancel{2}^{1}}{\cancel{3}_{1}} = \mathbf{\frac{3}{20}}$

**17.** $\dfrac{\frac{3}{3}\left(\frac{4}{5}\right) + \frac{5}{5}\left(\frac{1}{3}\right)}{\frac{5}{5}\left(\frac{5}{6}\right) - \frac{6}{6}\left(\frac{2}{5}\right)} = \dfrac{\frac{12}{15} + \frac{5}{15}}{\frac{25}{30} - \frac{12}{30}} = \dfrac{\frac{17}{15}}{\frac{13}{30}}$

Invert the fraction in the denominator and multiply:

$$\frac{17}{\cancel{15}^{1}}\times\frac{\cancel{30}^{2}}{13} = \frac{17\times 2}{1\times 13} = \mathbf{\frac{34}{13}}$$

**18.** $0.75\times 16 = 12$ or $\frac{3}{4}\times 16 = \mathbf{12}$

**19.** $\frac{22}{40}\times 100\% = \mathbf{55\%}$

**20.** First find the number of students who have not completed their assignments: 25 − 15 = 10. The percent who have not completed their assignments is 10 ÷ 25 = 0.4 = **40%**.

**21.** The discount = 0.25 × \$80 = \$20. The new price is \$80 − \$20 = **\$60**.

Alternatively, the new price = (1.00 − 0.25) × \$80 = (0.75) × \$80 = **\$60**.

**22.** In the ratio, the number of health experts is represented by 2 and the number of business leaders by 3; the total can be represented as 2 + 3 = 5. Therefore, the ratio of business leaders to total members is $\frac{3}{2+3} = \frac{3}{5}$. Find the number of business leaders: $\frac{3}{5}(25) = \mathbf{15}$.

**23.** $\frac{4}{3} = \frac{24}{x}$

$4x = 72$

$x = \mathbf{18}$

**24.** $\frac{\text{3 pints ginger ale}}{\text{2 quarts juice}} = \frac{x \text{ pints ginger ale}}{\text{10 quarts juice}}$

$\frac{3}{2} = \frac{x}{10}$

$2x = 30$

$x = \mathbf{15}$

**25.** Emma's age is part of both ratios. Multiply the ratios so that Emma's age is represented by the same number in each.

$\frac{\text{Anna}}{\text{Emma}} = \frac{3}{5}\left(\frac{3}{3}\right) = \frac{9}{15}$

$\frac{\text{Emma}}{\text{Nicholas}} = \frac{3}{5}\left(\frac{5}{5}\right) = \frac{15}{25}$

Anna:Emma:Nicholas = 9:15:25. Thus, the ratio of Anna's age to Nicholas's age is **9:25**.

Alternatively, multiply the ratios so the terms you're not interested in cancel out.

$\frac{\text{Anna}}{\text{Emma}} \times \frac{\text{Emma}}{\text{Nicholas}} = \frac{\text{Anna}}{\text{Nicholas}}$

So, $\frac{3}{5} \times \frac{3}{5} = \mathbf{\frac{9}{25}}$.

## Arithmetic and Number Properties Practice Set

**1. A**

Follow the order of operations (i.e., PEMDAS) and then combine like terms:

$$\begin{aligned}\left(3\sqrt{3}\right)\left(\sqrt{15}\right)+\sqrt{5} &= \\ 3\sqrt{45}+\sqrt{5} &= \\ 3\left(\sqrt{9}\right)\left(\sqrt{5}\right)+\sqrt{5} &= \\ 3(3)\left(\sqrt{5}\right)+\sqrt{5} &= \\ 9\sqrt{5}+\sqrt{5} &= \mathbf{10\sqrt{5}}\end{aligned}$$

**2. C**

Start with the numerator. Ignore the decimals and multiply the numbers as if they were whole numbers. Then count the total number of places to the right of the decimal point in both numbers and move the decimal point that many places to the left in the result.

$$\begin{aligned}&(0.02)\times(0.0003)\\ &2\times 3=6\\ &0.02 \qquad 0.0003\\ &2\text{ places}+4\text{ places}=6\text{ places}\\ &\text{so }(0.02)\times(0.0003)=0.000006\end{aligned}$$

To divide two decimals, move the decimal point in both numbers as many places to the right as necessary to make the number you're dividing by a whole number. Then divide:

$$\frac{0.000006}{0.002}=\frac{0.006}{2}=\mathbf{0.003}$$

An alternative way of solving this is to cancel a factor of 0.002 from the numerator and denominator. Since 0.02 is 10 times 0.002, rewrite the problem as 10 times 0.0003. Multiplying a decimal by 10 is the same as moving the decimal point one place to the right, so the result is **0.003**.

**3. B**

Multiply the numerator and denominator by the least common multiple of all the denominators in the fractions, 12:

$$\frac{12\left(\frac{1}{6}+\frac{1}{3}+2\right)}{12\left(\frac{3}{4}+\frac{5}{4}+3\right)}=\frac{2+4+24}{9+15+36}=\frac{30}{60}=\mathbf{\frac{1}{2}}$$

**4. E**

The fraction $\frac{10}{3}$ is the same as $3\frac{1}{3}$, and $\frac{62}{3}$ is the same as $20\frac{2}{3}$. The least odd integer greater than $3\frac{1}{3}$ is 5, and the greatest odd integer less than $20\frac{2}{3}$ is 19, so the odd integers in the specified range are 5, 7, 9, 11, 13, 15, 17, and 19. That's a total of **8**.

**5. D**

The simplest approach here is to pick an odd value for $n$, such as 3. Then try that value in each choice, eliminating those that are odd.

For (A), that is $\frac{3-1}{2} = \frac{2}{2} = 1$. Eliminate (A).

For (B), that is $\frac{3+1}{2} = \frac{4}{2} = 2$, which is even. Keep (B) for now.

Plug 3 into (C) to get $3^2 + 2(3) = 9 + 6 = 15$. Eliminate (C).

Plugging 3 into (D) yields $2(3) + 2 = 6 + 2 = 8$. Keep (D).

Finally, (E) is $3(3)^2 - 2(3) = 27 - 6 = 21$. Eliminate (E).

Since there are still two possible correct choices, try another value, such as 1. For (B), $\frac{1+1}{2} = \frac{2}{2} = 1$. This is odd, so **(D)** is correct.

**6. A**

The factor pairs for 130 are $1 \times 130$, $2 \times 65$, $5 \times 26$, and $10 \times 13$. Since there are no duplicates, there are **eight** different integers for which $\frac{130}{x}$ is an integer. You may have been tempted to use prime factors, but that would have involved finding not only the three prime factors of 130 (2, 5, and 13) but also all their combinations and remembering to include 1 and 130 as factors, too.

**7. B**

Call the three original integers $x$, $x + 1$, and $x + 2$. Their sum is 312, so $x + (x + 1) + (x + 2) = 312$ or $3x + 3 = 312$. The next three integers are $x + 3$, $x + 4$, and $x + 5$, which sum to $3x + 12$, which is 9 greater than $3x + 3$. So, $3x + 12 = 312 + 9$, or **321**.

**8. C**

Since $1\frac{3}{4} = \frac{7}{4}$, you can set up and solve a proportion with $x$ as the number of miles:

$$\frac{\frac{7}{4}}{x} = \frac{\frac{3}{4}}{1}$$

$$\frac{\frac{7}{4}}{x} = \frac{3}{4}$$

$$4\left(\frac{7}{4}\right) = 3x$$

$$7 = 3x$$

$$\frac{7}{3} = x$$

This is equivalent to $\mathbf{2\frac{1}{3}}$.

**9. B**

Every 8 pounds of the alloy has 6 pounds of copper and 2 pounds of tin. Therefore, $\frac{2}{8}$ or $\frac{1}{4}$ of the alloy is tin. To make 200 pounds of the alloy would require $\frac{1}{4} \times 200$, or **50** pounds of tin.

**10. C**

Set up an equation with $S$ as the September sales: $\left(1 + \frac{20}{100}\right)S = \$30{,}000$. So, $S = \frac{\$30{,}000}{1.2} = \mathbf{\$25{,}000}$.

**11. C**

Since the population increases by 50% every 50 years, the population in 1950 was 150%, or $\frac{3}{2}$ of the 1900 population. This means the 1900 population was $\frac{2}{3}$ of the 1950 population. Similarly, the 1850 population was $\frac{2}{3}$ of the 1900 population, and so on. Keep multiplying by $\frac{2}{3}$ until you get to a population of 160.

$$1950\text{: } 810 \times \frac{2}{3} = 540 \text{ in } 1900$$

$$1900\text{: } 540 \times \frac{2}{3} = 360 \text{ in } 1850$$

$$1850\text{: } 360 \times \frac{2}{3} = 240 \text{ in } 1800$$

$$1800\text{: } 240 \times \frac{2}{3} = 160 \text{ in } 1750$$

The population was 160 in **1750**.

**12. D**

To divide numbers with exponents, the numbers must have the same base. Since $2^2 = 4$, the simplest conversion is to restate the fraction as $\frac{4^3 - 4^2}{4^1}$. When dividing numbers with the same base, subtract the exponent of the denominator. Thus, the fraction becomes $4^{(3-1)} - 4^{(2-1)} = 4^2 - 4 = 16 - 4 = \mathbf{12}$.

Alternatively, since the calculations required aren't too tricky, you could just simplify following the order of operations.

$$\frac{4^3 - 4^2}{2^2} = \frac{64 - 16}{4} = \frac{48}{4} = \mathbf{12}$$

**13. C**

The simplest approach is to express both 9 and 27 with a common base. The most convenient base is 3, since $3^2 = 9$ and $3^3 = 27$. Then the equation becomes:

$$27^n = 9^4$$

$$\left(3^3\right)^n = \left(3^2\right)^4$$

$$3^{3 \cdot n} = 3^{2 \cdot 4}$$

$$3^{3n} = 3^8$$

If two terms with the same base are equal, the exponents must be equal. So, $3n = 8$ and $n = \mathbf{\frac{8}{3}}$.

**14. E**

Find the number of students who play on any sports team, then multiply by $\frac{1}{4}$ to find the number of students who play football. Of the 240 students, $\frac{2}{3}$ play some sport, or $\frac{2}{3} \times 240 = 160$ students. Then of these, $\frac{1}{4}$ play football; that equals $\frac{1}{4} \times 160$ or **40** students.

**15. D**

The maximum number of groups is obtained by making each group as small as possible. Each group must have at least 3 people and $3 \times 13 = 39$, so there can be 13 groups of 3 with 1 person left over. Put that extra person with one of the other groups. This yields 12 groups with 3 students each and 1 group with 4 students, for a total of **13** groups.

**16. A**

Set $p$ as the original price and write the equation $\left(1.00 - \frac{20}{100}\right)p = 800$. So, $0.8p = 800$ and $p = 1{,}000$. The amount of the discount is \$1,000 − \$800 = **\$200**.

**17. C**

A kilometer is 1,000 meters, so 5 kilometers is 5,000 meters. Set up a proportion, with $x$ representing the length of the street on the map: $\frac{x}{10} = \frac{750}{5{,}000}$. Cross multiply to get $5{,}000x = 7{,}500$. Dividing by 5,000 yields $x =$ **1.5**.

**18. D**

This is a Value question. To find the selling price after a 20% reduction, you need either the amount of the reduction or the original price.

Statement (1) provides the original price; this is sufficient. Eliminate (B), (C), and (E).

Statement (2) provides the amount of the reduction. Statement (2) is also sufficient. **(D)** is correct.

**19. D**

This is a Yes/No question, so you don't need to know the value of $n$, just whether $n + 3$ is divisible by 6. For $n + 3$ to be divisible by 6, it must be divisible by both the prime factors of 6, which are 3 and 2.

Statement (1) says that $n$ is even and divisible by 3. This means that $n + 3$ is odd. No odd number is divisible by 2, so Statement (1) is sufficient to answer no to the question. Eliminate (B), (C), and (E).

Statement (2) states that $n$ is divisible by 6, which means that it is even. Therefore, $n + 3$ is odd. The answer again is no. Statement (2) is also sufficient. **(D)** is correct.

**20. B**

This is a Yes/No question, so you don't need to be able to determine the exact number of sales employees. To determine whether there are more than 100 sales employees, information about either the total number of employees or the number of non-sales employees would enable you to calculate the number of females.

Statement (1) says that there are more than 150 total employees. If there were 155 employees, then 60% of that would be 93, so the answer would be no. However, if there were 200 total employees, 60% of that would be 120 and the answer would be yes. Statement (1) is insufficient. Eliminate (A) and (D).

Statement (2) gives the difference between the number of sales and non-sales employees. Since 60% are sales and 40% are non-sales, the difference must be 20% of the total number of employees. Thus, you could calculate the total number of employees; this makes Statement (2) sufficient. **(B)** is correct.

**21. A**

This is a Value question, so there must be sufficient information to determine an exact value for the current ratio. That would require knowing the current numbers of doctorates and nondoctorates and information about subsequent changes, or the present numbers of the two categories of researchers.

Statement (1) tells you that 50% more nondoctorates than doctorates were hired. Convert this to the ratio of 1 to 1.5 doctorates to nondoctorates. When doubled to get whole numbers, the ratio becomes 2:3, which is the same as the current ratio. Because no one left nor did any nondoctorates become doctorates, the ratio stayed the same, 2:3. Statement (1) is sufficient. Eliminate (B), (C), and (E).

Statement (2) provides the number of doctorates hired. However, you still lack the number of nondoctorates hired and the beginning numbers. Statement (2) is insufficient. **(A)** is correct.

**22. D**

This is a Yes/No question, so you don't need to find the value of the sum of the integers, only whether or not the sum is odd. If the first number is odd, then the sum will be odd + even + odd + even + odd. The sum of 3 odd numbers and 2 even numbers is odd. Likewise, if the first is even, the sum will be even. Just knowing whether one of the numbers is odd or even and its place in the sequence is enough information to determine if the sum is odd or even.

Statement (1) states that the first term is odd. This is sufficient, so eliminate (B), (C), and (E).

Statement (2) says that the average is odd. For a sequence of consecutive integers, the median is the average. Therefore, the third number is odd, which means that the first number is also odd. This is sufficient. **(D)** is correct.

**23. C**

This Yes/No question only asks if $xy$ is divisible by 4, so you won't need to determine an exact value. A number divisible by 4 has prime factors of 2 and 2. Any other factors do not matter.

Statement (1) states that $y + 2$ is divisible by 4; this is the same as saying 4 is a factor of $y + 2$. Thus, $y$ is 2 less than a multiple of 4, which is an even number, and all even numbers have a factor of 2. If $x$ is also even, then the answer is yes, but if $x$ is odd, the answer is no. Therefore, Statement (1) is insufficient. Eliminate (A) and (D).

Statement (2) is similar: if $x - 2$ is divisible by 4, then $x$ itself is even, but it is not a multiple of 4. However, the statement provides no information about $y$. Statement (2) is insufficient. Eliminate (B) and proceed to evaluate the statements together.

Combining the statements, both $x$ and $y$ are even numbers; therefore, they each have 2 as a factor. Since $xy$ then has at least two prime factors of 2, it is divisible by 4. So, both statements together are sufficient. **(C)** is correct.

**24. D**

This Value question asks for a specific quantity of flour rather than a ratio. Since the stem provides a complete three-part ratio, knowing the total quantity made with the recipe or the quantity of any of the three ingredients would be sufficient information to calculate the amount of flour.

Statement (1) tells you the amount of two ingredients needed to make three loaves. From this, you could calculate the amount needed for one loaf, so Statement (1) is sufficient. Eliminate (B), (C), and (E).

Statement (2) gives you the difference between the amounts for two of the terms in the ratio; this, too, is sufficient to derive each of the individual terms in the ratio. Statement (2) is also sufficient. **(D)** is correct.

**25. D**

This Value question gives an amount and asks what percent that amount is of an unknown quantity, the prior year's profit. Knowing that quantity, or being able to compute it, would be sufficient.

Statement (1) says that if the profit had decreased by $2 million, that equates to a 40% decrease. You could set up a ratio to find the percentage decrease for $1.5 million, so Statement (1) is sufficient. Eliminate (B), (C), and (E).

Statement (2) tells you this year's profits, from which you can derive last year's profits. Statement (2) is sufficient. **(D)** is correct.

CHAPTER 5

# Algebra

**LEARNING OBJECTIVES**

After studying this chapter, you will be able to:

- Describe which topics in algebra are tested on the GMAT
- Identify questions that feature algebra
- Apply the Kaplan Methods for Problem Solving and Data Sufficiency to questions testing various algebra skills

Many questions on the GMAT test your ability to use algebraic rules to manipulate unknown terms, or variables. Solving for variables in equations and inequalities is a necessary skill on the GMAT, and mastering frequently tested algebra concepts is a fundamental building block for Test Day success. Here are some of the concepts and skills the GMAT will test:

- Algebraic terminology
- Combining like terms
- Isolating variables
- Inequalities
- Systems of equations
- Functions and symbolism
- Sequences
- Polynomials and quadratics
- Linear equations in the coordinate plane

In this chapter, you will first see a set of drills that covers the concepts listed above. Work through the drills and then check your performance. Review the explanation of each question to see the steps taken to arrive at the correct answer.

As you review, assess your current ability. If you find that you struggled with certain drills and would like to refresh your understanding of the concepts tested, check out the Algebra section of Chapter 9: Math Reference before tackling the practice set at the end of this chapter.

If you instead feel comfortable with your performance on the drills and confident in your abilities, then proceed directly to the practice set of GMAT-style questions. You will see both Problem Solving and Data Sufficiency questions. Apply your knowledge of arithmetic and number properties to these questions and tackle them strategically, using the step-by-step approach outlined in the Kaplan Methods.

When you finish the practice set, fully review every question by reading through its explanation—even for the questions that you answered correctly. In any question where the explanation discusses concepts unfamiliar to you, use the Math Reference chapter to further your understanding.

# Algebra Drills

Try these drills to test your proficiency with algebra. Use the answer key and explanations at the end of the chapter to check your work.

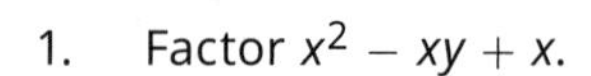

1. Factor $x^2 - xy + x$.

2. Simplify the expression $-4x + 5 - x + 9$.

3. Simplify $xyz\left(\frac{1}{xy} + \frac{1}{yz} + \frac{1}{xz}\right)$.

4. Solve for the value of $j$: $\frac{2}{3}j - \frac{1}{2} = \frac{1}{6}j + \frac{11}{2}$.

5. Isolate $b$: $A = \frac{1}{2}(a + b)h$.

6. Solve the following system of equations for the values of both variables:
   $2c = 14 + 4g$
   $3g = 2 - c$

7. Solve the following system of equations for the values of both variables:
   $4x + 3y = 10$
   $3x + 5y = 13$

8. Solve for $x$: $-\frac{1}{3}x > 5 - 2x$.

9. Solve for $x$: $\frac{3}{2}x - \frac{3}{4}x < \frac{7}{4}x - 1$.

10. Solve for $x$: $6 > x + 4 > 4$.

11. If $p \neq q$, simplify the expression $\frac{p^2 - q^2}{-5(q - p)}$.

12. Expand $(3x - 4)(2x + 5)$.

13. Factor $x^4 - 1$.

14. Solve for the roots of this equation:
    $3x^2 + 4x = x^2 + 5x + 3$.

15. $\left(\frac{zxy}{z}\right)\left(\frac{z^2y}{x}\right)\left(\frac{z}{y^2}\right) =$

16. What is the slope of the line that contains the points (3,6) and (−2,6)?

17. What is the slope of a line perpendicular to a line that contains the points (1,3) and (3,4)?

18. Does the point (−2,12) lie on the graph of $y = -2.5x + 7$?

19. 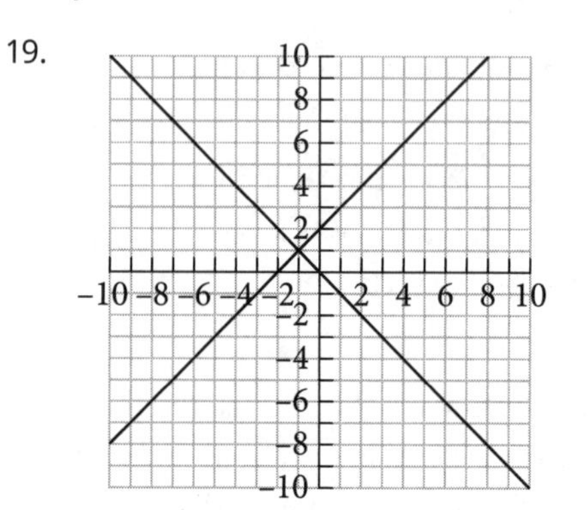


    What is the solution to the system shown on the coordinate plane above?

20. If $f(x) = cx^2 + 2$, where $c$ is a constant, and $f(-3) = 29$, what is the value of $c$?

21. What is $h(-4)$ if $h(x) = x^3 + 3x^2 + x$?

22.

| $x$ | 4 | 5 | 6 | −4 | −5 | −6 |
|---|---|---|---|---|---|---|
| $f(x)$ | 25 | 31 | 37 | −23 | −29 | −35 |

The above table shows the function $f(x)$ throughout its domain. Express the relationship between $x$ and $f(x)$ algebraically.

23. If $g(a) = a^2 - 1$ and $f(a) = a + 4$, what is $g(f(-4))$?

24. If, for all nonzero $p$ and $n$, $n \ast p = \frac{p}{2n}$, what is $7 \ast 28$?

25. If $m ❖ n$ is defined by the equation $m ❖ n = \frac{m^2 - n + 1}{mn}$ for all nonzero $m$ and $n$, then what is $3 ❖ 1$?

Once you've completed these drills, check your performance by reviewing the answers and explanations at the end of this chapter. If you feel confident in your algebra skills, try the realistic GMAT-style questions in the next practice set. If you want a refresher, check out the Algebra section in the Math Reference chapter at the end of the book.

# Algebra Practice Set

Try the following questions, using the Kaplan Method for Problem Solving and looking for opportunities to use picking numbers and backsolving. Answers and explanations are at the end of this chapter.

1. If $5a + 3b = 30$ and $b = 17 - 4a$, what is the value of $a + 2b$?

   - O 7
   - O 11
   - O 13
   - O 15
   - O 20

2. If $x^2 = 7x - 10$ and $x > 2$, what is the value of $x - 2$?

   - O −2
   - O 0
   - O 2
   - O 3
   - O 5

3. Given that $\#(x) = \frac{5x}{2} - 3$ and $@@(x) = 2x + 1$, if $\#(x) = @@(x)$, then $x =$

   - O −4
   - O 2
   - O 4
   - O 5
   - O 8

4. Marketing Service A charges \$3.00 for the first text message a customer sends each week and \$0.50 for each additional message. Marketing Service B charges \$2.00 for the first text message each week and \$0.70 for each additional message. If the cost of sending $x$ messages a week, where $x$ is a positive integer, is \$15.00 more with Marketing Service B than with Marketing Service A, what is the value of $x$?

   - O 56
   - O 60
   - O 77
   - O 80
   - O 81

5. Point $A$ (4,6) lies on a line with slope $-\frac{3}{4}$. Point $B$ lies on the same line and is 5 units from point $A$. Which of the following could be the coordinates of point $B$?

   - O (−1,1)
   - O (−4,12)
   - O (8,3)
   - O (1,10)
   - O (9,0)

6. Given that $\triangle a = 5 - a^2$ and $\Phi b = \frac{3}{b} + 2$, if $\Phi(\triangle x) = 5$, which of the following is a possible value of $x$?

   - O −20
   - O −5
   - O 2
   - O 5
   - O 7

7. If Juanita gives half of her rare stamps in a 1:2 ratio to Pat and Svetlana, respectively, then Pat will have one-fourth as many stamps as will Svetlana, who will in turn have twice as many stamps as will Juanita. If Pat currently has 2 stamps, then how many more stamps does Juanita currently have than Svetlana?

   - O 8
   - O 12
   - O 20
   - O 22
   - O 24

8. Between 1950 and 1960, the population of Country A increased by 3.5 million people. If the increase between 1960 and 1970 was 1.75 million more than the increase between 1950 and 1960, what was the total amount of increase in population of Country A between 1950 and 1970?

   - O 1.75 million
   - O 3.5 million
   - O 5.25 million
   - O 7 million
   - O 8.75 million

9. At Garage A, it costs \$8.75 to park a car for the first hour and \$1.25 for each additional hour. At Garage B, it costs \$5.50 for the first hour and \$2.50 for each additional hour. What is the difference between the cost of parking a car for 5 hours at Garage A and the cost of parking a car for 5 hours at Garage B?

   - O \$1.50
   - O \$1.75
   - O \$2.25
   - O \$2.75
   - O \$3.25

10. In a typical month, $\frac{1}{2}$ of the UFO sightings in the state are attributable to airplanes and $\frac{1}{3}$ of the remaining sightings are attributable to weather balloons. If there were 108 UFO sightings during one typical month, how many would be attributable to weather balloons?

    - O 18
    - O 24
    - O 36
    - O 54
    - O 72

11. Doris spent $\frac{2}{3}$ of her savings on a used car, and she spent $\frac{1}{4}$ of her remaining savings on a new carpet. If the carpet cost her \$250, how much were Doris's original savings?

    - O \$1,000
    - O \$1,200
    - O \$1,500
    - O \$2,000
    - O \$3,000

12. Gheri is *n* years old. Carl is 6 years younger than Gheri and 2 years older than Jean. What is the sum of the ages of all three?

    - O $3n + 16$
    - O $3n + 4$
    - O $3n - 4$
    - O $3n - 8$
    - O $3n - 14$

13. In a certain baseball league, each team plays 160 games. After playing half of their games, Team A has won 60 games and Team B has won 49 games. If Team A wins half of its remaining games, how many more games must Team B win to have the same record as Team A at the end of the season?

   - O 48
   - O 49
   - O 50
   - O 51
   - O 52

14. If a sequence of consecutive integers of increasing value has a sum of 63 and a first term of 6, how many integers are in the sequence?

   - O 11
   - O 10
   - O 9
   - O 8
   - O 7

15. A recent graduate earns $N$ dollars a month and spends $S$ dollars a month on rent. If this individual spends $\frac{3}{8}$ of the remaining money on food, how much, in dollars, is available to pay for other expenses, in terms of $N$ and $S$?

   - O $\frac{3}{8}(N-S)$
   - O $\frac{3}{8}(N+S)$
   - O $\frac{5}{8}(N-S)$
   - O $\frac{5}{8}(N+S)$
   - O $\frac{8}{3}(N-S)$

16. The kinetic energy $K$, in joules, provided by the mass of a particle $m$, in kilograms, with a velocity of $v$ meters per seconds, is given by the equation $K=\frac{1}{2}mv^2$. If a particle has a velocity of 4 meters per second and a kinetic energy of 144 joules, then what is the mass, in kilograms, of this particle?

   - O 16
   - O 18
   - O 24
   - O 44
   - O 64

17. A vault holds 8-ounce tablets of gold and 5-ounce tablets of silver. If there are 130 ounces of gold and silver in total, what is the greatest amount of gold that can be in the vault, in ounces?

   - O 40
   - O 80
   - O 120
   - O 128
   - O 130

Try the following questions using the Kaplan Method for Data Sufficiency and looking for opportunities to pick numbers, solve without algebra, and guess strategically. Answers and explanations are at the end of this chapter.

*Note:* Because the Data Sufficiency answer choices are always the same and should be memorized, we have omitted them here. If you need a refresher on the choices or the 12TEN mnemonic, review Chapter 3 on Data Sufficiency.

18. If $x$ is an integer, what is the value of $x$?

    (1) $14 < 2x < 18$

    (2) $5 < x < 10$

19. What is the value of the fraction $\frac{x}{y}$?

    (1) $x - y = 14$

    (2) $2x = 5y$

20. What is the price of 5 apples and 5 pears?

    (1) The cost of 2 apples and 10 pears is $0.90.

    (2) The cost of 2 apples and 2 pears is $0.50.

21. If $x$ and $y$ are positive integers such that $xy = 30$, what is the value of $x + y$?

    (1) $1 < \frac{x}{y} < 2$

    (2) $x > y$

22. Point *A*, with coordinates (1,2), point *B*, with coordinates (1,5), and point *C*, with coordinates ($x$,2) in the *xy*-plane, are connected to form triangle *ABC*. If $x > 1$, what is the value of $x$?

    (1) The area of triangle *ABC* is 6.

    (2) The length of the hypotenuse of triangle *ABC* is 5.

23. For all integers $n$, $n^* = n(n - 1)$. What is the value of $x^*$?

    (1) $x^* = x$

    (2) $(x - 1)^* = x - 2$

24. Both $x$ and $y$ are integers, and $x > y + 8 > 16$. What is the remainder when $x^2 - y^2$ is divided by 8?

    (1) The remainder when $x + y$ is divided by 8 is 7.

    (2) The remainder when $x - y$ is divided by 8 is 5.

25. If $s_n = s_{n-1} + a$, what is the value of $s_4$?

    (1) $a = 2$

    (2) $s_9 = 35$

Answers follow on the next page. ▶ ▶ ▶

# Answer Key

## Algebra Drills

1. $x(x - y + 1)$
2. $-5x + 14$
3. $z + x + y$
4. $j = 12$
5. $b = \frac{2A}{h} - a$ or $b = \frac{2A - ah}{h}$
6. $c = 5$ and $g = -1$
7. $x = 1$ and $y = 2$
8. $x > 3$
9. $x > 1$
10. $2 > x > 0$ or $0 < x < 2$
11. $\frac{p+q}{5}$
12. $6x^2 + 7x - 20$
13. $(x^2 + 1)(x + 1)(x - 1)$
14. $\frac{3}{2}, -1$
15. $z^3$
16. 0
17. $-2$
18. Yes
19. $(-1,1)$ or $x = -1, y = 1$
20. 3
21. $-20$
22. $f(x) = 6x + 1$
23. $-1$
24. 2
25. 3

## Algebra Practice Set

1. C
2. D
3. E
4. E
5. C
6. C
7. A
8. E
9. B
10. A
11. E
12. E
13. D
14. E
15. C
16. B
17. C
18. A
19. B
20. B
21. A
22. D
23. B
24. C
25. C

# Answers and Explanations

## Algebra Drills

**1.** Use the distributive property to factor $x$ from each term $x^2 - xy + x = \mathbf{x(x - y + 1)}$. You can check your work by multiplying the $x$ by each term in the parentheses, yielding the same expression you started with.

**2.** Combine like terms: $-4x - x = -5x$ and $5 + 9 = 14$. So $-4x + 5 - x + 9 = \mathbf{-5x + 14}$.

**3.** Distribute $xyz$ across the terms in parentheses. Then cancel common factors in the numerator and denominator of each fraction.

$$xyz\left(\frac{1}{xy} + \frac{1}{yz} + \frac{1}{xz}\right) = \frac{xyz}{xy} + \frac{xyz}{yz} + \frac{xyz}{xz} = \mathbf{z + x + y}$$

**4.** Begin by multiplying each expression by the least common denominator of all the fractions, which is 6.

$$6 \times \left(\frac{2}{3}j - \frac{1}{2}\right) = 6 \times \left(\frac{1}{6}j + \frac{11}{2}\right)$$
$$4j - 3 = j + 33$$
$$4j - j - 3 + 3 = j - j + 33 + 3$$
$$3j = 36$$
$$j = \mathbf{12}$$

**5.** Start by clearing the fraction by multiplying both sides of the equation by 2.

$$A = \frac{1}{2}(a + b)h$$
$$2 \times A = 2 \times \frac{1}{2}(a + b)h$$
$$2A = (a + b)h$$

Now divide both sides of the equation by $h$.

$$\frac{2A}{h} = \frac{(a + b)h}{h}$$
$$\frac{2A}{h} = a + b$$

Subtract from both sides to isolate $b$.

$$\frac{2A}{h} - a = a - a + b$$
$$\mathbf{\frac{2A}{h} - a} = b$$

This can also be written as

$$\mathbf{\frac{2A - ah}{h}}.$$

**6.** You could opt to use combination. Rearrange the second equation so that like terms are "stacked."

$$2c = 14 + 4g$$
$$c = 2 - 3g$$

Multiply the second equation by 2 so the $c$ terms have the same coefficient. Then subtract the second equation from the first, eliminating the $c$ terms.

$$\begin{array}{r} 2c = \ \ 14 + 4g \\ -[2c = \ \ \ 4 - 6g] \\ \hline 0 = 10 + 10g \end{array}$$

Then $10g = -10$ and $g = \mathbf{-1}$.

Now use $g = -1$ to solve for $c$.

$$2c = 14 + 4g$$
$$2c = 14 + 4(-1)$$
$$c = 7 + 2(-1)$$
$$c = \mathbf{5}$$

If you use substitution, you can begin by solving for $c$ in terms of $g$:

$$2c = 14 + 4g$$
$$\frac{2c}{2} = \frac{14 + 4g}{2}$$
$$c = 7 + 2g$$

Substitute $7 + 2g$ for $c$ in the second equation.

$$3g = 2 - c$$
$$3g = 2 - (7 + 2g)$$
$$3g = 2 - 7 - 2g$$
$$3g = -5 - 2g$$
$$3g + 2g = -5 - 2g + 2g$$
$$5g = -5$$
$$\frac{5g}{5} = \frac{-5}{5}$$
$$g = \mathbf{-1}$$

And, as above in the combination approach, plug in $-1$ for $g$ into either equation and solve for $c$, which is **5**.

**7.** The most efficient way to solve is with combination. Multiply to give the $x$ term the same coefficient. Then, subtract one equation from the other.

$$\begin{aligned} 3(4x+3y)=3(10) \rightarrow &\quad 12x+9y=30 \\ 4(3x+5y)=4(13) \rightarrow &\; -[12x+20y=52] \\ \hline &\quad -11y=-22 \\ &\quad \frac{-11y}{-11}=\frac{-22}{-11} \\ &\quad y=\mathbf{2} \end{aligned}$$

Substitute 2 for $y$ in one of the equations.

$$\begin{aligned} 4x+3y&=10 \\ 4x+3(2)&=10 \\ 4x+6&=10 \\ 4x+6-6&=10-6 \\ 4x&=4 \\ \frac{4x}{4}&=\frac{4}{4} \\ x&=\mathbf{1} \end{aligned}$$

**8.** Begin by multiplying each term by 3 to clear the fraction.

$$\begin{aligned} 3\times\left(-\frac{1}{3}x\right) &> 3\times(5-2x) \\ -x &> 15-6x \\ 5x &> 15 \\ \boldsymbol{x} &> \mathbf{3} \end{aligned}$$

**9.** Remember to reverse the direction of the inequality when you multiply or divide by a negative number.

$$\begin{aligned} \frac{3}{2}x-\frac{3}{4}x &< \frac{7}{4}x-1 \\ 4\times\left(\frac{3}{2}x-\frac{3}{4}x\right) &< 4\times\left(\frac{7}{4}x-1\right) \\ 6x-3x &< 7x-4 \\ 3x &< 7x-4 \\ -4x &< -4 \\ \frac{-4x}{-4} &> \frac{-4}{-4} \\ \boldsymbol{x} &> \mathbf{1} \end{aligned}$$

**10.** In the given inequality, the $x$ term is added to 4. To isolate $x$, subtract 4 from each term.

$$\begin{array}{ccccc} 6-4 & > & x+4-4 & > & 4-4 \\ 2 & > & x & > & 0 \end{array}$$

The answer is $\mathbf{2 > \boldsymbol{x} > 0}$ or $\mathbf{0 < \boldsymbol{x} < 2}$.

**11.** The expression in the numerator is a commonly seen quadratic pattern known as the difference of squares. Begin by factoring it. In the denominator, apply the negative sign to the factor with variables, allowing you to cancel out $(p - q)$.

$$\frac{p^2 - q^2}{-5(q-p)} = \frac{(p-q)(p+q)}{5(-1)(q-p)} = \frac{\cancel{(p-q)}(p+q)}{5\cancel{(p-q)}} = \frac{\mathbf{p+q}}{\mathbf{5}}$$

**12.** Multiply the terms by each other, using the FOIL mnemonic to keep track of the arithmetic.

- First: $3x(2x)$
- Outside: $3x(5)$
- Inside: $-4(2x)$
- Last: $-4(5)$

Multiply and then combine like terms: $6x^2 + 15x - 8x - 20 = \mathbf{6x^2 + 7x - 20}$.

**13.** This is a commonly seen quadratic pattern, the difference of squares. This is the product of the sum and difference of the square roots of the two terms: $\sqrt{x^4} = x^2$ and $\sqrt{1} = 1$. So $x^4 - 1 = (x^2 + 1)(x^2 - 1)$. Then the second factor is another difference of squares (the square roots of the two terms are $x$ and 1), so it can be expanded: $\mathbf{(x^2 + 1)(x + 1)(x - 1)}$.

**14.** Begin by placing all the terms on one side of the equal sign, leaving zero on the other side. Then factor the quadratic.

$$3x^2 + 4x = x^2 + 5x + 3$$
$$2x^2 - x - 3 = 0$$
$$(2x-3)(x+1) = 0$$

$$2x - 3 = 0 \qquad x + 1 = 0$$
$$2x = 3 \qquad x = \mathbf{-1}$$
$$x = \mathbf{\frac{3}{2}}$$

**15.** Multiply all the numerators and multiply all the denominators. When you multiply exponents with the same base, add the exponents. When you divide exponents with the same base, subtract exponents.

$$\left(\frac{zxy}{z}\right)\left(\frac{z^2y}{x}\right)\left(\frac{z}{y^2}\right) = \left(\frac{\cancel{z^4}^{z^3}\,\cancel{xy^2}}{\cancel{z}\,\cancel{xy^2}}\right) = \mathbf{z^3}$$

**16.** Because the $y$-coordinates of the points are the same, this is a horizontal line and thus has a slope of zero. You can also calculate the slope using the slope formula:

$$\text{Slope} = \frac{y_2 - y_1}{x_2 - x_1} = \frac{6-6}{-2-3} = \frac{0}{-5} = \mathbf{0}$$

**17.** Slope $= \frac{4-3}{3-1} = \frac{1}{2}$

The given line has a slope of $\frac{1}{2}$, and a perpendicular line has a slope that is the negative reciprocal, or **−2**.

**18.** Points on a line have coordinates that satisfy the line's equation when plugged in for $x$ and $y$.

$$\begin{aligned} y &= -2.5x + 7 \\ 12 &= -2.5(-2) + 7 \\ 12 &= 5 + 7 \\ 12 &= 12 \end{aligned}$$

The values satisfy the equation, so **yes**, the point lies on the graph.

**19.** The point of intersection of the two lines is the solution to the system of linear equations. Thus, the solution is **(−1,1)** or $\mathbf{x = -1, y = 1}$.

**20.** There's an expression defining $f(x)$ in terms of $c$, and a value, 29, is given for $f(-3)$. So, plug −3 in for $x$ and set it equal to 29: $f(-3) = c(-3)^2 + 2 = 29$. Thus, $9c = 27$ and $c = \mathbf{3}$.

**21.** Substitute −4 for $x$ in the expression $x^3 + 3x^2 + x$:

$$\begin{aligned} h(-4) &= (-4)^3 + 3(-4)^2 + (-4) \\ h(-4) &= -64 + 3(16) + (-4) \\ h(-4) &= -64 + 48 - 4 \\ h(-4) &= \mathbf{-20} \end{aligned}$$

**22.** This question is asking you to describe a function using an algebraic equation. Note that in the table, every change of 1 unit in $x$ is accompanied by a change of 6 units in $f(x)$, suggesting a consistent linear relationship. Indeed, if you treat $f(x)$ as $y$ in the formula for the slope of a line and use any two points to calculate the slope, you find that it equals 6.

$$m = \frac{\text{Change in } y}{\text{Change in } x} = \frac{31-25}{5-4} = \frac{6}{1} = 6$$

Then choose any point from the table and the slope-intercept formula for a line to find the $y$-intercept. In this example, (4,25) is used.

$$\begin{aligned} y &= mx + b \\ 25 &= (6)(4) + b \\ 25 &= 24 + b \\ b &= 1 \end{aligned}$$

Substitute the slope and the slope-intercept into the slope-intercept formula, using $f(x)$ in place of $y$: $\mathbf{f(x) = 6x + 1}$.

**23.** Replace $a$ in $f(a)$ with −4: $f(-4) = -4 + 4 = 0$. Then replace $a$ in $g(a)$ with the value of $f(-4)$, which is 0: $g(f(-4)) = g(0) = (0)^2 - 1 = \mathbf{-1}$.

**24.** Plug in 7 for $n$ and 28 for $p$ in the given expression:

$$\frac{p}{2n} = \frac{28}{2(7)} = \frac{28}{14} = \mathbf{2}$$

**25.** Plug in 3 for $m$ and 1 for $n$ in the given expression:

$$3 ❖ 1 = \frac{3^2 - 1 + 1}{3 \times 1} = \frac{9 - 1 + 1}{3} = \frac{9}{3} = \mathbf{3}$$

## Algebra Practice Set

**1. C**

Rearrange $b = 17 - 4a$ to $4a + b = 17$ so that the format matches $5a + 3b = 30$. Since the question asks for the value of $a + 2b$ rather than the value of an individual variable, you might be able to answer this without determining the values of each variable. Note that $5a - 4a = a$ and $3b - b = 2b$, so you can get the desired result by subtracting the rearranged second equation from the first:

$$\begin{array}{r} 5a + 3b = 30 \\ -(4a + b = 17) \\ \hline a + 2b = \mathbf{13} \end{array}$$

**2. D**

Rearrange $x^2 = 7x - 10$ so that the right side is 0 by adding 10 to both sides and subtracting $7x$ from both sides; this means $x^2 - 7x + 10 = 0$. Factor this equation using reverse FOIL to get $(x - 5)(x - 2) = 0$, so $x$ could be either 2 or 5. However, the stem limits $x$ to values greater than 2, so $x = 5$ and $x - 2 = \mathbf{3}$. Choice (E), 5, is a trap answer because it is $x$ rather than $x - 2$.

**3. E**

Set the two symbolic functions, # and @@, equal to each other and solve for $x$: $\frac{5x}{2} - 3 = 2x + 1$. Multiplying both sides by 2 to clear the fraction yields $5x - 6 = 4x + 2$. Thus, $x = \mathbf{8}$.

**4. E**

The cost of sending $x$ messages a week with Service A is $3 + 0.5(x - 1)$ dollars. The cost of $x$ messages with Service B is $2 + 0.7(x - 1)$ dollars. Since the cost of $x$ messages a week with Service B is \$15.00 more than with Service A, write the equation $2 + 0.7(x - 1) = 3 + 0.5(x - 1) + 15$. Solve this equation for $x$.

$$\begin{aligned} 2 + 0.7x - 0.7 &= 3 + 0.5x - 0.5 + 15 \\ 1.3 + 0.7x &= 17.5 + 0.5x \\ 0.2x &= 16.2 \end{aligned}$$

Therefore, $x = 5 \times 16.2 = \mathbf{81}$.

**5. C**

By definition, the formula for the slope of this line is $\frac{y_2 - y_1}{x_2 - x_1} = -\frac{3}{4}$. The distance between two points in the $xy$-coordinate plane can be calculated as the hypotenuse of a right triangle. Given the slope, $-\frac{3}{4}$, and a distance of 5, the legs of the triangle are 3 units vertically and 4 units horizontally, with opposite signs. One point that is 5 units away from (4,6) is $(4 - 4, 6 + 3) = (0,9)$. The other is $(4 + 4, 6 - 3) =$ **(8,3)**.

**6. C**

Set the expression equal to 5 and substitute the given functions into the expression, starting from the inside and working out. Don't be distracted by the different letters used for the variables; whether the variable is $a$ or $b$ or $x$, it just represents the value input to the function. Because $\triangle a = 5 - a^2$, you know that $\triangle x = 5 - x^2$. This becomes the input for $\Phi b$, so write $\Phi(5 - x^2) = \frac{3}{5 - x^2} + 2$. Now set this equal to 5, which gives $\frac{3}{5 - x^2} + 2 = 5$, so $\frac{3}{5 - x^2} = 3$. Divide both sides by 3, yielding $\frac{1}{5 - x^2} = 1$. Multiply both sides by $5 - x^2$ to get $1 = 5 - x^2$. Subtract 5 from both sides: $-4 = -x^2$. Then $x^2 = 4$ and $x = \pm 2$. The possible value of $x$ among the answer choices is **2**.

**7. A**

Let $J$, $P$, and $S$ represent the number of stamps initially in the hands of Juanita, Pat, and Svetlana, respectively. If Juanita gives half of her stamps away, she'll have $\frac{J}{2}$ stamps left. If Pat and Svetlana receive Juanita's stamps in a 1:2 ratio, that means Pat will receive one-third of those stamps and Svetlana will receive the remaining two-thirds. Thus, Pat will receive one-third of one-half, or one-sixth, of Juanita's stamps, or $\frac{J}{6}$. Svetlana will receive two-thirds of one-half, or $\frac{2}{3} \times \frac{1}{2} = \frac{1}{3}$ of Juanita's stamps, or $\frac{J}{3}$. After Juanita makes the gift, she will have $\frac{J}{2}$ stamps, Pat will have $P + \frac{J}{6}$, and Svetlana will have $S + \frac{J}{3}$. You're told that Pat's total will be one-fourth of Svetlana's. Thus:

$$P + \frac{J}{6} = \frac{1}{4}\left(S + \frac{J}{3}\right)$$

Multiply this equation by 12 to eliminate the fractions, then simplify as much as you can:

$$12P + 2J = 3\left(S + \frac{J}{3}\right)$$

$$12P + 2J = 3S + J$$

$$12P = 3S - J$$

You're also told that, after the gift, Svetlana's total will be double Juanita's. Thus:

$$S + \frac{J}{3} = 2\left(\frac{J}{2}\right)$$

$$S + \frac{J}{3} = J$$

$$S = J - \frac{J}{3}$$

$$S = \frac{2}{3}J$$

$$3S = 2J$$

Substitute $2J$ in place of $3S$ in the earlier equation to get:

$$12P = 3S - J$$
$$12P = 2J - J$$
$$12P = J$$

Finally, you can make use of the fact that Pat has 2 stamps. This means that Juanita has $12(2) = 24$ stamps. Because $3S = 2J$, it follows that $S = \frac{2}{3}J$, and Svetlana has $\frac{2(24)}{3} = 2(8) = 16$ stamps. The question asks how many more stamps Juanita has than Svetlana, so the answer is $24 - 16 =$ **8**.

If the question had asked for one value (say, Juanita's number of stamps), then backsolving would be a terrific way to bypass most of the work on this complex translation question. Unfortunately, the question asks for the difference between two values, so backsolving won't work. Algebra it is!

**8. E**

In Country A, the population increase between 1960 and 1970 was 1.75 million more than the increase between 1950 and 1960, so the increase between 1960 and 1970 is 1.75 million + 3.5 million = 5.25 million. The total growth in population over the two decades is thus 3.5 million + 5.25 million = **8.75 million.**

**9. B**

The total cost for parking at Garage A $= 8.75 + (5 - 1)1.25 = 8.75 + 5.00 = \$13.75$. The total cost for parking at Garage B $= 5.50 + (5 - 1)2.50 = 5.50 + 10.00 = \$15.50$. The difference in cost is $15.50 - 13.75 =$ **$1.75.**

**10. A**

The total number of UFO sightings is 108. Of these, $\frac{1}{2}$ turn out to be airplanes: $\frac{1}{2} \times 108 = 54$. If $\frac{1}{2}$ are airplanes, $\frac{1}{2}$ are not, so 54 sightings remain that are not attributable to airplanes. Of these 54, $\frac{1}{3}$ are attributable to weather balloons: $\frac{1}{3} \times 54 =$ **18.**

**11. E**

The $250 that Doris spent on the carpet is one-quarter of the one-third of Doris's savings that's left over after she buys the car, or $\frac{1}{4} \times \frac{1}{3} = \frac{1}{12}$ of her original savings. Therefore, her original savings must have been $12 \times \$250$, or **$3,000.**

**12. E**

Gheri is $n$ years old, so Carl is $n - 6$ years old. Carl is 2 years older than Jean, so Jean is $(n - 6) - 2 = n - 8$ years old. The sum of their ages is $n + (n - 6) + (n - 8) =$ **$3n - 14$** years.

**13. D**

Since the season is half over, there are 80 games left in the season. If Team A wins half of the remaining games, that's another 40 games, for a total of 60 + 40, or 100 games. Team B has won 49 games so far, so in order to tie Team A, it must win another 100 − 49, or **51** games.

**14. E**

Using the counting formula for sequences of consecutive integers, the last value will be the first value plus the number of terms minus one. The formula for the sum of a series of consecutive integers is $\text{Sum} = \frac{\text{First} + \text{Last}}{2}(\#\text{ of terms})$. Using $n$ for the number of values, substitute the given values and state "last" in terms of "first," which results in $63 = \frac{6 + (6 + n - 1)}{2}(n) = \frac{11 + n}{2}(n)$. At this point, you can backsolve, starting with (D): $\frac{11 + 8}{2}(8) = \frac{19}{2}(8) = 19(4) = 76$. Thus, 8 is too large, so the answer must be **7**.

**15. C**

The recent graduate has $N - S$ left for things other than rent. This person spends $\frac{3}{8}$ of this amount on food, so what's left for other expenses is $(N - S) - \frac{3}{8}(N - S) = \mathbf{\frac{5}{8}(N - S)}$.

**16. B**

You don't need to know anything about physics to answer this one. Just rearrange the equation to get $m$ on one side.

$$K = \frac{1}{2}mv^2$$
$$2K = mv^2$$
$$\frac{2K}{v^2} = m$$

Now substitute the given values for $K$ and $v$:

$$\begin{aligned} m &= \frac{2 \cdot 144}{(4)^2} \\ &= \frac{288}{16} \\ &= \mathbf{18} \end{aligned}$$

**17. C**

Not all of the 130 ounces can be gold, since 130 is not a multiple of 8. There must be some silver as well. The largest multiple of 8 less than 130 is $16 \times 8$, or 128, but this can't be the amount of gold either, since this leaves only $130 - 128 = 2$ ounces for the silver, and each silver tablet weighs 5 ounces. Look at the multiples of 8 less than 128 until you find one that leaves a multiple of 5 when subtracted from 130. The next smallest multiple of 8, which is $15 \times 8 = 120$, leaves $130 - 120 = 10$ ounces of silver, and since $2 \times 5 = 10$, this amount works. Therefore, **120** ounces is the greatest possible amount of gold. If you had chosen to backsolve, you would have started with (D) because the question asks for the greatest amount. The logic that followed would have been essentially the same as that above.

**18. A**

There's nothing to simplify in this Value question.

Statement (1) simplifies to $7 < x < 9$. Because $x$ must be an integer, the only possible value is 8, so this statement is sufficient. Eliminate (B), (C), and (E).

Statement (2) only advises that $x$ is between 5 and 10. There is more than one integer in this range, so the second statement is insufficient. **(A)** is correct.

**19. B**

This is a Value question, so you'll need an exact numerical value of the fraction. To get that, you need either the individual values of $x$ and $y$ or the ratio of $x$ to $y$.

Statement (1) does not give the values, nor enough information to manipulate the equation to find the ratio of $x$ to $y$. It is not sufficient. Eliminate (A) and (D).

Statement (2) does not provide the individual values either, but you can manipulate the equation to find the ratio. Divide both sides by $y$, to get $\frac{2x}{y} = 5$, and then divide by 2 to see that $\frac{x}{y} = \frac{5}{2}$.

Statement (2) is sufficient. **(B)** is correct.

**20. B**

This is a Value question, so you need either the price per apple and the price per pear or some other information that will allow you to find the price of 5 apples and 5 pears.

Statement (1) gives neither enough information to find the individual cost per fruit nor enough to find the cost of 5 apples and 5 pears. Eliminate (A) and (D).

Statement (2) gives the cost of 2 apples and 2 pears. You could multiply this by 2.5 to find the cost of 5 apples and 5 pears. Statement (2) is sufficient. **(B)** is correct.

**21. A**

This Value question states the product of two positive integers and asks for their sum. Thus, the integers are limited to being the factor pairs of 30.

Statement (1) limits $\frac{x}{y}$ to a value between 1 and 2. The factor pairs are $1 \times 30$, $2 \times 15$, $3 \times 10$, and $5 \times 6$. The only division with these pairs that yields an answer between 1 and 2 is $\frac{6}{5}$. Statement (1) is sufficient. Eliminate (B), (C), and (E).

Statement (2) tells you that $x$ is greater than $y$; this doesn't pin down the factor pairs any further. Statement (2) is insufficient. **(A)** is correct.

**22. D**

To get the value of $x$, you need to know the length of side $AC$. The length of side $AB$ is $5 - 2 = 3$; since the $x$-coordinates of points $A$ and $B$ are both 1, this is a vertical line. The length of side $AC$ is $x - 1$; since the $y$-coordinates of points $A$ and $C$ are both 2, this is a horizontal line. Thus, $AB$ and $AC$ are the legs of a right triangle. The limitation that $x > 1$ means that leg $AC$ extends to the right from point $A$.

Statement (1) gives the area of the triangle. Since the area of a right triangle is half the product of the lengths of the legs, you could use this value to calculate the length of $AC$, from which you could get the value of $x$. Statement (1) is sufficient. Eliminate (B), (C), and (E).

Statement (2) gives the length of the hypotenuse, which is $BC$. Knowing the length of one leg and the hypotenuse enables you to calculate the length of the other leg using the Pythagorean theorem. Statement (2) is also sufficient. **(D)** is correct.

**23. B**

This is a Value question that asks for the value of a variable when it is plugged into a function symbolized by $x^* = x(x - 1) = x^2 - x$.

Statement (1) means that $x^2 - x = x$. Before you divide by $x$, note that $x = 0$ is a solution to the equation. Now divide all terms by $x$ to get $x - 1 = 1$. So, $x$ could also be 2. Statement (1) is insufficient. Eliminate (A) and (D).

Statement (2) gives the value of the function for $(x - 1)$. Plug in $(x - 1)$ for $n$ in the original function, set that equal to $x - 2$, and solve for $x$:

$$x - 2 = (x - 1)(x - 1 - 1)$$
$$x - 2 = (x - 1)(x - 2)$$
$$x - 2 = x^2 - 3x + 2$$
$$0 = x^2 - 4x + 4$$
$$0 = (x - 2)^2$$

So, $x = 2$. Statement (2) is sufficient. **(B)** is correct.

**24. C**

First, evaluate the inequality. Since $x$ and $y$ are integers, $y \geq 9$ and $x \geq 18$. As for the expression $x^2 - y^2$, it is a difference of squares and can be rewritten as $(x + y)(x - y)$.

From Statement (1), all that you can determine is that $x + y = 8m + 7$, where $m$ is a positive integer. So, Statement (1) is insufficient. Eliminate (A) and (D).

Similarly, all that Statement (2) tells you is that $x - y = 8n + 5$, where $n$ is a positive integer. So, Statement (2) is also insufficient. Eliminate (B).

Combine the statements by multiplying them: $(x + y)(x - y) = (8m + 7)(8n + 5)$. After multiplying, this becomes $x^2 - y^2 = 64mn + 40m + 56n + 35$. To determine the remainder when $x^2 - y^2$ is divided by 8, divide the right side by 8 to get $8mn + 5m + 7n + \frac{35}{8}$. The first three terms are all integers, so their sum is an integer, and $\frac{35}{8}$ is 4 with a remainder of 3. So, taken together, the statements are sufficient to determine that the remainder when $x^2 - y^2$ is divided by 8 is 3. **(C)** is correct.

Alternatively, you could attack this by picking numbers. Choose $y = 9$, the smallest allowable value for $y$. The remainder when 9 is divided by 8 is 1. In order for $x + y$ to have a remainder of 7, the remainder when $x$ is divided by 8 must be $7 - 1 = 6$. While 14 would work for that requirement, 14 is not more than 8 greater than 9, so use $14 + 8 = 22$. Test these numbers. For Statement (1), $22 + 9 = 31$, which, when divided by 8, is 3 with a remainder of 7. For Statement (2), $22 - 9 = 13$, which, when divided by 8, is 1 with a remainder of 5. These values work in both statements, so plug the values into the expression in the question stem: $x^2 - y^2 = 484 - 81 = 403$, and $403 \div 8 = 50$ with a remainder of 3.

**25. C**

This is a Value question that asks for the value of the fourth number in a series. The equation for the series tells you that this is an arithmetic series since each value is the previous value plus some number $a$. To determine the value of $s_4$, the statements will need to provide both a value in the sequence (along with which term in the sequence it is) and the value of the constant $a$.

Statement (1) defines $a$. Knowing that $a = 2$ is enough to fully define the relationship, but without a value for a specific term in the series, it's not possible to determine the value for $s_4$.

Statement (2) states the value of the ninth term in the sequence, but nothing about the value of $a$. This is insufficient, so proceed to evaluate the statements together.

Taken together, the statements are sufficient because they provide both the relationship, $s_n = s_{n-1} + 2$, and a starting point, $s_9 = 35$. **(C)** is correct.

CHAPTER 6

# Formulas, Statistics, and Data Analysis

**LEARNING OBJECTIVES**

After studying this chapter, you will be able to:

- Describe which topics in formulas, statistics, and data analysis are tested on the GMAT
- Identify questions that feature formulas, statistics, and data analysis
- Apply the Kaplan Methods for Problem Solving and Data Sufficiency to questions testing various formulas, statistics, and data analysis skills

In addition to questions involving arithmetic and algebra, the GMAT presents questions that test certain formulas. Learning these formulas and then using them fluently on Test Day will significantly boost your GMAT Quantitative score. You will also need to be familiar with certain statistics and data analysis concepts. Specifically, it will be important to know:

- Rates
- Work formula
- Average formula
- Median, mode, and range
- Combinations and permutations
- Probability
- How to deal with word problems
- Logic problems
- Tables, graphs, and charts

In this chapter, you will first see a set of drills that covers the concepts listed above. Work through the drills and then check your performance. Review the explanation of each question to see the steps taken to arrive at the correct answer.

As you review, assess your current ability. If you find that you struggled with certain drills and would like to refresh your understanding of the concepts tested, check out the Formulas, Statistics, and Data Analysis section of Chapter 9: Math Reference before tackling the practice set at the end of this chapter.

If you instead feel comfortable with your performance on the drills and confident in your abilities, then proceed directly to the practice set of GMAT-style questions. You will see both Problem Solving and Data Sufficiency questions. Apply your knowledge of formulas, statistics, and data analysis to these questions and tackle them strategically, using the step-by-step approach outlined in the Kaplan Methods.

When you finish the practice set, fully review every question by reading through its explanation—even for the questions that you answered correctly. In any question where the explanation discusses concepts unfamiliar to you, use the Math Reference chapter to further your understanding.

# Formulas, Statistics, and Data Analysis Drills

Try these drills to test your proficiency with formulas, statistics, and data analysis. Use the answer key and explanations at the end of the chapter to check your work.

1. What is the average of $y$, $y + 2$, $y + 4$, and $y + 6$ in terms of $y$?

2. In how many different ways can the letters of the word MEXICO be arranged?

3. At a high school, 300 students are members of the band, chess club, or both. If 200 students are members of the band only and 50 students are members of both the band and chess club, what is the probability that a student chosen at random is a member of only the chess club?

4. The daily attendance of an art exhibit for the past 8 days was 90, 95, 77, 78, 87, 81, 85, and 93. What are the mean, median, and mode of these attendance numbers?

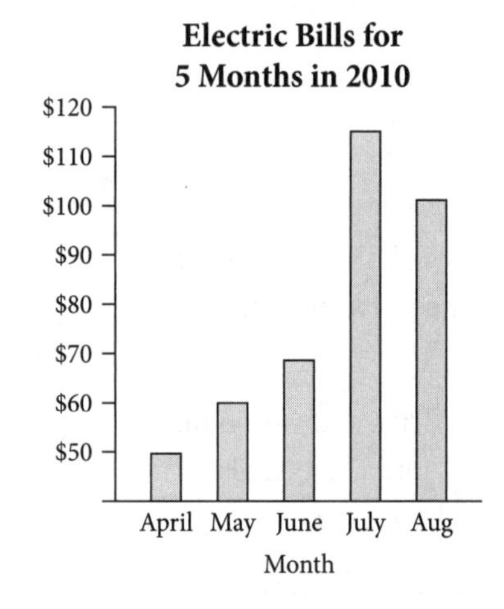


5. If the electric bill in September is half of the bill in August, will it be more or less than the bill in May?

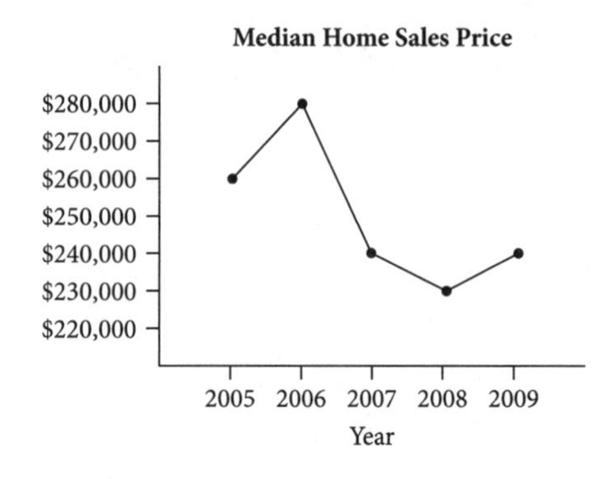


6. If the median home sales price increased the same amount between 2009 and 2010 as it did between 2008 and 2009, what was the median sales price in 2010?

7. At an animal shelter, there are 8 puppies and 12 kittens. If a staff member randomly chooses 3 pets to be featured in this Saturday's adoption fair, what is the probability that all 3 will be puppies?

8. If a fair coin is tossed 3 times, what is the probability that the coin will land heads up exactly 2 times?

9. If a fair six-sided die with faces numbered 1 through 6 is tossed three times, what is the probability of getting a 1 or a 2 on all three tosses?

10. What is the average speed for a 24-mile bicycle trip if half the distance was covered at 12 miles per hour and half at 24 miles per hour?

11. Determine the time to drain a tank using two pipes if one pipe could drain the tank in 4 hours by itself and the other could drain the tank in 5 hours by itself.

12. Find the number of ways in which 4 different figurines can be lined up in a row.

13. Calculate the number of balls with no stripes if, out of a total of 100 balls, 60 have a red stripe, 50 have a blue stripe, and 25 have both stripes. No balls have any stripes other than red or blue.

14. How long does it take to pump $30 worth of gasoline if the fuel costs $3 per gallon and a pump dispenses 4 gallons per minute?

15. Find the average of $\frac{1}{2}$, $\frac{1}{3}$, $\frac{1}{4}$, $\frac{1}{5}$, and $\frac{13}{60}$.

16. What is the increase in the range if the number 15 is added to the set {2, 6, –1, 3, 9, 0}?

17. Determine the time it takes Machine B to produce a batch of Product X if Machine A can produce a batch of Product X in 30 minutes and the two machines working together can produce a batch of Product X in 20 minutes.

18. Calculate the number of combinations of 3 objects that can be selected from 7 distinct objects.

19. Find the difference in speed, in miles per hour, between a car that travels 15 miles in 30 minutes at a constant speed and another car that travels 30 miles in 40 minutes at a constant speed.

20. Sets *A* and *B* together contain a total of 50 objects. If 30 of the objects are in set *B* and 20 objects are in both sets, how many objects are in set *A* only?

21. What is the number of different ways 3 objects out of 5 distinct objects can be arranged?

22. What is the probability of flipping exactly 2 heads in 4 tosses of a fair coin?

23. What is the median of the set {0, 7, –3, –8, 4, 5}?

24. Express the average overall speed for a trip of *m* miles at *a* miles per hour plus *n* miles at *b* miles per hour.

25. Students in a class take 5 equally weighted tests. If a student's scores on the first four tests are 86, 92, 80, and 94, what score does the student need on the fifth test to earn an overall average of 90?

Once you've completed these drills, check your performance by reviewing the answers and explanations at the end of this chapter. If you feel confident in your skill with formulas, statistics, and data analysis drills, try the realistic GMAT-style questions in the next practice set. If you want a refresher, check out the Formulas, Statistics, and Data Analysis section in the Math Reference chapter at the end of the book.

## Formulas, Statistics, and Data Analysis Practice Set

Try the following questions, using the Kaplan Method for Problem Solving and looking for opportunities to use picking numbers and backsolving. Answers and explanations are at the end of this chapter.

1. If Carol can finish a job in 5 hours and Steve can finish the same job in 10 hours, how many minutes will it take both of them to finish the job together?

   - O 160
   - O 180
   - O 200
   - O 210
   - O 220

2. To determine how far to move their pieces on a board, players of a game generate a "movement value" using a fair five-sided die with the numbers 1 through 5 and a fair six-sided die with the numbers 1 through 6. Both dice are rolled simultaneously. The number rolled on the five-sided die is the tens digit of the movement value, and the number rolled on the six-sided die is the ones digit of the movement value. What is the probability of rolling a value of 45 or greater on a single roll of the two dice?

   - O $\frac{1}{30}$
   - O $\frac{1}{5}$
   - O $\frac{1}{4}$
   - O $\frac{4}{15}$
   - O $\frac{1}{3}$

3. Two cars travel away from each other in opposite directions at 24 miles per hour and 40 miles per hour respectively. If the first car travels for 20 minutes and the second car for 45 minutes, how many miles apart will they be at the end of their trips?

   - O 22
   - O 24
   - O 30
   - O 38
   - O 42

4. Phil is making a 40-kilometer canoe trip. If he travels at 30 kilometers per hour for the first 10 kilometers and then at 15 kilometers per hour for the rest of the trip, how many minutes longer will it take him than if he makes the entire trip at 20 kilometers per hour?

   - O 15
   - O 20
   - O 35
   - O 45
   - O 50

5. What is the range of $x$ consecutive multiples of 3, where $x$ is a positive integer greater than 2?

   - O $2x$
   - O $3x$
   - O $3x - 1$
   - O $3(x - 1)$
   - O $x + 3$

6. Three mowers are cutting the grass in a park. One of the mowers could mow the entire park in 9 hours. Another smaller mower could mow it in 12 hours. A third mower is slower and would take 18 hours to mow the grass in the park. If the three mowers work simultaneously and independently at the above rates, how many hours would it take them to mow all the grass in the park?

   - O 4
   - O 5
   - O 6
   - O 7
   - O 8

7. Tammy bikes the course of a race at 30 miles per hour then returns home along the same route at 10 miles per hour. If the total time it takes her to travel the course and return home is 2 hours, and if the time spent turning around is negligible, what is the length, in miles, of the racecourse?

   - O 15
   - O 20
   - O 25
   - O 30
   - O 35

8. The sum of the current ages of Kendra, Mike, and Raj is 32 years. Raj is 1 year older than Mike. In 3 years, Kendra's age will be two-thirds of Mike's age. How old was Mike 4 years ago?

   - O 7
   - O 8
   - O 12
   - O 13
   - O 15

9. John buys $R$ pounds of cheese to feed $N$ guests at a party. If $N + P$ guests come to the party, how many more pounds of cheese must John buy in order to feed each guest the originally planned amount?

   - O $\frac{NP}{R}$
   - O $\frac{N}{RP}$
   - O $\frac{N+P}{R}$
   - O $\frac{P}{NR}$
   - O $\frac{PR}{N}$

10. Ahmed finds that by wearing different combinations of the jackets, shirts, and pairs of trousers that he owns, he can make up 90 different outfits. If he owns 5 jackets and 3 pairs of trousers, how many shirts does he own?

    - O 3
    - O 6
    - O 12
    - O 18
    - O 30

11. Robert purchased $2,000 worth of U.S. savings bonds. If bonds are sold in $50 or $100 denominations only, which of the following CANNOT be the number of U.S. savings bonds that Robert purchased?

    - O 20
    - O 27
    - O 30
    - O 40
    - O 50

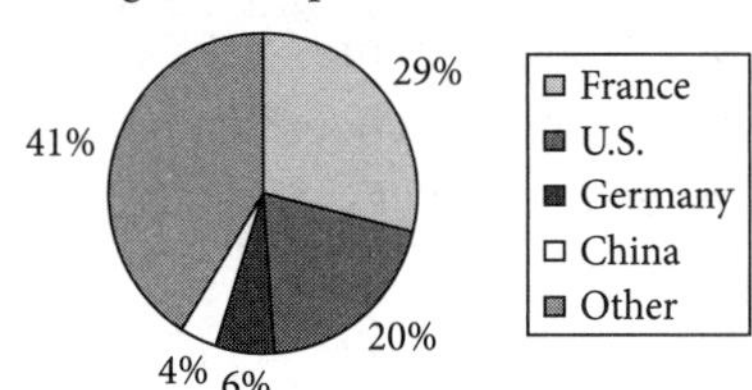


12. If Madagascar's exports totaled $1.3 billion in 2009, approximately what was the value, in millions of dollars, of the country's exports to China?

   - O 52
   - O 78
   - O 100
   - O 325
   - O 520

**Grocery Store Employees, by Department**

| Department | Hourly | Salaried |
|---|---|---|
| Bakery and Deli | 14 | 4 |
| Dairy | 19 | 8 |
| Frozen Foods | 6 | 5 |
| Health and Beauty | 11 | 3 |
| Meat and Seafood | 14 | 5 |
| Packaged Foods | 32 | 9 |
| Produce | 10 | 4 |
| Total | 106 | 38 |

13. What is the ratio of the number of hourly employees working in Packaged Foods to the number of hourly employees working in Frozen Foods?

   - O 5:6
   - O 8:3
   - O 9:5
   - O 13:6
   - O 16:3

14. Steve takes an average of 15 minutes to analyze the contents of a Petri dish, and Rosie can analyze the contents of 6 Petri dishes per hour on average. Working together at their average rates, how long will it take Steve and Rosie to analyze the contents of 40 Petri dishes?

   - O $2\frac{1}{2}$ hours
   - O 4 hours
   - O $6\frac{2}{3}$ hours
   - O 8 hours
   - O 10 hours

15. A certain mule travels at $\frac{2}{3}$ the speed of a certain horse. If it takes the horse 6 hours to travel 20 miles, how many hours will the trip take the mule?

   - O 4
   - O 8
   - O 9
   - O 10
   - O 30

16. In how many different ways can 3 sophomores, 3 juniors, and 4 seniors be standing in a line if the 3 sophomores are in 3 consecutive locations, the 3 juniors are in 3 consecutive locations, and the 4 seniors are in 4 consecutive locations?

   - O 864
   - O 5,184
   - O 6,048
   - O 7,560
   - O 8,640

17. Events A and B are independent. The probability that Event A occurs is 0.6, and the probability that neither Event A nor Event B occurs is 0.06. What is the probability that Event B occurs?

   - O 0.34
   - O 0.65
   - O 0.72
   - O 0.76
   - O 0.85

Try the following questions, using the Kaplan Method for Data Sufficiency and looking for opportunities to pick numbers, solve without algebra, and guess strategically. Answers and explanations are at the end of this chapter.

*Note:* Because the Data Sufficiency answer choices are always the same and should be memorized, we have omitted them here. If you need a refresher on the choices or the 12TEN mnemonic, review Chapter 3 on Data Sufficiency.

18. If Joe and Sam completed a job in 2 hours working together, what fraction of the job was done by Joe?

    (1) If Joe had worked alone, he would have completed the job in 3 hours.

    (2) Sam did one-third of the job.

19. In Papersville, 6,000 people read at least one of the two papers, the *Herald* or the *Tribune*. How many people read both newspapers?

    (1) Of the people in Papersville, 2,000 read the *Herald* only.

    (2) Of the people in Papersville, 2,500 read the *Tribune* only.

20. During July, an online retailer received 3,300 orders for amounts less than or equal to $100 and 1,100 orders for amounts greater than $100. What was the average dollar amount of an order in July?

    (1) The gross sales from the orders for amounts less than or equal to $100 equaled the gross sales from the orders for amounts greater than $100.

    (2) The orders for amounts less than or equal to $100 accounted for $134,000 in gross sales.

21. $S$ is a set of positive integers such that if $x$ is a member of $S$, then both $x^2$ and $x^3$ are also in $S$. If the only member of $S$ that is neither the square nor the cube of another member of $S$ is called the source integer, is 8 in $S$?

    (1) 4 is in $S$ and is not the source integer.

    (2) 64 is in $S$ and is not the source integer.

22. What is the value of the median of the data set $\{-3, 0, 1, 4, x\}$?

    (1) $x \geq 1$

    (2) $x \leq 1$

23. What is the average production cost of a single X-car?

    (1) A total of 100 X-cars and 100 Y-cars cost $2.2 million to produce.

    (2) The average X-car costs $2,000 more to produce than the average Y-car.

24. Mr. Daniels deposits $10,000 in a savings certificate earning $p$ percent annual interest compounded quarterly. What is the value of $p$?

    (1) During the term of the certificate, he earns $18 more than he would if the interest were not compounded.

    (2) He withdraws all the money six months after depositing it.

List L: $v, w, x, y, z$

List M: $v + 12, w + 12, x + 12, y + 12, z + 12$

List N: $8v, 8w, 8x, 8y, 8z$

25. What is the standard deviation of the numbers in List $L$?

    (1) The standard deviation of the numbers in List $M$ is 3.5.

    (2) The standard deviation of the numbers in List $N$ is 28.

# Answer Key

## Formulas, Statistics, and Data Analysis Drills

1. $y + 3$
2. 720
3. $\frac{1}{6}$
4. Mean: 85.75
   Median: 86
   Mode: none
5. Less
6. $250,000
7. $\frac{14}{285}$
8. $\frac{3}{8}$
9. $\frac{1}{27}$
10. 16 miles per hour
11. $2\frac{2}{9}$ hours
12. 24
13. 15
14. 2 minutes 30 seconds or $2\frac{1}{2}$ minutes
15. $\frac{3}{10}$ or 0.3
16. 6
17. 60 minutes
18. 35
19. 15 miles per hour
20. 20
21. 60
22. $\frac{3}{8}$
23. 2
24. $\frac{m+n}{\frac{m}{a}+\frac{n}{b}}$
25. 98

## Formulas, Statistics, and Data Analysis Practice Set

1. C
2. D
3. D
4. B
5. D
6. A
7. A
8. B
9. E
10. B
11. E
12. A
13. E
14. B
15. C
16. B
17. E
18. D
19. C
20. C
21. A
22. A
23. C
24. C
25. D

# Answers and Explanations

## Formulas, Statistics, and Data Analysis Drills

**1.** $\frac{(y)+(y+2)+(y+4)+(y+6)}{4}=\frac{4y+12}{4}=y+3$

**2.** There are no repeated letters, so you can solve this as $6! = 6 \times 5 \times 4 \times 3 \times 2 \times 1 =$ **720.**

**3.** Set up the overlapping sets formula, where Total = Band + Chess − Both, so 300 = (200 + 50) + Chess − 50. Solve for Chess to find there are 100 members of the Chess club. Of these, 50 are in both clubs, so Chess only = 300 − 200 − 50 = 50. Probability $= \frac{50}{300} = \mathbf{\frac{1}{6}}$.

**4.** Put the numbers in order: 77, 78, 81, 85, 87, 90, 93, 95.

$$\text{Mean} = \frac{\text{Sum of values}}{\text{Number of values}} = \frac{77+78+81+85+87+90+93+95}{8} = \frac{686}{8} = \mathbf{85.75}$$

Median is the average of the middle two values: $(85 + 87) \div 2 =$ **86.**

All of the numbers appear with equal frequency, so there is **no mode** for this data set.

**5.** The August bill is a little over $100. The September bill will be about $50 if it is half of the August bill. This is **less than** the May bill of $60.

**6.** From 2008 to 2009, the increase is $240,000 − $230,000 = $10,000. For 2010, the median sales price is thus $240,000 + $10,000 = **$250,000.**

**7.** To begin with, there are 20 total baby animals and 8 puppies, so the probability of getting a puppy the first time is $\frac{8}{20}$. When the second animal is chosen, there are only 19 pets to choose from and only 7 puppies, so that probability is $\frac{7}{19}$. And then for the last pick, the probability is $\frac{6}{18}$. Multiply the probabilities together:

$$\left(\frac{8}{20}\right)\left(\frac{7}{19}\right)\left(\frac{6}{18}\right) = \left(\frac{2}{5}\right)\left(\frac{7}{19}\right)\left(\frac{1}{3}\right) = \mathbf{\frac{14}{285}}$$

**8.** With each toss, there are 2 possible outcomes. Since there are three tosses, there are $2 \times 2 \times 2 = 8$ total possible outcomes. Use the combinations formula to find the number of combinations of tosses with exactly 2 heads: $\frac{3!}{2!(3-2)!} = \frac{3 \times 2 \times 1}{2 \times 1 \times 1} = \frac{6}{2} = 3$. Probability $= \mathbf{\frac{3}{8}}$.

Alternatively, just list out all the possible results (there are 8 of them) and count those with exactly 2 heads: HTH, HHT, THH. That's **3 out of 8.**

**9.** The probability of getting a 1 or a 2 on a single toss $= \frac{2}{6} = \frac{1}{3}$. Because the tosses are independent (they don't affect each other), the probability of a 1 or a 2 on all three tosses is $\frac{1}{3} \times \frac{1}{3} \times \frac{1}{3} = \mathbf{\frac{1}{27}}$.

**10.** The average speed for the whole trip is total distance divided by total time. The time for the first half of the trip is $\frac{12 \text{ mi}}{12 \text{ mi/hr}} = 1$ hr. The time for the second half: $\frac{12 \text{ mi}}{24 \text{ mi/hr}} = \frac{1}{2}$ hr. Thus, the average rate for the entire tip is $\frac{24 \text{ mi}}{1.5 \text{ hr}} = \mathbf{16\ mi/hr}$.

**11.** If $T$ is the time it takes the pipes to drain the tank when they are both in use, then $\frac{1}{T} = \frac{1}{4} + \frac{1}{5} = \frac{20}{20}\left(\frac{1}{4}\right) + \frac{20}{20}\left(\frac{1}{5}\right) = \frac{5+4}{20} = \frac{9}{20}$. Cross multiplying yields $9T = 20$, so $T = \frac{20}{9} = \mathbf{2\frac{2}{9}}$.

Alternatively, use the combined work formula derived from the above math: $T = \frac{ab}{a+b} = \frac{4(5)}{4+5} = \frac{20}{9} = \mathbf{2\frac{2}{9}}$.

**12.** The first figurine could be any of the 4, so there are 4 options for that position. Once that figurine is placed, there are only 3 options for the next position, and so on. Multiply the number of possibilities for each position to find the total ways of arranging the figurines: $4! = 4 \times 3 \times 2 \times 1 = \mathbf{24}$.

**13.** Total = Group A + Group B − Both + Neither: 100 = 60 + 50 − 25 + Neither. So, Neither = 100 − 60 − 50 + 25 = **15**.

**14.** You are asked for a time, so set up the ratios so that when multiplied, the units you're not interested in (dollars and gallons) cancel out:

$$\cancel{\$}30 \times \frac{1 \cancel{\text{gal}}}{\cancel{\$}3} \times \frac{1 \text{ min}}{4 \cancel{\text{gal}}} = \frac{30 \text{ min}}{12} = \mathbf{2.5 \text{ or } 2\frac{1}{2} \text{ minutes}}$$

This can also be expressed as **2 minutes 30 seconds.**

**15.** To find the average, you need the sum of the numbers. Add up the values by setting their denominators equal to their least common denominator: $\frac{30}{60} + \frac{20}{60} + \frac{15}{60} + \frac{12}{60} + \frac{13}{60} = \frac{90}{60} = \frac{3}{2}$.

Now divide the sum by the number of elements, 5, to find the average:

$$\frac{\frac{3}{2}}{\frac{5}{1}} = \frac{3}{2} \times \frac{1}{5} = \mathbf{\frac{3}{10} \text{ or } 0.3}$$

**16.** Range is the largest value minus the smallest value. The original range is $9 - (-1) = 10$. The new range is $15 - (-1) = 16$. So, the increase is $16 - 10 = \mathbf{6}$.

**17.** Convert the rates to fractions and use the fact that the total rate of the two machines is the sum of their individual rates: $\frac{1}{20} = \frac{1}{30} + \frac{1}{b}$. So, $\frac{3}{60} = \frac{2}{60} + \frac{1}{b}$ and $b =$ **60 minutes**.

**18.** $\frac{7!}{3!(7-3)!} = \frac{7 \times 6 \times 5 \times 4 \times 3 \times 2 \times 1}{3 \times 2 \times 1 \times 4 \times 3 \times 2 \times 1} = \frac{7 \times 6 \times 5}{3 \times 2 \times 1} = \mathbf{35}$

**19.** Converting the two speeds into miles per hour yields $\frac{15}{\frac{30}{60}} = 15 \times \frac{60}{30} = 30$ and $\frac{30}{\frac{40}{60}} = 30 \times \frac{60}{40} = 45$.

The difference in speeds is 45 − 30 = **15 miles per hour.**

**20.** You can use logic to solve. There are 30 objects in set $B$, but 20 objects are in both sets $A$ and $B$, so there are $30 - 20 = 10$ objects only in set $B$. Since there are 10 objects only in set $B$ and 20 objects in both sets, that's 30 objects. To have a total of 50 objects, there must be $50 - 30 = 20$ objects only in set $A$.

You can also use the overlapping sets formula to solve: Total = Group A + Group B − Both groups + Neither group. Thus, $50 = A + 30 - 20 + 0$, and $A = 40$. However, this is the total number of objects in set $A$. You know that 20 objects are in both sets, so $40 - 20 =$ **20** objects only in set $A$.

**21.** Since this question asks for the number of arrangements, use the permutation formula:

$$\frac{5!}{(5-3)!} = \frac{5 \times 4 \times 3 \times 2 \times 1}{2 \times 1} = \mathbf{60}$$

Alternatively, you can use the "slots" approach. In this question, there are three slots for objects. When you put an object in the first slot, there are 5 objects to choose from. For the second slot, there are only 4 possible objects. And for the third slot, there are only 3 possibilities. Multiply the number of possibilities for each slot: $5 \times 4 \times 3 =$ **60** total possible arrangements.

**22.** There are 2 possible outcomes (heads or tails) for each toss, and there are 4 tosses. Thus, the total possible outcomes $= 2^4 = 16$. It may be most efficient to simply list the desired outcomes: HHTT, HTHT, HTTH, THHT, THTH, TTHH = 6. The probability of getting 2 heads is $\frac{6}{16} = \mathbf{\frac{3}{8}}$.

Alternatively, for situations such as coin tosses where there are two possibilities for each event, you can use the combinations formula to find the number of desired outcomes:

$${}_4C_2 = \frac{4!}{2!(4-2)!} = \frac{4 \times 3 \times 2 \times 1}{2 \times 1 \times 2 \times 1} = 6$$

So again, of the total 16 possible outcomes, 6 have two heads: that's $\frac{6}{16} = \mathbf{\frac{3}{8}}$.

**23.** Arranged in order, the set is $\{-8, -3, 0, 4, 5, 7\}$. There is an even number of values in the set, so the median is the average of the two middle values: $\frac{0+4}{2} =$ **2**.

**24.** The average overall speed is the total distance divided by the total time. The total distance is $m + n$. The time for the first part is distance divided by rate, or $\frac{m}{a}$, and the time for the second part is $\frac{n}{b}$. The average speed for the trip is thus $\mathbf{\dfrac{m+n}{\frac{m}{a}+\frac{n}{b}}}$.

**25.** Because the numbers in this question are fairly large and the average is given, it is most efficient to use the balance method, which relies on the fact that all the values in a group will "balance out" around the average. First, find the difference between the four given scores and the desired average. Those differences are −4, +2, −10, and +4. These differences sum to −8. To bring the values "into balance," the fifth test must be 8 greater than the average, or $90 + 8 =$ **98**.

## Formulas, Statistics, and Data Analysis Practice Set

**1. C**

Since you only need to consider two rates, use the shortcut combined work formula where $A$ and $B$ represent the two times.

$$\frac{AB}{A+B} = \frac{5 \times 10}{5+10} = \frac{50}{15} = \frac{10}{3} \text{ hours}$$

Working together, it would take them $\frac{10}{3}$ hours. But the question asks for the number of minutes. Since there are 60 minutes in one hour, multiply the number of hours by 60.

$$\frac{10}{3} \times 60 = \frac{600}{3} = \mathbf{200} \text{ minutes}$$

**2. D**

There are two ways to get a value of 45 or greater. If the five-sided die roll is a 5, the result of the roll of the other die doesn't matter, because the value is definitely greater than 45. The probability of this occurring is $\frac{1}{5}$. The other way to get 45 or greater is to roll a 4 on the five-sided die and a 5 or 6 on the six-sided die. The probability of rolling a 4 is $\frac{1}{5}$, and the probability of rolling a 5 or 6 is $\frac{2}{6} = \frac{1}{3}$. The probability that both these events occur is $\frac{1}{5} \times \frac{1}{3} = \frac{1}{15}$. Add the probabilities of the two ways to roll 45 or greater to get the total probability: $\frac{1}{5} + \frac{1}{15} = \frac{3}{15} + \frac{1}{15} = \mathbf{\frac{4}{15}}$.

**3. D**

Since the cars are traveling in opposite directions, the distance between the two cars equals the sum of the distances each car travels. The first car travels 20 minutes, or a third of an hour, so it goes only $\frac{1}{3}$ the distance it would travel in an hour, or $\frac{1}{3}$ of 24 miles $= 8$ miles. The second car travels 45 minutes, or $\frac{3}{4}$ of an hour. It goes $\frac{3}{4}$ of the distance it would go in an hour, or $\frac{3}{4}$ of $40 = 30$ miles. The two cars are then $8 + 30 = \mathbf{38}$ miles apart.

**4. B**

First, find how long the trip takes him at the two different rates, using the formula:

$$\text{Time} = \frac{\text{Distance}}{\text{Rate}}$$

Phil travels the first 10 km at 30 km per hour, so he takes $\frac{10}{30} = \frac{1}{3}$ hour for this portion of the journey.

Phil travels the remaining 30 km at 15 km per hour, so he takes $\frac{30}{15} = 2$ hours for this portion of the journey. So, the whole journey takes him $2 + \frac{1}{3} = 2\frac{1}{3}$ hours. Now compare this to the amount of time it would take to make the same trip at a constant rate of 20 km per hour. If he traveled the whole 40 km at 20 km per hour, it would take $\frac{40}{20} = 2$ hours.

This is $\frac{1}{3}$ hour, or **20** minutes, shorter.

**5. D**

Pick numbers to find the correct choice. Try $x = 3$ and the numbers 3, 6, and 9. The range is $9 - 3 = 6$. Choices (A), (D), and (E) all match. Try $x = 4$, using 3, 6, 9, and 12. Now the range is 9 and only **(D), 3(4 − 1)**, matches.

**6. A**

Since three mowers will be working, you cannot use the simplified formula for the combined work of two entities. Instead, convert the completion times to rates and add the fractions. The fastest mower can mow the park in 9 hours, so that is a rate of $\frac{1}{9}$ park per hour. The other reciprocals are $\frac{1}{12}$ and $\frac{1}{18}$. If the time for all three mowers to complete the task is $T$, then $\frac{1}{T} = \frac{1}{9} + \frac{1}{12} + \frac{1}{18}$. Convert the fractions to a common denominator of 36 to get $\frac{1}{T} = \frac{4}{36} + \frac{3}{36} + \frac{2}{36} = \frac{9}{36}$. Therefore, $T = \frac{36}{9} = \mathbf{4}$.

**7. A**

If you can find how long either leg of the journey takes, you can use that time and the speed to find the distance. Since Tammy traveled 3 times as fast to the end of the racecourse as she traveled back home, it took her 3 times as long to return. If she took $x$ hours to complete the course and $3x$ hours to return, then her total time is $x + 3x = 4x$. The question says that her total time is 2 hours, so $4x = 2$ hours. Therefore, $x$ is $\frac{1}{2}$. In $\frac{1}{2}$ hour at 30 miles per hour, Tammy traveled **15** miles.

**8. B**

Translate the words in the problem into equations. There are 3 variables, so you'll need at least 3 equations. Set Kendra's, Mike's, and Raj's ages as $k$, $m$, and $r$, respectively.

The sum of the three people's ages is 32, so $k + m + r = 32$. Raj is one year older than Mike, so $r = m + 1$. In 3 years, Kendra's age will be two-thirds of Mike's, so $k + 3 = \frac{2}{3}(m + 3)$. Substitute $m + 1$ for $r$ in the first equation to get $k + m + m + 1 = 32$, or $k + 2m = 31$. Now you have 2 equations and 2 variables. Substitute $31 - 2m$ for $k$ in the remaining equation to get $31 - 2m + 3 = \frac{2}{3}(m + 3)$. Solve this for $m$:

$$3(31 - 2m + 3) = 3\left(\frac{2}{3}\right)(m + 3)$$
$$93 - 6m + 9 = 2m + 6$$
$$96 = 8m$$
$$12 = m$$

The question asks for Mike's age 4 years ago, so that would be $12 - 4 = \mathbf{8}$.

**9. E**

If John buys $R$ pounds for $N$ people, he is planning on feeding his guests cheese at a rate of $\frac{R}{N}$ pounds per person.

You need to figure out how much additional cheese John must buy for the extra $P$ people. If John is buying $\frac{R}{N}$ pounds of cheese for each person, then he will need $P \times \frac{R}{N}$, or $\frac{PR}{N}$ pounds for the extra $P$ people. You can check the answer by seeing if the units cancel out:

$$P \cancel{\text{people}} \times \frac{R \text{ pounds}}{N \cancel{\text{people}}} = \frac{PR}{N} \text{pounds}$$

The other approach here is to pick numbers. Say John buys 10 pounds of cheese for 5 people (that is, $R = 10$ and $N = 5$). Then everyone gets 2 pounds of cheese. (That's a ridiculous amount of cheese per person, but the numbers just have to be mathematically permissible and easy to work with. They don't have to make real-world sense!) Now say 2 more people come than expected (that is, $P = 2$), so 7 people attend the party. Now John needs 14 pounds to have enough for all his guests to consume 2 pounds of cheese. Since he already bought 10 pounds, he must buy an additional 4 pounds. Therefore, the correct answer choice will equal 4 when you substitute 10 for $R$, 5 for $N$, and 2 for $P$:

(A) $\frac{(5)(2)}{10} \neq 4$ Discard

(B) $\frac{5}{(10)(2)} \neq 4$ Discard

(C) $\frac{5+2}{10} \neq 4$ Discard

(D) $\frac{2}{(5)(10)} \neq 4$ Discard

(E) $\frac{(2)(10)}{5} = 4$ Correct

Since only **(E)** gives 4, that must be the correct choice.

**10. B**

Ahmed owns 3 pairs of trousers and 5 jackets. So, for every pair of trousers, he can wear 5 different jackets, giving 5 different combinations for each pair of trousers, or $3 \times 5 = 15$ different combinations of trousers and jackets. With each of these combinations, he can wear any of his different shirts. The different combinations of shirts, jackets, and trousers is (number of shirts) $\times$ 15. You're told this equals 90, so the number of shirts $= 90 \div 15 =$ **6**.

**11. E**

This is best solved intuitively. The maximum number of bonds that can be bought is when all the bonds are in \$50 denominations. Since Robert bought \$2,000 worth of bonds, the maximum number of bonds he could buy is $\frac{\$2{,}000}{\$50} = 40$ bonds. If he bought fifty \$50 bonds, he would spend $50 \times \$50 = \$2{,}500$. This is too much. If he bought any \$100 bonds, he would spend even more money. So, it is impossible to buy \$2,000 worth of bonds by purchasing **50** bonds in any combination of the two denominations.

**12. A**

Exports to China are 4% of all of Madagascar's exports. The dollar amount for Madagascar's exports is $1.3 billion, but be aware that the question asks for millions of dollars. Multiply $1.3 billion by 1,000 to get the number of millions, or 1,300 million. Then, multiply 1,300 by 0.04 (4%) to get **$52 million**.

**13. E**

To find the ratio of the numbers of hourly employees working in Packaged Foods and Frozen Foods, use the given table. The Packaged Foods department has 32 hourly employees, and the Frozen Foods department has 6 hourly employees. That means the ratio is 32:6, which simplifies to **16:3**. Note that (C) is a trap answer; 9:5 is the ratio of salaried employees in the two departments, not hourly employees.

**14. B**

Because the time it takes each person to analyze one dish is a fraction of an hour, the most efficient way to answer this question is to define each person's rate in terms of analyses per hour, which is an integer (rather than using the two-person combined rate formula $t = \frac{ab}{a+b}$, which would require you to plug in times). For Rosie, that rate is given as 6 per hour. Since Steve analyzes the contents of one dish in 15 minutes (a quarter hour), his average rate is 4 per hour. Thus, working together, the two can analyze the contents of $6 + 4 = 10$ Petri dishes per hour. This means they can analyze $4 \times 10 = 40$ dishes in **4 hours**.

**15. C**

The mule covers $\frac{2}{3}$ of the distance the horse does in any given amount of time, so if the horse goes the whole distance in 6 hours, the mule goes $\frac{2}{3}$ of the distance in the same time, with $\frac{1}{3}$ of the distance to go. It takes 6 hours to get $\frac{2}{3}$ of the way, so it will take half this, or 3 hours, to get the remaining $\frac{1}{3}$ of the way. Therefore, the whole journey takes the mule $6 + 3 = 9$ hours.

Alternatively, consider finding the mule's rate by taking two-thirds of the horse's rate. The horse travels 20 miles in 6 hours; therefore, the horse's speed is $\frac{20 \text{ miles}}{6 \text{ hours}}$. The mule travels at $\frac{2}{3}$ this speed:

$$\frac{2}{3} \times \frac{20 \text{ miles}}{6 \text{ hours}} = \frac{20 \text{ miles}}{9 \text{ hours}}$$

Thus, the mule needs **9** hours to travel 20 miles.

**16. B**

This is a "groups of groups" question. The three groups (sophomores, juniors, and seniors) can be arranged in $3! = 6$ different ways. Within the sophomores grouped together and the juniors grouped together, they can each be arranged in $3! = 6$ different ways. The seniors can line up in $4! = 24$ different ways. Thus, the total number of different ways the 10 students can be arranged is $6 \times 6 \times 6 \times 24 = 5{,}184$ ways. Since you don't have a calculator, you can approximate the calculations as $6 \times 6 = 36$. Multiply that by 6 and the result is slightly more than 200 (216 to be exact). Finally, $200 \times 24 = 4{,}800$, so the result is a bit more than 4,800; only **5,184** is close.

**17. E**

The probability of all the outcomes of two independent events can be expressed as $P_A + P_B - P_{Both} + P_{Neither} = 1$. The stem provides the values for $P_A$ and $P_{Neither}$. The probability of both Event A and Event B occurring is the product of their individual probabilities, so $P_{Both} = 0.6P_B$. Plug these values into the equation to get $0.6 + P_B - 0.6P_B + 0.06 = 1.00$. Thus, $0.4P_B = 0.34$, and $P_B =$ **0.85**.

**18. D**

You know the time it takes Joe and Sam together to finish a job, so see if the statements provide information that would help establish the time it takes Joe to complete the job alone.

Statement (1) gives Joe's time alone; from that you can find what fraction of the job he did. Statement (1) is sufficient.

Statement (2) establishes what fraction Sam did; Joe must have done the rest of the job, so Statement (2) is also sufficient. Each statement alone is sufficient, so choose **(D)**.

**19. C**

You're given the total number who read at least one of the two papers. Keep in mind that this includes people who read both papers. With the number of people who read exactly one of each of the two papers, you'd be able to find the number who read both.

Statement (1) gives the number who read only the *Herald.* But you can't find what you need: the number who read both papers. The first statement is insufficient, so eliminate (A) and (D).

Statement (2) is similar to Statement (1); it, too, gives you information on only one paper, while you need information on both, so it's insufficient as well. Eliminate (B). If you use both statements together, though, you have the number reading each paper and the total number. You could add each of the individual numbers to get the total number of people who read exactly one of the papers. Then, you could subtract this from the total number of people who read at least one of the papers to get the number of people who read both. Thus, the statements are sufficient together, and **(C)** is correct.

**20. C**

To find the average order, you'd need the number of orders and the total income. You already know the number of orders for amounts \$100 or less and the number of orders for amounts greater than \$100; the total number of orders is just the sum of these two. So, what you need from the statements is the total income.

Statement (1) tells you the totals from the two types of sales were equal; however, you still need the actual numbers. This is not sufficient.

Statement (2) gives the income for orders for amounts \$100 or less; this still leaves you in the dark about the income for orders for amounts greater than \$100. Using the statements together, you know the two types of sales account for equal income, you know the income from one type, and you know the total number of sales. This is sufficient to find the average dollar amount of an order. Both statements together are sufficient; choose **(C)**.

**21. A**

First consider Statement (1). If 4 is in $S$, and it is not the source integer, then it must be the square or cube of another integer in $S$. Since 4 is not the cube of any positive integer, and it is the square of 2, then 2 must be in $S$. The square and cube of every integer in $S$ is also in $S$; thus, 4 and 8 would be in $S$. Statement (1) by itself is sufficient to answer the question. Eliminate (B), (C), and (E).

Now look at Statement (2). The statement "64 is in $S$ and is not the source integer" must be considered in two cases:

1. If 64 is in $S$ because it represents the square of 8, then 8, 64, and 512 are in $S$. In this case, 8 would be in $S$.

   OR

2. If 64 is in $S$ because it represents the cube of 4, then you only know for sure that 4, 16, and 64 are in $S$. In this case, you cannot prove that 8 is in $S$.

Therefore, Statement (2) is insufficient to answer this question. The correct choice is **(A)**.

**22. A**

This Value question lists a set of 5 values, including the variable $x$, and asks for the value of the median. When placed in ascending order, the set is $\{-3, 0, 1, 4, x\}$, with $x$ arbitrarily placed at the end. In order to determine the value of the median, you will need to know more about the value of $x$.

Statement (1) limits $x$ to values greater than or equal to 1. If $x = 1$, then the data set is $\{-3, 0, 1, 1, 4\}$, so the median is 1. If $x > 1$, then the data set is $\{-3, 0, 1, x, 4\}$ or $\{-3, 0, 1, 4, x\}$. In either case, the median is 1. Statement (1) is sufficient. Eliminate (B), (C), and (E).

Statement (2) limits $x$ to values less than or equal to 1. From the analysis of Statement (1), if $x = 1$, the median is 1. However, if $x < 0$, the data set is $\{-3, x, 0, 1, 4\}$ or $\{x, -3, 0, 1, 4\}$, either of which will result in a median of 0. Statement (2) is insufficient. **(A)** is correct.

**23. C**

The stem asks for the average production cost of an $x$-car but provides no other information, so look to the statements to see what information they might give to establish that price. Statement (1) tells you the cost of producing a group of $x$-cars and $y$-cars; since there is no way to determine how much of the money is due to the x-cars, Statement (1) is insufficient. Eliminate (A) and (D).

Statement (2) only gives the difference in cost between producing an X-car and a Y-car with nothing to establish the actual costs; this is also insufficient, so eliminate (B). Putting the statements together, you have the total cost of 100 X-cars and 100 Y-cars, and you have the difference in cost between the two types of cars. Express this information in equation form as

1. $100x + 100y = 2.2$ million
2. $x = 2{,}000 + y$

This gives two linear equations with two unknowns; thus, this system of equations is solvable. Both statements together are sufficient, and **(C)** is correct.

**24. C**

To find the value of $p$, you need the amount of the interest and the length of time over which that interest was earned. Statement (1) gives you some information about the interest, but since you still don't know how long the term of the certificate is, you cannot find the interest from Statement (1). Eliminate (A) and (D).

Statement (2) gives the term of the certificate, but there's no information about the interest, so it is insufficient. Eliminate (B). If you consider both statements together, you know how much less the certificate would earn if it were not compounded, and you know how long the money was earning this interest. The interest accrued in the first quarter is the same regardless of whether the interest is compounded; the difference is the second quarter interest. This extra interest is one-quarter of $p$ percent of the interest earned in the first quarter. The first quarter interest is one-quarter of $p$ percent of \$10,000; therefore:

$$18 = \frac{p}{4} \text{ percent of } \frac{p}{4} \text{ percent of } \$10{,}000$$

This is a bit of a nasty equation, but it's a linear equation with one variable, so it can be solved for $p$. Both statements together are sufficient—that's **(C)**.

**25. D**

Standard deviation is a measure of the spread of a data set. Since the lists have variables, the standard deviation can only be calculated if actual values are given or, possibly, some comparison to a known standard deviation.

Statement (1): Each value in List $M$ is 12 greater than each value in List $L$, so the spread between the numbers in the two lists is identical, even though the mean of List $M$ is greater. Statement (1) is sufficient.

Statement (2): Each value in List $N$ is 8 times each value in List $L$. Therefore, the spread between the numbers is 8 times as great and the standard deviation is also 8 times as great. Statement (2) is also sufficient. Since each statement is sufficient on its own, **(D)** is correct.

CHAPTER 7

# Geometry

**LEARNING OBJECTIVES**

After studying this chapter, you will be able to:

- Describe which topics in geometry are tested on the GMAT
- Identify questions that feature geometry
- Apply the Kaplan Methods for Problem Solving and Data Sufficiency to questions testing various geometry skills

The GMAT will test your ability to solve questions dealing with geometric shapes and figures. Thankfully, only a finite set of geometry concepts are tested on the GMAT. Learning a handful of rules and principles will give you a solid foundation for success on these questions in the Quantitative section. Here is a list of geometry concepts that the GMAT might test:

- Lines and angles
- Polygons
- Triangles
- Right triangles
- Distances and right triangles in coordinate geometry
- Quadrilaterals
- Circles
- Solids
- Multiple figures

In this chapter, you will first see a set of drills that covers the concepts listed above. Work through the drills and then check your performance. Review the explanation of each question to see the steps taken to arrive at the correct answer.

As you review, assess your current ability. If you find that you struggled with certain drills and would like to refresh your understanding of the concepts tested, check out the Geometry section of Chapter 9: Math Reference before tackling the practice set at the end of this chapter.

If you instead feel comfortable with your performance on the drills and confident in your abilities, then proceed directly to the practice set of GMAT-style questions. You will see both Problem Solving and Data Sufficiency questions. Apply your knowledge of geometry to these questions and tackle them strategically, using the step-by-step approach outlined in the Kaplan Methods.

When you finish the practice set, fully review every question by reading through its explanation—even for the questions that you answered correctly. In any question where the explanation discusses concepts unfamiliar to you, use the Math Reference chapter to further your understanding.

## Geometry Drills

Try these drills to test your proficiency with geometry. Use the answer key and explanations at the end of the chapter to check your work.

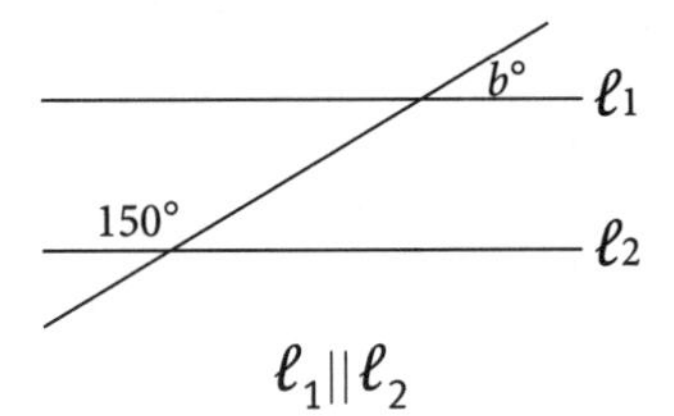


1. What is the value of *b*?

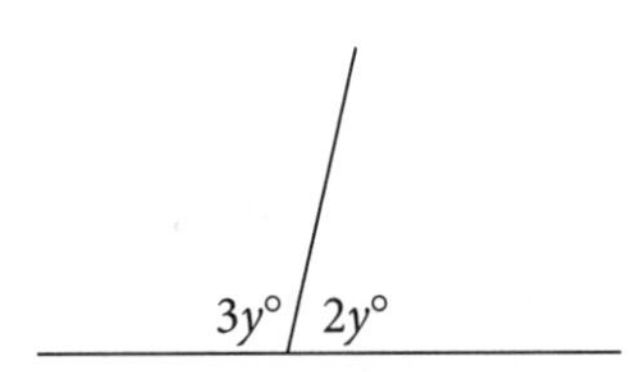


2. What is the value of *y*?

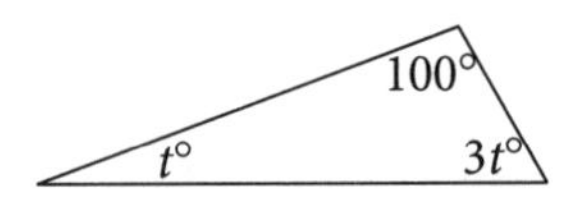


3. What is the value of *t*?

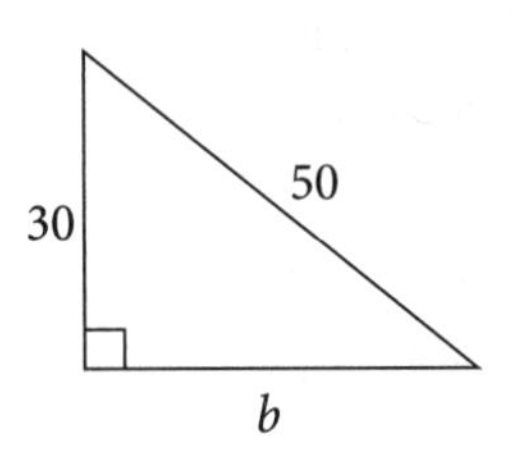


4. What is the value of *b*?

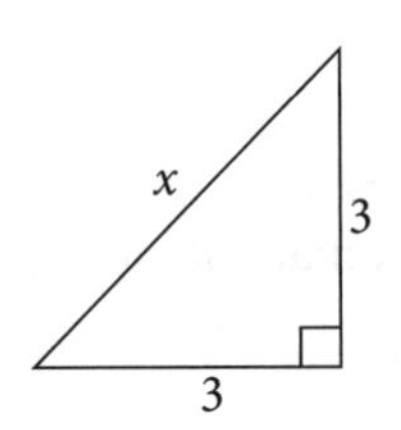


5. What is the value of *x*?

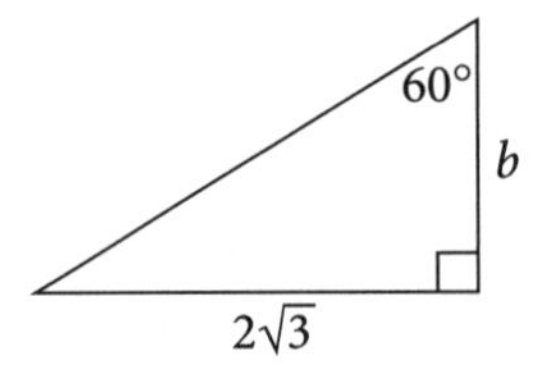


6. What is the value of *b*?

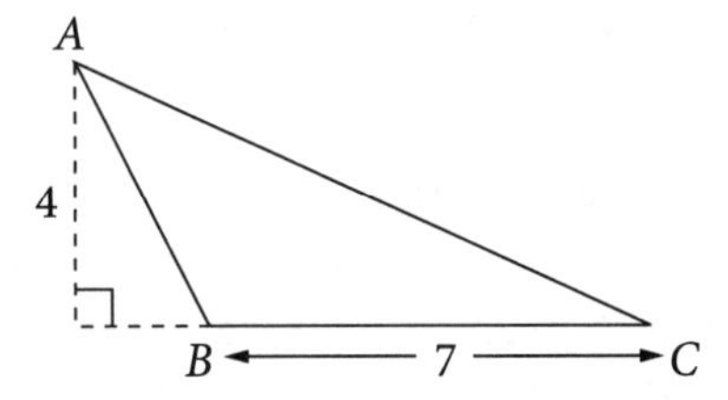


7. What is the area of triangle *ABC*?

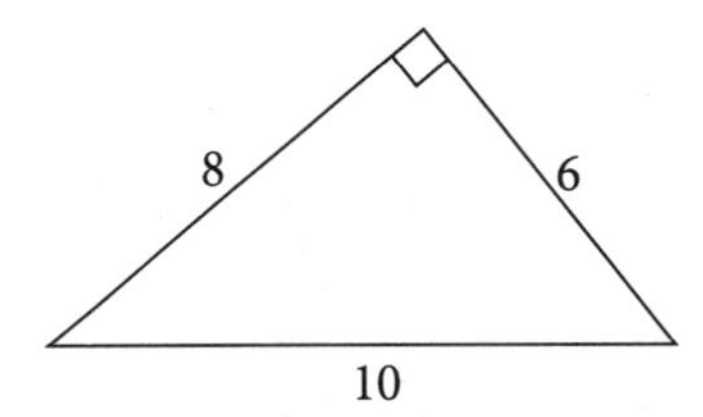


8. What is the area of the triangle above?

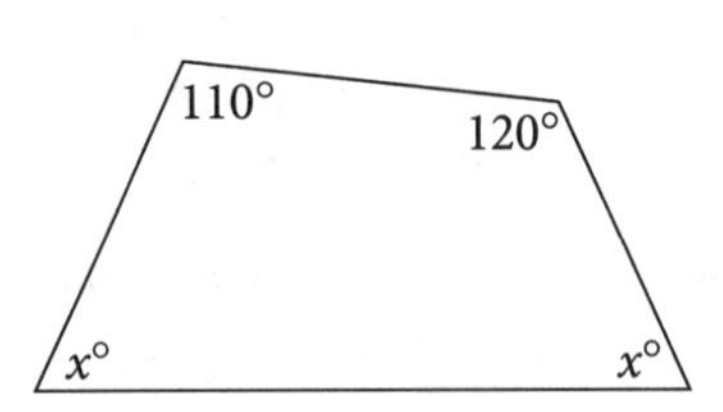


9. What is the value of *x*?

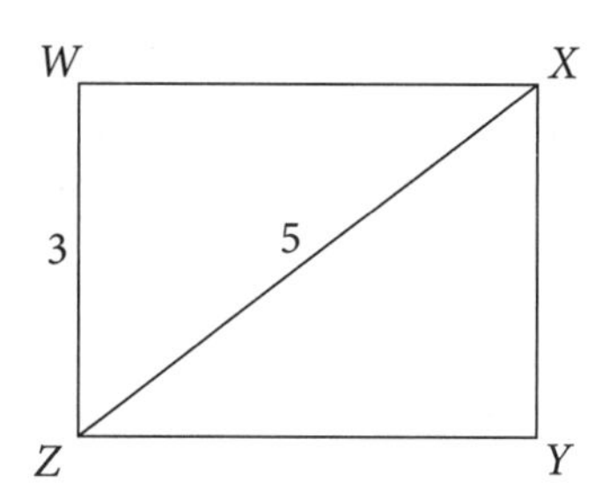


10. What is the area of rectangle *WXYZ*?

11. What is the circumference of a circle with diameter $\frac{3}{4\pi}$?

12. What is the area of a circle with radius $\sqrt{2}$?

13. What is the diameter of a circle with area $49\pi$?

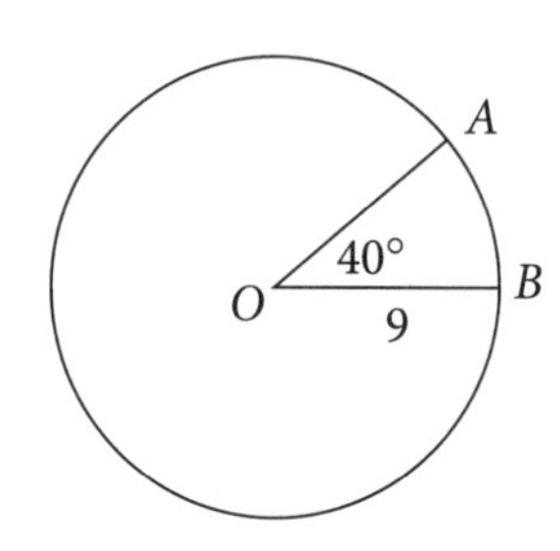


Arc $AB = ?$

14. Find the length of minor arc *AB*.

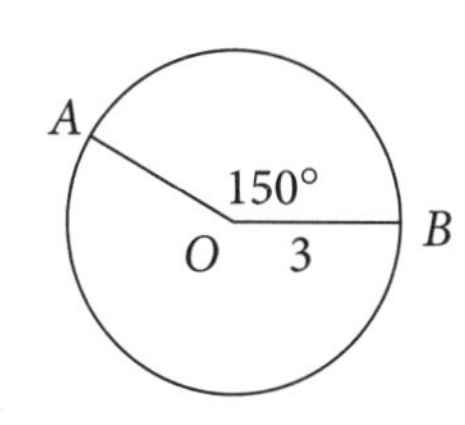


15. Find the area of sector *AOB*.

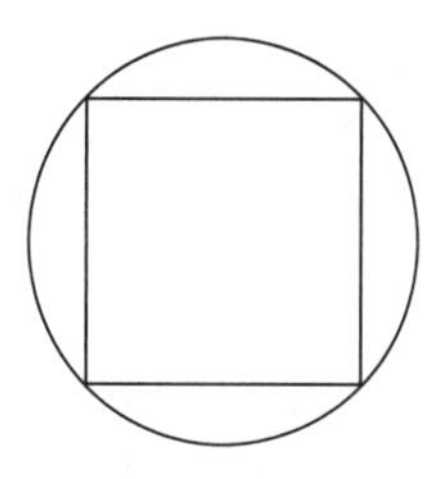

16. If the area of the square above is 4, what is the area of the circle?

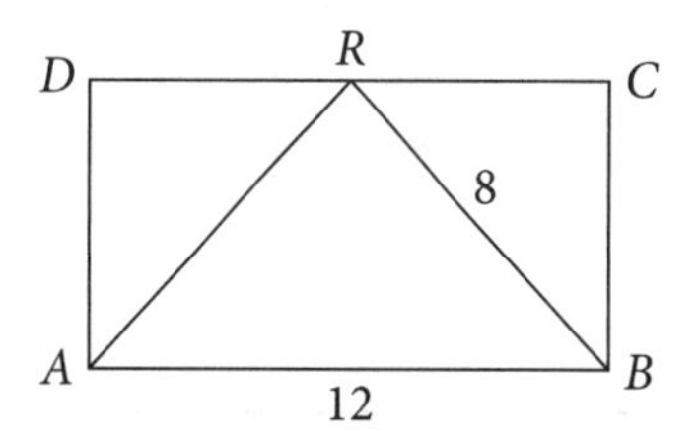


17. In the figure shown above, *AB* is the base of isosceles triangle *ABR* and a side of rectangle *ABCD*. What is the area of rectangle *ABCD*?

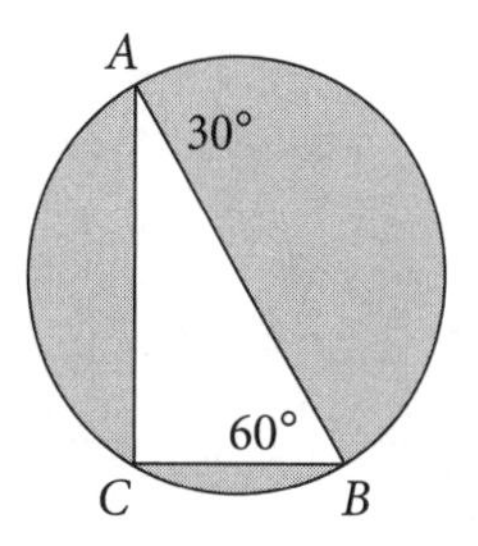


18. The hypotenuse of right triangle *ABC* is the diameter of the circle. If the diameter of the circle is 18, what is the area of the shaded region?

19. What are the volume and surface area of a cylinder with height 12 and radius 6?

20. What are the volume and surface area of a rectangular solid with dimensions 3, 4, and 12?

21. For two similar triangles, the ratio of their corresponding sides is 2:3. What is the ratio of their perimeters?

22. Triangle *ABC* is congruent to triangle *DEF*, and $AC = 8$, $AB = 10$, and $BC = 15$. The corresponding sides are *AB* and *DE*, *AC* and *DF*, and *BC* and *EF*. What is *EF*?

23. The diameter of a circle on the coordinate plane is formed by the line joining points (5, –2) and (–5, 3). Find the circumference of the circle.

24. If the radius of a circle is tripled, the circle's area is multiplied by what amount?

25. The length of a rectangle is $2x - 1$. The width is $3x + 5$. The perimeter is 38. What is the value of $x$?

Once you've completed these drills, check your performance by reviewing the answers and explanations at the end of this chapter. If you feel confident in your skill with geometry, try the realistic GMAT-style questions in the next practice set. If you want a refresher, check out the Geometry section in the Math Reference chapter at the end of the book.

# Geometry Practice Set

Try the following questions, using the Kaplan Method for Problem Solving and looking for opportunities to use picking numbers and backsolving. Answers and explanations are at the end of this chapter.

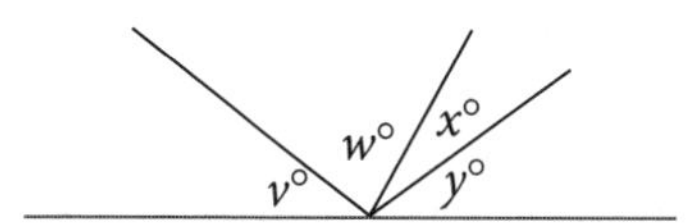


1. In the figure above, $2v = w$, $w = 4x$, and $x = \frac{y}{3}$. What is the value of $y$?

   - 18
   - 36
   - 45
   - 54
   - 60

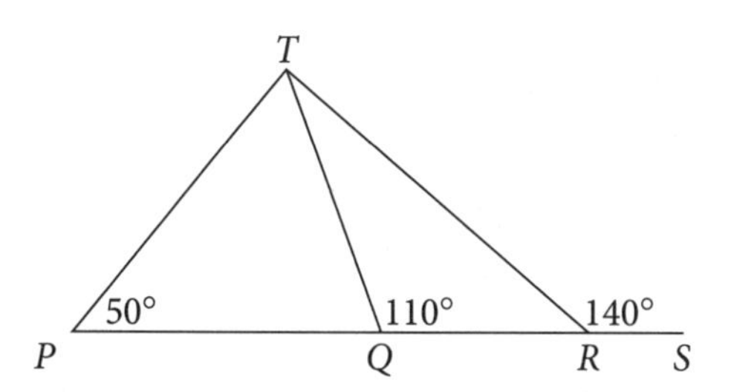


2. In the figure above, what is the measure of $\angle PTR$?

   - 30°
   - 50°
   - 65°
   - 70°
   - 90°

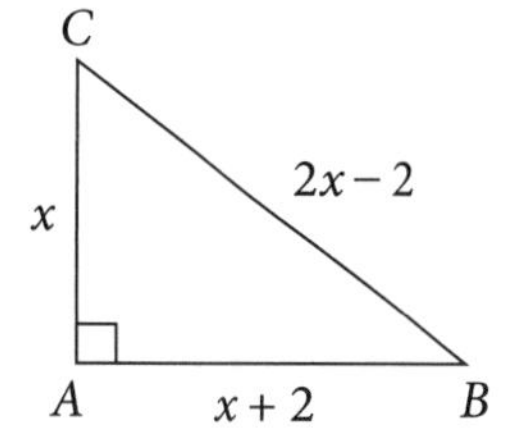


3. In right triangle $ABC$ above, $x =$

   - 6
   - 8
   - $6\sqrt{2}$
   - 10
   - 13

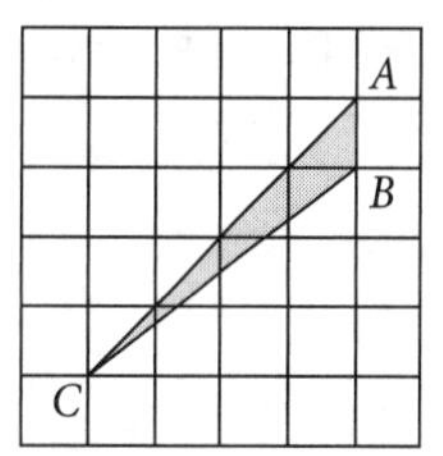


4. The figure shown above consists of 36 squares, each with a side of 1. What is the area of $\Delta ABC$?

   - 8
   - 6
   - 4
   - 2
   - $\frac{1}{2}$

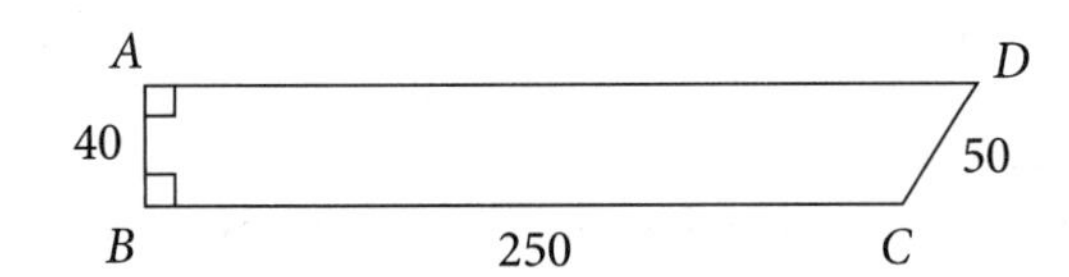


5. In the figure above, $AD \parallel BC$. What is the perimeter of quadrilateral $ABCD$?

- 590
- 600
- 620
- 640
- 680

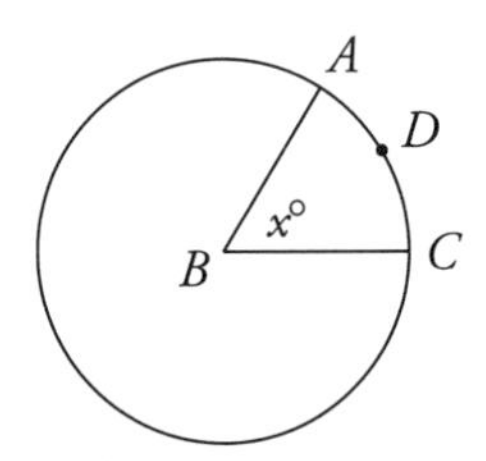


6. In the figure above, the ratio of the circumference of circle $B$ to the length of arc $ADC$ is 8:1. What is the value of $x$?

- 30
- 45
- 60
- 75
- 90

7. A line segment joining two points on the circumference of a circle is one inch from the center of the circle at its closest point. If the circle has a two-inch radius, what is the length of the line?

- 1
- $\sqrt{2}$
- 2
- $2\sqrt{2}$
- $2\sqrt{3}$

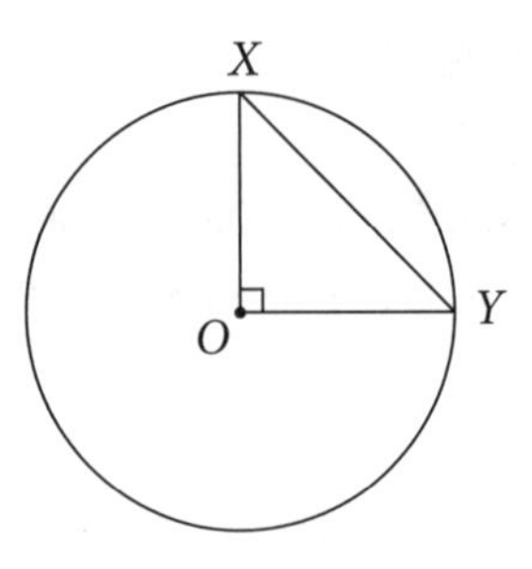


8. In the figure above, $O$ is the center of the circle. If the area of triangle $XOY$ is 25, what is the area of the circle?

- $25\pi$
- $25\pi\sqrt{2}$
- $50\pi$
- $50\pi\sqrt{3}$
- $625\pi$

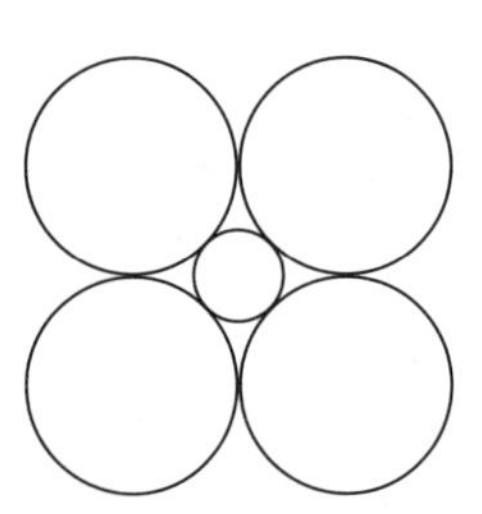

9. The total area of the four equal circles in the figure above is $36\pi$, and the circles are all tangent to one another. What is the diameter of the small circle?

- $6\sqrt{2}$
- $6+\sqrt{2}$
- $3\sqrt{2}-3$
- $6\sqrt{2}-6$
- $6\sqrt{2}+6$

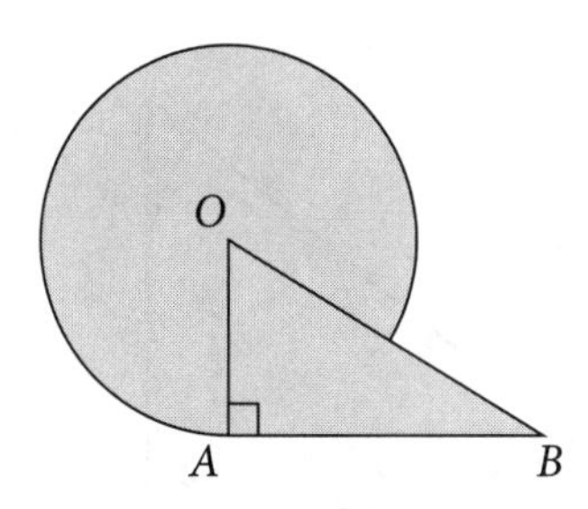


10. In the figure above, if radius $OA$ is 8 and the area of right triangle $OAB$ is 32, what is the area of the shaded region?

   - $64\pi + 32$
   - $60\pi + 32$
   - $56\pi + 32$
   - $32\pi + 32$
   - $16\pi + 32$

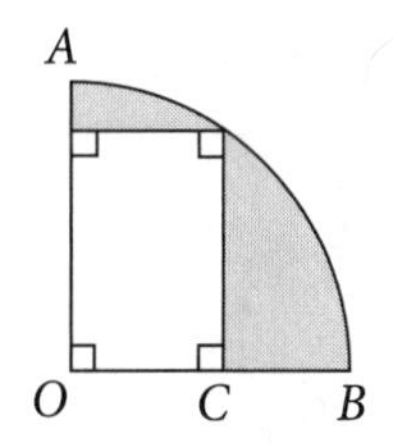


11. In the figure above, $AB$ is an arc of a circle with center $O$. If the length of arc $AB$ is $5\pi$ and the length of $CB$ is 4, what is the sum of the areas of the shaded regions?

   - $25\pi - 60$
   - $25\pi - 48$
   - $25\pi - 36$
   - $100\pi - 48$
   - $100\pi - 36$

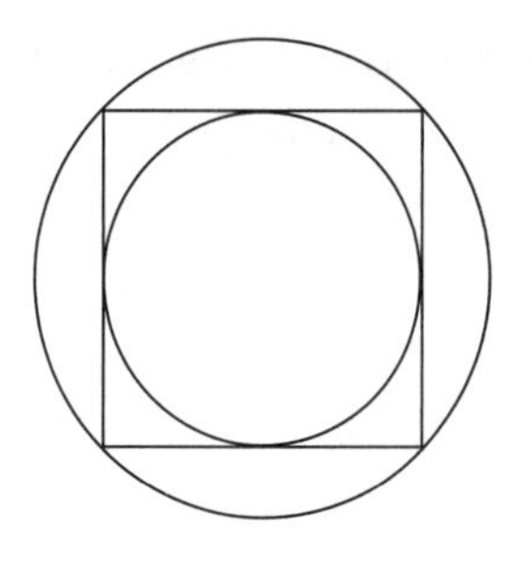

12. In the figure above, the smaller circle is inscribed in the square, and the square is inscribed in the larger circle. If the length of each side of the square is $s$, what is the ratio of the area of the larger circle to the area of the smaller circle?

   - $2\sqrt{2}:1$
   - $2:1$
   - $\sqrt{2}:1$
   - $2s:1$
   - $s\sqrt{2}:1$

13. A motor scooter has an empty rectangular gas tank with dimensions of $4 \times 8 \times 10$ inches. The tank is filled completely with gasoline from a cylindrical container with a diameter of 8 inches. If the gasoline in the cylindrical container is originally filled to a height of 20 inches before it is used to fill the gas tank, how high, in inches, is the gasoline in the cylindrical container after the tank is filled?

   - $\frac{20}{\pi}$
   - $80(4\pi - 3)$
   - $10$
   - $\frac{5(\pi - 1)}{4}$
   - $\frac{20(\pi - 1)}{\pi}$

14. What is the radius of the largest sphere that can be placed inside a cube of volume 64?

   - $6\sqrt{2}$
   - 8
   - 4
   - $2\sqrt{2}$
   - 2

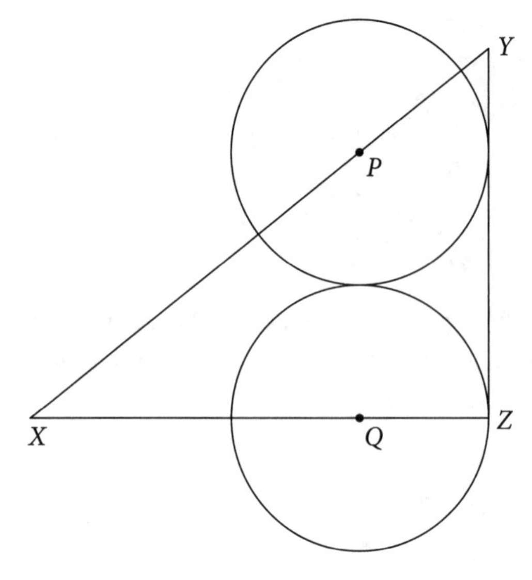


15. Circles $P$ and $Q$ each have a circumference of $10\pi$ and are each tangent to $YZ$. If $XZ = 17$, then $YZ =$

   - 10
   - $\frac{85}{6}$
   - $\frac{43}{3}$
   - 15
   - 17

Try the following questions, using the Kaplan Method for Data Sufficiency and looking for opportunities to pick numbers, solve without algebra, and guess strategically. Answers and explanations are at the end of this chapter.

*Note:* Because the Data Sufficiency answer choices are always the same and should be memorized, we have omitted them here. If you need a refresher on the choices or the 12TEN mnemonic, review Chapter 3 on Data Sufficiency.

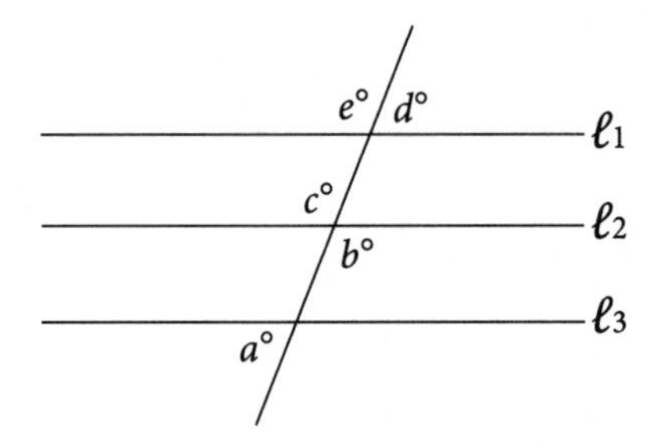


16. What is the value of $a + b + c + d + e$?

   (1) $\ell_1$ is parallel to $\ell_2$, and $\ell_2$ is parallel to $\ell_3$.

   (2) $e = 150$

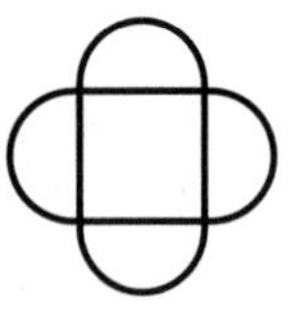

17. What is the area of the figure above formed by a square and four semicircles?

   (1) The perimeter of the figure is $12\pi$.

   (2) The perimeter of the square is 24.

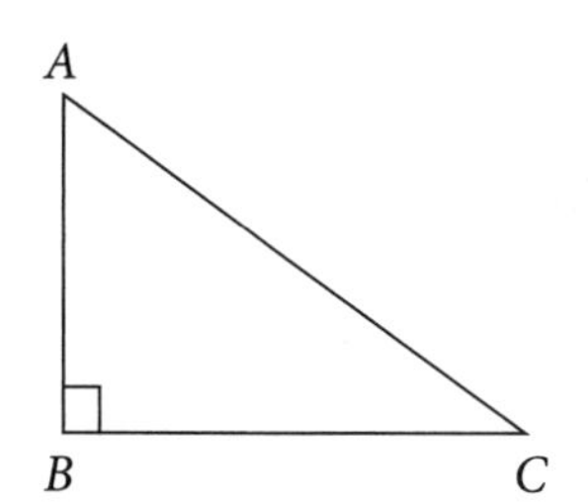


18. In $\Delta ABC$ above, what is the length of segment $AB$?

    (1) $AC = \sqrt{2}$

    (2) $AB = BC$

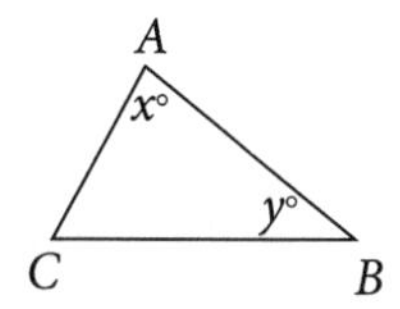


19. What is the length of side $AC$ of triangle $ABC$?

    (1) $AB = 13$ and $BC = 5$

    (2) $x + y = 90$

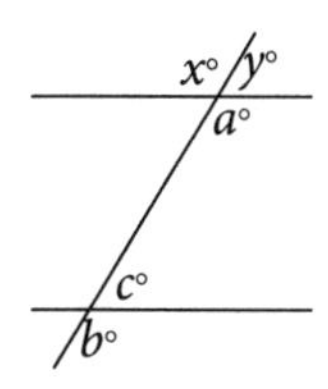


20. In the figure above, does $a = b$?

    (1) $x = y$

    (2) $c = x$

21. What is the perimeter of rectangle $ABCD$?

    (1) The area of $ABCD$ is 12 square inches.

    (2) The length of $AB$, in inches, is an integer.

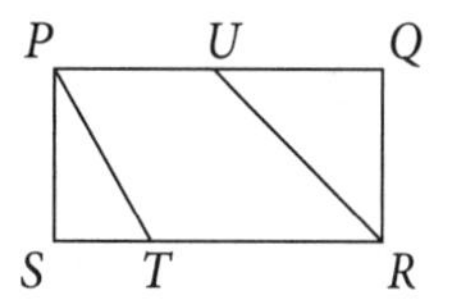


22. What is the area of triangle $PST$ shown above?

    (1) The area of rectangle $PQRS$ is 40.

    (2) The area of parallelogram $PTRU$ is 32.

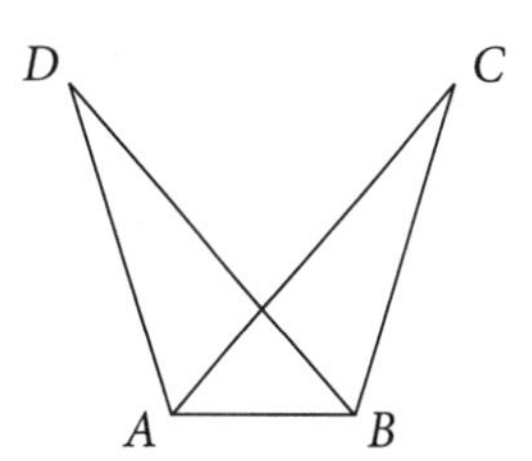


23. In the figure above, what is the ratio of the area of triangle $ABC$ to the area of triangle $ABD$?

    (1) The ratio of the height of triangle $ABD$ to the height of triangle $ABC$ is 4:3.

    (2) $AB = 8$

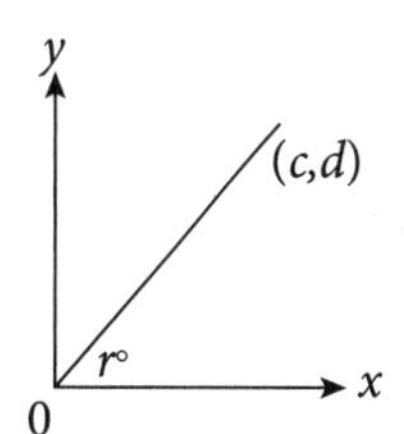


24. In the figure above, what is the value of $r$?

    (1) $c = 2$

    (2) $c = d$

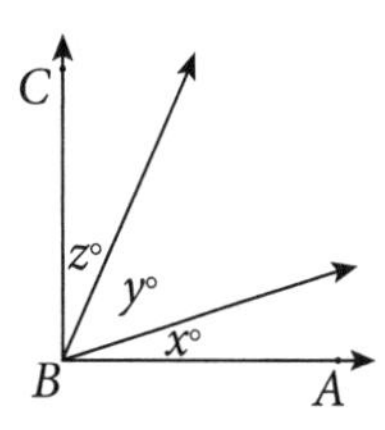


25. In the given diagram, $\angle ABC$ is a right angle. What is the value of $z$?

    (1) The value of $y$ is three times the value of $z$.

    (2) The value of $x$ is $\frac{1}{2}$ the value of $z$.

## Answer Key

### Geometry Drills

1. 30
2. 36
3. 20
4. 40
5. $3\sqrt{2}$
6. 2
7. 14
8. 24
9. 65
10. 12
11. $\frac{3}{4}$
12. $2\pi$
13. 14
14. $2\pi$
15. $\frac{15}{4}\pi$
16. $2\pi$
17. $24\sqrt{7}$
18. $81\pi - \frac{81\sqrt{3}}{2}$
19. $V = 432\pi$; $SA = 216\pi$
20. $V = 144$; $SA = 192$
21. 2:3
22. 15
23. $5\pi\sqrt{5}$
24. 9
25. 3

### Geometry Practice Set

1. D
2. E
3. A
4. D
5. C
6. B
7. E
8. C
9. D
10. C
11. B
12. B
13. E
14. E
15. B
16. C
17. D
18. C
19. C
20. C
21. E
22. C
23. A
24. B
25. C

# Answers and Explanations

## Geometry Drills

**1.** The angle to the right of 150° is $180° - 150° = 30°$; this angle corresponds to angle $b$, so $b = \mathbf{30}$.

**2.** Angles that form a straight line together measure 180°, so $3y + 2y = 180$. Thus, $5y = 180$. Dividing each side of the equation by 5 yields $y = \mathbf{36}$.

**3.** The interior angles of a triangle sum to 180°, so $t + 3t + 100 = 180$. Combining like terms yields $4t = 80$, and dividing both sides of the equation by 4 gives $t = \mathbf{20}$.

**4.** Recognize that the given sides are components of the 3:4:5 Pythagorean triple multiplied by 10, which means $b$ is $4 \times 10 = \mathbf{40}$. Alternatively, use the Pythagorean theorem to solve for $b$: $30^2 + b^2 = 50^2$, so $b^2 = 1{,}600$, which means $b = \mathbf{40}$.

**5.** Use the Pythagorean theorem: $3^2 + 3^2 = x^2 = 18$. Then $x = \sqrt{18} = \sqrt{9}\sqrt{2} = \mathbf{3\sqrt{2}}$.

Alternatively, use the fact that the legs of this right triangle are of equal length to deduce that the opposite angles equal 45°. The side ratio for a 45-45-90 triangle is $1{:}1{:}\sqrt{2}$, which here is multiplied by 3, or $3{:}3{:}3\sqrt{2}$. The hypotenuse is $\mathbf{3\sqrt{2}}$.

**6.** The side ratio for a 30-60-90 triangle is $1{:}\sqrt{3}{:}2$. Here, the side opposite the 60° angle is $2\sqrt{3}$, so multiply each part of the side ratio by 2 to get $2{:}2\sqrt{3}{:}4$. The side with length $b$ is opposite the 30° angle, so $b = \mathbf{2}$.

**7.** The area of a triangle is $\frac{1}{2}(\text{Base})(\text{Height})$. Here that's $\frac{1}{2}(4)(7) = \mathbf{14}$.

**8.** The area of a triangle is $\frac{1}{2}(\text{Base})(\text{Height})$. The legs of a right triangle form its base and height, so that's $\frac{1}{2}(6)(8) = \mathbf{24}$.

**9.** The interior angles of a quadrilateral sum to 360°, so $x + x + 110 + 120 = 360$. Combining like terms yields $2x = 130$, and dividing each side of the equation by 2 gives $x = \mathbf{65}$.

**10.** Triangle $ZWX$ is a 3:4:5 triangle, so $WX = 4$. The area of a rectangle is Length × Width, so the area of this rectangle is $3 \times 4 = \mathbf{12}$.

**11.** The circumference of a circle is Diameter($\pi$), so this circumference $= \pi\left(\frac{3}{4\pi}\right) = \mathbf{\frac{3}{4}}$.

**12.** The area of a circle is Radius$^2(\pi)$, so the area of this circle $= \pi(\sqrt{2})^2 = \mathbf{2\pi}$.

**13.** The area of a circle is Radius$^2(\pi)$. First find the radius: $49\pi = \pi r^2$, so $r^2 = 49$ and $r = 7$. The diameter is twice the radius, or $2(7) = \mathbf{14}$.

**14.** The central angle, arc length, and area of the sector of a circle are proportional to the corresponding measures of the whole circle. There are 360° in a circle, so the sector bounded by arc $AB$ is $\frac{40}{360} = \frac{1}{9}$ of the circle. Because the radius is 9, the circumference is $(2)(9)(\pi) = 18\pi$. Finally, $\left(\frac{1}{9}\right)(18\pi) = \mathbf{2\pi}$.

**15.** The central angle, arc length, and area of the sector of a circle are proportional to the corresponding measures of the whole circle. There are 360° in a circle, so sector *AOB* is $\frac{150}{360} = \frac{5}{12}$ of the circle. Because the radius is 3, the area of the circle is $3^2\pi$, or $9\pi$. Finally, the area of the sector $= \left(\frac{5}{12}\right)(9\pi) = \mathbf{\frac{15}{4}\pi}$.

**16.** Because the area of the square is 4, its sides have length $\sqrt{4} = 2$. The diagonal of the square would form two 45-45-90 triangles and, per the side ratios for these triangles, is thus $2\sqrt{2}$. The diagonal of a square inscribed in a circle is also the diameter of the circle.

$$\text{diameter} = 2\sqrt{2}$$
$$\text{radius} = \sqrt{2}$$
$$\text{area} = \pi(\sqrt{2})^2 = \mathbf{2\pi}$$

**17.** To find the area of a rectangle, you need the length and width. The length of this rectangle is 12. Triangle *RCB* is a right triangle with a hypotenuse of 8. *RC* is $\left(\frac{1}{2}\right)12 = 6$. Use the Pythagorean theorem to solve for leg *BC*: $6^2 + BC^2 = 8^2$, so $36 + BC^2 = 64$. Thus, $BC^2 = 28$ and $BC = \sqrt{28} = \sqrt{4 \times 7} = 2\sqrt{7}$.

Now find the area: $12 \times 2\sqrt{7} = \mathbf{24\sqrt{7}}$.

**18.** The area of the shaded region is the area of the whole circle minus the area of the inscribed right triangle. The area of the circle is $\pi r^2 = \pi(9)^2 = 81\pi$. Because the hypotenuse of the triangle is also the circle's diameter, its length is 18. Per the side ratios of a 30-60-90 triangle, the legs have lengths of 9 and $9\sqrt{3}$. Now find the area of the triangle:

$$\left(\frac{1}{2}\right)(\text{base})(\text{height}) = \left(\frac{1}{2}\right)(9)\left(9\sqrt{3}\right) = \frac{81\sqrt{3}}{2}.$$

Finally, the shaded area is $\mathbf{81\pi - \frac{81\sqrt{3}}{2}}$.

**19.** The volume of a cylinder is the area of the circular base times the height. The area of this cylinder's base is $\pi r^2 = (6^2)\pi = 36\pi$. Thus, the volume $= 36\pi \times 12 = \mathbf{432\pi}$.

The surface area of a cylinder is the areas of its two circular bases plus the area of its sides. Think of the sides as a soup can label; when unrolled, it is a rectangle with a length that is the circumference of the can and a width that is the height of the can. The area of each base is $36\pi$, so together they have an area of $2 \times 36\pi = 72\pi$. The area of the sides is $(2\pi \times 6)(12) = 144\pi$. Thus, the surface area of the cylinder is $72\pi + 144\pi = \mathbf{216\pi}$.

**20.** The volume of a rectangular solid is Length × Width × Height. Therefore, the volume of this solid is $3 \times 4 \times 12 =$ **144**.

The surface area of a rectangular solid is the area of each of its six rectangular faces:

- $3 \times 4 = 12$
- $4 \times 12 = 48$
- $3 \times 12 = 36$

Each of these faces is matched with an identical face on the opposite side of the solid, so add their areas and multiply by 2: $(12 + 48 + 36) \times 2 = 96 \times 2 =$ **192**.

**21.** The ratio of the perimeters of two similar triangles equals the ratio of the corresponding sides, which is **2:3** in this case.

**22.** The word *congruent* means "identical in every way." Since $EF$ is the corresponding side to $BC$ and $BC = 15$, $EF =$ **15**.

**23.** Make a quick sketch, drawing a line from (5,–2) to (–5,3) and then two more lines to make a right triangle. Find the lengths of the legs of the triangle and then use the Pythagorean theorem to solve for the hypotenuse, which is the distance between the points (and the diameter of the circle).

One leg has length $|5-(-5)| = 10$. The other leg has length $|-2-3| = 5$.

$$(10)^2 + (5)^2 = d^2$$
$$100 + 25 = d^2$$
$$d = \sqrt{125} = \sqrt{25}\sqrt{5} = 5\sqrt{5}$$

The diameter is $5\sqrt{5}$, so the circumference is $\mathbf{5\pi\sqrt{5}}$.

**24.** If the original circle has radius $r$, then its area is $\pi r^2$. The area after the radius is tripled would be $\pi(3r)^2 = 9\pi r^2 = 9 \times \pi r^2$. Thus, the area is multiplied by **9**.

**25.** The perimeter of a rectangle is the sum of the lengths of its sides, or 2(Length) + 2(Width). In this case, $38 = 2(2x - 1) + 2(3x + 5)$. Multiply: $38 = 4x - 2 + 6x + 10$. Combine like terms: $38 = 10x + 8$. And solve for $x$: $30 = 10x$; $x =$ **3**.

## Geometry Practice Set

**1. D**

The sum $v + w + x + y$ must equal 180 since the angles with these measures together form a straight line. Since the question asks for the value of $y$, define all variables in terms of $y$. If $w = 4x$ and $x = \frac{y}{3}$, then $w = \frac{4y}{3}$. Similarly, $2v = w$, so $v = \frac{4y}{3} \div 2$, or $\frac{4y}{6}$, which reduces to $\frac{2y}{3}$. Substitute the angles in terms of $y$ into the equation:

$$v + w + x + y = 180$$
$$\frac{2y}{3} + \frac{4y}{3} + \frac{y}{3} + y = 180$$
$$\frac{10y}{3} = 180$$
$$10y = 540$$
$$y = \mathbf{54}$$

**2. E**

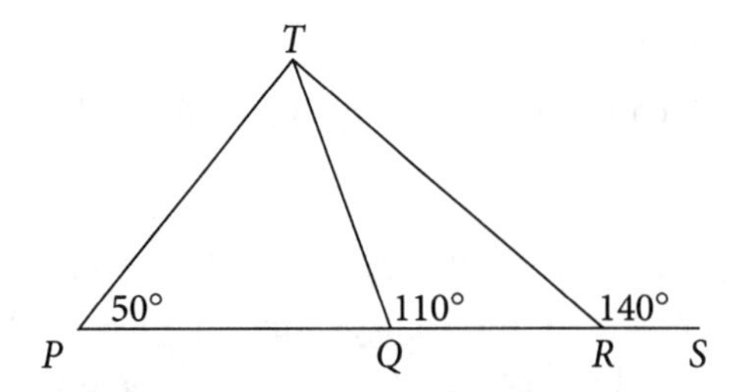


The two interior angles of $\Delta PRT$ that are remote to the exterior angle $\angle TRS$ will be equal to the measure of that exterior angle, or 140°. $\angle TPR$ with measure 50° is one of these angles and $\angle PTR$, whose measure you're trying to find, is the other. Since 50° plus the measure of $\angle PTR$ must sum to 140°, the measure of $\angle PTR = 140° - 50°$, or 90°. Alternatively, you could notice that $\angle PRT$ is supplementary to $\angle TRS$, which means it must equal 40°. Since $\angle RPT$ is equal to 50° and interior angles of a triangle must add up to 180°, $\angle PTR = 180° - 50° - 40° = \mathbf{90°}$.

**3. A**

This problem involves as much algebra as geometry. The Pythagorean theorem states that the sum of the squares of the legs is equal to the square of the hypotenuse, or, in this case:

$$x^2 + (x+2)^2 = (2x-2)^2$$

From here on in, it's a matter of algebra:

$$x^2 + x^2 + 4x + 4 = 4x^2 - 8x + 4$$
$$2x^2 + 4x + 4 = 4x^2 - 8x + 4$$
$$2x^2 - 12x = 0$$
$$2x(x-6) = 0$$

When the product of two factors is 0, one of them must equal 0. Thus, either $2x = 0$ and $x = 0$, or $x - 6 = 0$ and $x = 6$. Since $x$ is the length of one side of a triangle, it must be a positive number, and $x$ must equal **6** (which makes this a 6:8:10 triangle).

Another way to do this problem is to try plugging each answer choice into the expression for $x$ to see which one gives side lengths that work in the Pythagorean theorem. **(A)** yields 6, 8, and 10 (a Pythagorean triple) for the three sides of the triangle, so it must be the answer.

**4. D**

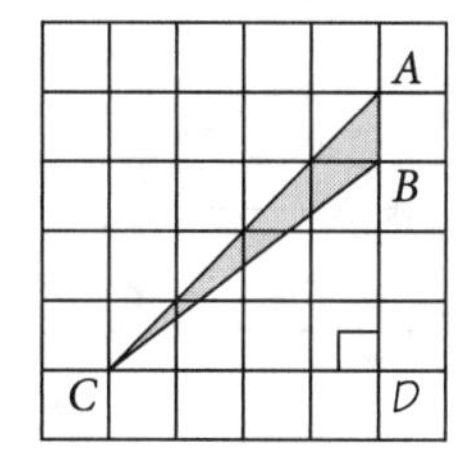


Note that point *D* has been added for clarity.

The area of a triangle is $\frac{1}{2} \times \text{base} \times \text{height}$. If you treat *AB* as the base of $\Delta ABC$, then the triangle's height is *CD*. Each square has a side length of 1, so you can just count the squares. $AB = 1$, $CD = 4$, so the area is $\frac{1}{2} \times 1 \times 4 = \mathbf{2}$.

**5. C**

You're given the lengths of three of the four sides of *ABCD*; all you need to find is the length of side *AD*. Drop a perpendicular line from point *C* to side *AD* and call the point where this perpendicular line meets side *AD* point *E*; this divides the figure into rectangle *ABCE* and right triangle *CDE*.

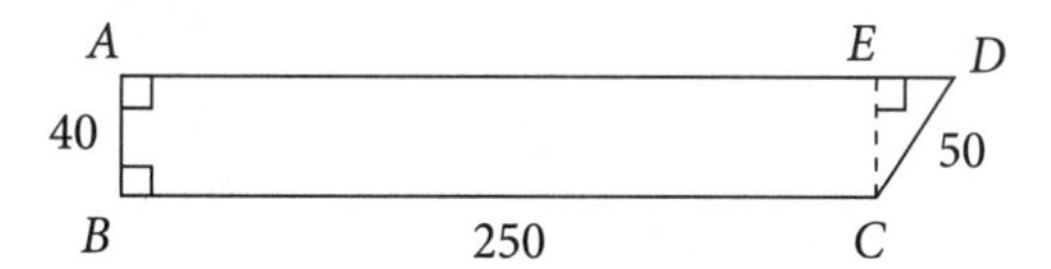


Since *ABCE* is a rectangle, *AE* has the same length as *BC*: 250. Similarly, *EC* has the same length as *AB*: 40. Now, find the length of *ED*: it is a leg of a right triangle with hypotenuse 50 and other leg 40. This is just 10 times as big as a 3:4:5 right triangle; therefore, *ED* must have a length of $10 \times 3$, or 30. So *AD*, which is $AE + ED$, is $250 + 30$, or 280. Finally, the perimeter is equal to $AB + BC + CD + AD$, or $40 + 250 + 50 + 280 = \mathbf{620}$.

**6. B**

Use the following ratio:

$$\frac{\text{Length of arc}}{\text{Circumference}} = \frac{\text{Measure of arc's central angle}}{360^\circ}$$

The measure of the arc's central angle is marked *x* degrees, and since the ratio of the circumference to the arc length is 8:1, the length of the arc is $\frac{1}{8}$ of the circumference. So,

$$\frac{1}{8} = \frac{x}{360}$$

$$8x = 360$$

$$x = \mathbf{45}$$

**7. E**

Sketch a diagram:

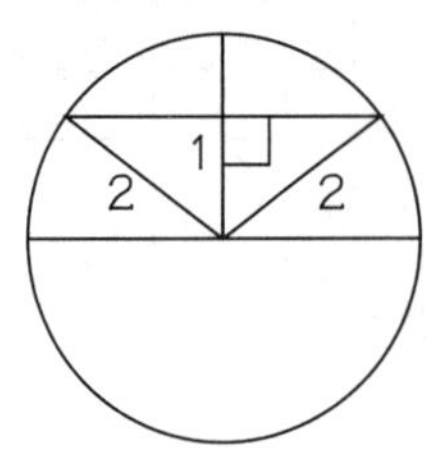


Since the radius of the circle is 2, the endpoints of the line are both 2 inches from the center. The line can be seen as the legs of two right triangles, each of which has a hypotenuse of 2 and a leg of 1. Each of the legs that make up the line must have a length equal to $\sqrt{2^2 - 1^2}$, or $\sqrt{3}$. The total length of the line is twice this, or $\mathbf{2\sqrt{3}}$.

**8. C**

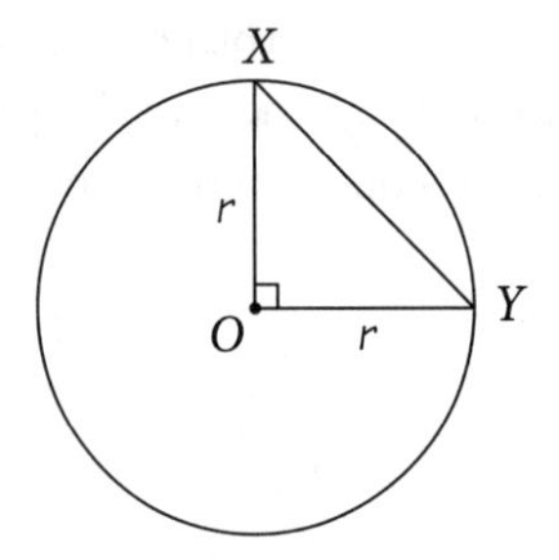


Each leg of right triangle *XOY* is also a radius of circle *O*. If the radius is *r*, then the area of $\Delta XOY$ is $\frac{1}{2}(r)(r) = \frac{r^2}{2}$.

At the same time, the area of circle *O* is $\pi r^2$. So, you can use the area of $\Delta XOY$ to find $r^2$, and then multiply $r^2$ by $\pi$ to get the area of the circle.

$$\text{Area of } \Delta XOY = \frac{r^2}{2} = 25$$

$$r^2 = 50$$

$$\text{Area of circle } O = \pi r^2 = \pi(50) = \mathbf{50\pi}$$

Note that it's unnecessary (and extra work) to find the actual value of *r*, since the value of $r^2$ is sufficient to find the area.

**9. D**

Connect the centers of the circles $O$, $P$, and $Q$ as shown below. Each leg in this right triangle consists of two radii. The hypotenuse consists of two radii plus the diameter of the small circle.

Since the total area of the four large circles is $36\pi$, each large circle has area $9\pi$. Since the area of a circle is $\pi r^2$, the radii of the large circles are all equal to 3.

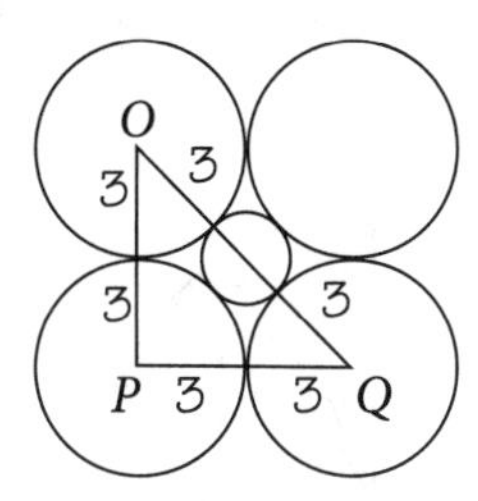


Therefore, each leg in the isosceles right triangle $OPQ$ is 6. The hypotenuse then has length $6\sqrt{2}$. (The hypotenuse of an isosceles right triangle is always $\sqrt{2}$ times the length of a leg.) The hypotenuse is equal to two radii plus the diameter of the small circle, so $6\sqrt{2} = 2(3) +$ diameter, or diameter $=$ $\mathbf{6\sqrt{2} - 6}$.

**10. C**

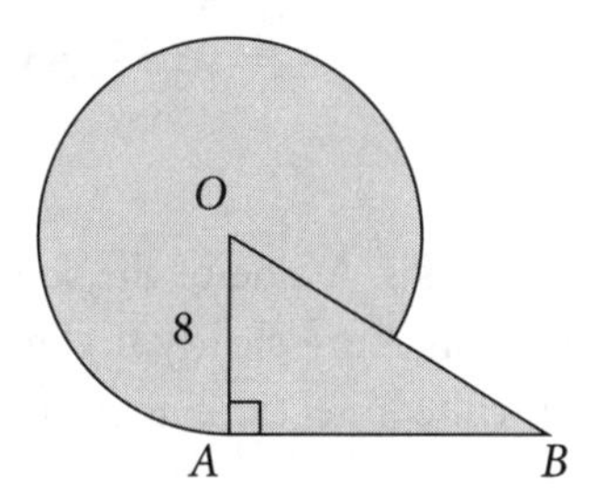


The total area of the shaded region equals the area of the circle plus the area of the right triangle minus the area of overlap. The area of circle $O$ is $\pi(8)^2$, or $64\pi$. You're told that the area of right triangle $OAB$ is 32. So, you just need to find the area of overlap, the area of right triangle $OAB$ inside circle $O$, which forms a sector of the circle.

The area of right triangle $OAB$ is 32, and the height is the radius. So $\frac{1}{2}(8)(AB) = 32$, or $AB = 8$. Since $AB = OA$, $\Delta OAB$ is an isosceles right triangle. Therefore, $\angle AOB$ has a measure of 45°. So, the area of the sector is $\frac{45}{360}(64\pi)$, or $8\pi$. Now you can get the total area of the shaded region:

$$64\pi + 32 - 8\pi = \mathbf{56\pi + 32}$$

**11. B**

Since angle $AOB$ is a right angle, or one-quarter of 360°, the shape $OAB$ is a quarter-circle. The total area of the shaded regions equals the area of this quarter-circle minus the area of the rectangle. Since the length of arc $AB$ (a quarter of the circumference of circle $O$) is $5\pi$, the whole circumference equals $4 \times 5\pi$, or $20\pi$. Thus, the radius $OE$ in the diagram below has length 10. (Point $E$ has been added to the diagram for clarity.) Since $OB$ also equals 10, $OC = 10 - 4$, or 6. This tells you that $\Delta OEC$ is a 3:4:5 right triangle multiplied by 2 and $EC = 8$.

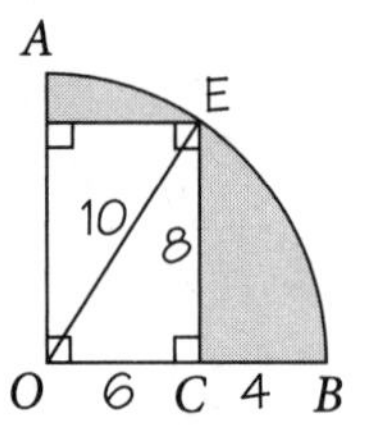


Now you know the dimensions of the rectangle, so find its area: $l \times w = 8 \times 6 = 48$. Finally, use this to get the total area of the shaded regions:

$$\text{Area of shaded regions} = \frac{1}{4} \times \pi \times (10)^2 - 48$$
$$= \mathbf{25\pi - 48}$$

**12. B**

The length of each side of the square is given as $s$. A side of the square has the same length as the diameter of the smaller circle. (You can see this more clearly if you draw the vertical diameter in the smaller circle. The diameter you draw will connect the upper and lower tangent points where the smaller circle and square intersect.)

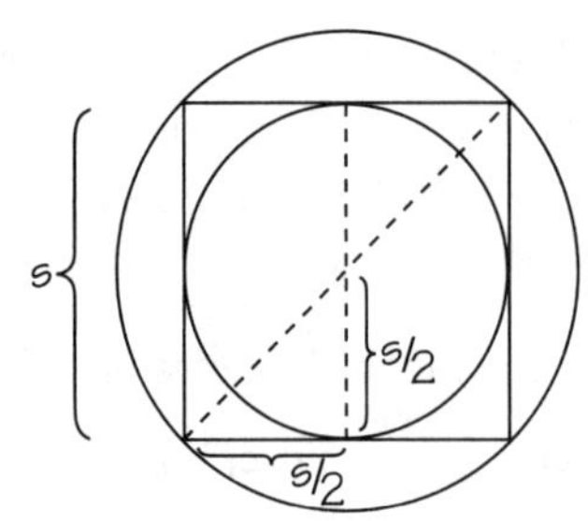


This means that the radius of the smaller circle is $\frac{s}{2}$, so its area is $\left(\frac{s}{2}\right)^2 \pi$, or $\frac{s^2}{4}\pi$. Now draw a diagonal of the square, and you'll see that it's the diameter of the larger circle. The diagonal breaks the square up into two isosceles right triangles, where each leg has length $s$ as in the diagram above. So, the diagonal must have length $s\sqrt{2}$. Therefore, the radius of the larger circle is $\frac{s\sqrt{2}}{2}$, and its area is $\left(\frac{s\sqrt{2}}{2}\right)^2 \pi$, or $\frac{2s^2}{4}\pi$, or $\frac{s^2}{2}\pi$. This is twice the area of the smaller circle, so the ratio of their sizes is **2:1**.

**13. E**

This problem may seem difficult, but it is quite manageable if you approach it step-by-step. Gasoline is poured from a cylindrical container into a rectangular tank, so the first step is to find the volume of each solid. The volume of a solid is the area of its base multiplied by its height. In the case of the gas tank, that's $4 \times 8 \times 10 = 320$ cubic inches.

Now find the volume of gasoline in the cylinder in a similar way. The base of the cylinder has a diameter of 8, so its radius is 4. The area of the base is therefore $16\pi$. You're told that the gasoline reached a height of 20 inches before the tank was filled, so the cylinder began with $16\pi \times 20 = 320\pi$ cubic inches of gasoline.

After filling the tank, the cylindrical container has $(320\pi - 320)$ cubic inches of gasoline remaining. Since $v = \pi r^2 h$, then $h = \frac{v}{\pi r^2}$. The base of the cylinder is $16\pi$, so the new height is

$$\frac{320\pi - 320}{16\pi} = \frac{320(\pi - 1)}{16\pi} = \frac{\mathbf{20(\pi - 1)}}{\boldsymbol{\pi}}$$

**14. E**

It may be helpful to draw a quick diagram, like this one:

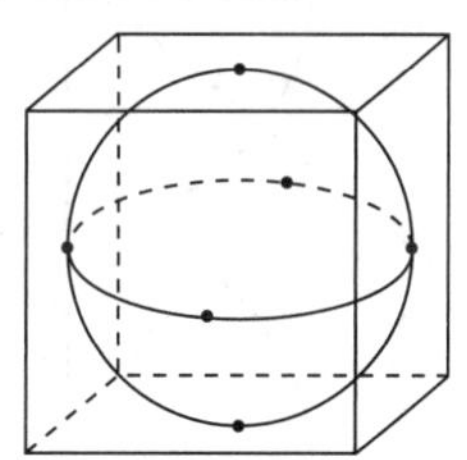

The sphere will touch the cube at six points. Each point will be an endpoint of a diameter and will be at the center of one of the cubic faces. So, the diameter extends directly from one face of the cube to the other, and is perpendicular to both faces that it touches. This means that the diameter must have the same length as an edge of the cube. The cube's volume is 64, so each edge has length $\sqrt[3]{64}$, or 4. Thus, the diameter of the sphere is 4, which means that the radius is **2**.

**15. B**

Take a moment to analyze the figure. You know the circumference of both circles, so you can easily find their radii:

$$C = 2\pi r = 10\pi$$
$$2r = 10$$
$$r = 5$$

Next, you know that *YZ* is tangent to both circles. This means that angle *Z* is a right angle, so triangle *XYZ* is a right triangle. This leaves a lot of unknowns in the diagram, however. Whenever a complex figure seems to be missing a lot of information, a good strategy is to look for hidden right triangles. Here, add line segment *PQ* to create right triangle *PQX*, because it forms two radii and you know the length of the radius:

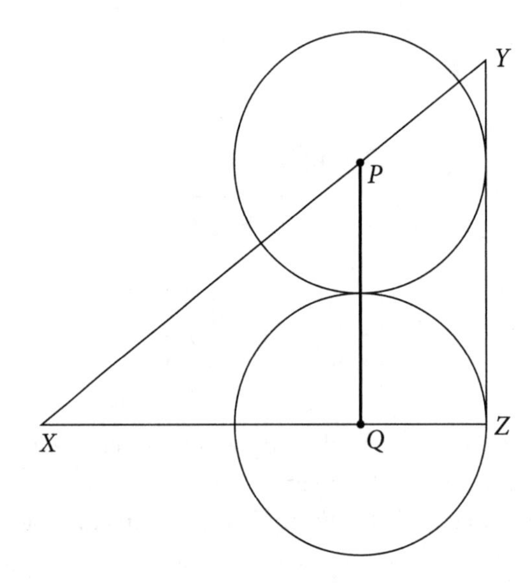


Consider the dimensions of this new right triangle. Leg *PQ* is equal to two radii of the circles, or $2 \times 5 = 10$. Leg *XQ* is equal to $XZ - QZ$. The question states that $XZ = 17$, and you know that *QZ* is a radius, so it's 5. Thus, $XQ = 17 - 5 = 12$. Now, since triangles *XPQ* and *XYZ* are similar (they're both right triangles and they share angle *X*), their sides must be proportional. Set up a proportion and solve:

$$\frac{YZ}{PQ} = \frac{XZ}{XQ}$$
$$\frac{YZ}{10} = \frac{17}{12}$$
$$YZ = \frac{17 \times 10}{12} = \frac{170}{12} = \mathbf{\frac{85}{6}}$$

**16. C**

This Value question asks for the sum of five angle measures found in a figure that looks like three parallel lines crossed by a transversal. Although the lines may look parallel, you cannot assume they are. In Data Sufficiency, figures will comport with the information given in the question stem but may otherwise not be to scale. However, you can deduce from the figure that $c = b$, since they are vertical angles. To have sufficient information to calculate the sum, you would need either the values for each of the variables involved or some relationship tying their values together from which you could deduce the value of their sum.

Statement (1) tells you that $\ell_1$, $\ell_2$, and $\ell_3$ are all parallel to one another. Remember, when parallel lines are cut by a transversal, all acute angles formed by the transversal are equal, all obtuse angles are equal, and any acute angle is supplementary to any obtuse angle. You can get two pairs of supplementary angles from the five marked angles:

$$\underbrace{a+b}_{180}+\underbrace{c+d}_{180}+e$$

You're left with $360 + e$. Since you don't know the value of $e$, you cannot find the sum. Statement (1) is insufficient, so eliminate (A) and (D).

Statement (2) gives the value of $e$. Since angles $e$ and $d$ form a straight line, they add up to 180, which means $d = 30$. However, no information is given about any of the other values in the sum (remember: you are considering Statement (2) by itself, so you have to forget the lines are parallel). So Statement (2) alone is also insufficient. Eliminate (B).

The only missing piece of information when evaluating Statement (1) was the value of $e$, which is provided in Statement (2). Therefore, both statements together are sufficient, and **(C)** is correct.

**17. D**

Each of the semicircles has an area equal to half of that of a circle with the same diameter. The area of a circle can be found with the diameter (or radius), and the area of a square can be found with the side length. Since the diameter of each of the semicircles is the same as a side of the square, you can find the area of the whole figure if the statements give you enough information to establish that shared measurement.

Statement (1) gives the perimeter of the figure. The perimeter is made up of four semicircles; from the perimeter of the figure you can find the perimeter of each semicircle, from which you can find the diameters and all the areas. Statement (1) is sufficient, so the answer is either choice (A) or (D).

Statement (2) gives the perimeter of the square; this is four times the length of a side, so it's sufficient to find the area of the square. The length of a side of the square is the same as a diameter of one of the semicircles, so from the perimeter of the square you can find the area of both the square and the semicircles, which gives you the area of the whole figure. Each statement alone is sufficient, so **(D)** is correct.

**18. C**

You know that *ABC* is a right triangle, but not what specific kind of right triangle. Look for either the type of triangle and one of the side lengths, from which you can find the other sides, or the lengths of two of the sides, from which you can use the Pythagorean theorem to find the third side.

Statement (1) gives the length of one side, but not the side you want. This is insufficient. Eliminate (A) and (D).

From Statement (2), you learn that two of the sides are equal. Thus, this is an isosceles right triangle with side lengths in the ratio of $x{:}x{:}x\sqrt{2}$; however, this only gives you the relationship between the sides, not any of their lengths. Statement (2) is also insufficient. Using both statements together, you know *ABC* is an isosceles right triangle, and you know the length of one side. Using this information, you can find the length of any other side. Both statements together are sufficient, and **(C)** is correct.

**19. C**

To find the length of the side, you need some information about the triangle, and some information about the other sides. Statement (1) provides the lengths of two of the sides; however, without knowing it's a right triangle, that's not sufficient to find the length of the third side. The most you can deduce is a range of values for *AC*, which is not enough. Statement (1) is insufficient. Eliminate (A) and (D).

Statement (2) gives us the sum of two of the angles. You can deduce from this that the other angle must have measure $180° - 90° = 90°$; therefore, *ABC* is a right triangle. However, Statement (2) tells you nothing about any side lengths; it is insufficient. Using both statements together, you know that it is a right triangle, you know which angle is the right angle, and you know the lengths of two of the sides. You can use the Pythagorean theorem to find the length of the third side. Both statements together are sufficient—that's **(C)**.

**20. C**

If the two lines are parallel, then $a$ and $b$ will be equal, as they would be corresponding angles created by a transversal. Statement (1) doesn't tell you whether the lines are parallel; if $x$ and $y$ are equal, then they must each be right angles, since together they form a straight line. That means that $a$ is also a right angle, since it's a vertical angle with $x$, but that tells you nothing about $b$ or whether the two lines are parallel. Statement (1) is insufficient. Eliminate (A) and (D).

Statement (2) is not sufficient either. The angles $x$ and $c$ could each be 60° angles, for instance, in which case the lines would not be parallel; or they could be 90° angles, in which case the lines would be parallel. Statement (2) is also insufficient. Using both statements together, you'll find that $x$ and $y$ are right angles, as are $a$ and $c$. Since $c$ is a right angle, $b$ must be a right angle, and $a$ and $b$ are equal. Both statements together are sufficient, so choose **(C)**.

**21. E**

This Value question asks for the perimeter of a rectangle, which is $2L + 2W$. There is nothing to simplify in the question stem.

Statement (1) provides the area of the rectangle, which is $L \times W$. There is an infinite number of pairs of values of $L$ and $W$ whose product is 12. To name just a few, the dimensions could be 1 by 12, 2 by 6, or 3 by 4. Each yields a different perimeter. Thus, this statement is insufficient. Eliminate (A) and (D).

Statement (2) limits the value of side *AB* to integers. This is of no help in finding the perimeter, as it says nothing about the length of side *AB* or of the other side. Statement (2) is also insufficient. Eliminate (B) and evaluate the statements together.

Considering both statements, you know that the area is 12 and that one of the sides is an integer. However, all the dimensions listed in the analysis of Statement (1) would still work, as well as many others. For example, side *AB* could have the integer length 5, and the adjacent sides could have the non-integer length 2.4. Even taken together, the statements are insufficient. **(E)** is correct.

**22. C**

You are given a figure, quadrilateral *PQRS*, but you do not know what kind of quadrilateral it is. To find the area of *PST*, you'll need the height and the base of the triangle, but keep in mind that the length of *QR* is not necessarily the same as that of *PS* and that *PS* is not necessarily the height of the triangle, because it may not be perpendicular to the base.

Statement (1) says that *PQRS* is a rectangle, and you're given the area of the rectangle. This tells you nothing about the area of one part of the rectangle, the triangle. This is insufficient. Eliminate (A) and (D).

Statement (2) gives information about part of the large quadrilateral: *PTRU* is a parallelogram. You also now know the area of the parallelogram, but this says nothing about the triangle. Statement (2) is also insufficient. If you consider both statements together, a clearer picture results. Since *PTRU* is a parallelogram, *PT* and *UR* are of the same length, as are *PU* and *TR*. Since *PQRS* is a rectangle, *PQ* and *SR* are of equal length, and *PS* and *QR* are equal. So what you have is parallelogram *PTRU* and triangles *PST* and *RQU*. The triangles have sides of equal length, so they are congruent and have equal area. The sum of their areas is the difference of the area of the rectangle and the area of the parallelogram; dividing this by 2 gives the area of one triangle. Both statements together are sufficient; **(C)** is correct.

**23. A**

The two triangles share a base; since the area is one-half the product of the base and height, if you find the ratio of the heights of the triangles, you'll know the ratio of the areas. Statement (1) tells you exactly what you need: the ratio of the heights. Therefore, it is sufficient. Eliminate (B), (C), and (E).

Statement (2) only gives us the length of the base; this is insufficient. Since only Statement (1) is sufficient, **(A)** is correct.

**24. B**

Angle $r$ is formed by the $x$-axis and the line segment with point $(c,d)$ on it. To find the measure of angle $r$, you need some information about the line segment—specifically its equation. Statement (1) gives the value of $c$, but you still need the value of $d$ to find anything about the line. Statement (1) is insufficient. Eliminate (A) and (D).

Statement (2) says that the coordinates of the point are equal; this is enough to tell you the line has the equation $y = x$. Thus, the point $(c,d)$ is the same distance from the $x$-axis as it is from the $y$-axis; you could drop a perpendicular from the point to the $x$-axis and get an isosceles right triangle. This means the angle is a 45° angle. Only Statement (2) is sufficient, so choose **(B)**.

**25. C**

Statement (1) compares the values of $y$ and $z$. Because these values are not compared to $x$, and no exact values are provided for either $y$ or $z$, there are many possibilities for $y$ and $z$. Given only Statement (1), the values of $y$ and $z$ respectively could be 30° and 10°, 33° and 11°, 36° and 12°, etc. Since you cannot pinpoint an exact value for $z$, Statement (1) is insufficient. Eliminate (A) and (D).

The same reasoning holds true for Statement (2). It only compares the values of $x$ and $z$ and does not provide any exact value of any of the three variables. Statement (2) alone is also insufficient.

Taking both statements together, however, you can set up three equations and solve by substitution:

$$y = 3z$$

$$x = \frac{z}{2}$$

$$x + y + z = 90$$

This is a system of three linear equations in terms of three variables, which means each variable can be solved for, so you can find the value of $z$. Statements (1) and (2) taken together are sufficient. The answer is **(C)**.

PART THREE

# Putting It All Together

CHAPTER 8

# Quantitative Practice Sections

**LEARNING OBJECTIVE**

After this chapter, you will be able to:

- Strategically and efficiently answer GMAT Quantitative questions on a number of math topics

This chapter contains two 31-question practice sections. You'll see both Problem Solving and Data Sufficiency questions, and you'll encounter questions that test a variety of math concepts. Following each section, you'll find an answer key, as well as complete explanations for every question.

## How to Use These Practice Sections

While these practice sections contain the same number and type of questions you'll see on a real GMAT Quantitative section, there is one key difference between these practice sections and the real thing: these are on paper, while the actual GMAT is a computer-adaptive test.

Your goal in tackling these practice sections, then, is to get practice and engage in self-assessment. See what it feels like to tackle 31 questions in 62 minutes. Do you feel rushed when there's a timer ticking? How does it feel to move back and forth between Problem Solving and Data Sufficiency questions? Are you able to quickly remember key arithmetic and algebra principles? Can you recall and use important formulas and geometric properties? Did you use the Kaplan Methods and approach each question strategically?

We recommend that you first take Practice Section 1, then review your performance by reading through the explanations of all questions—even the ones you answered correctly. As you review, do you notice that you still struggle with certain concepts or formulas? If so, consult Chapter 9: Math Reference to brush up on any material in which you want more guidance.

Use what you learned from your review to set a game plan for Practice Section 2. What will you do differently to improve your performance? How can you be more strategic in your approach to Problem Solving questions—can you do a better job of using alternative strategies like backsolving and picking numbers? And for Data Sufficiency questions, are you evaluating the statements efficiently and effectively?

After you complete Practice Set 2, again review your performance by reading through the explanations and determining areas in which you still need to improve. For continued practice, consult your online resources, where you will encounter realistic, test-like questions in an online interface.

# Practice Section 1

62 Minutes—31 Questions

Answers and explanations are at the end of the chapter.

*Note:* Because the Data Sufficiency answer choices are always the same and should be memorized, we have omitted them here. If you need a refresher on the choices or the 12TEN mnemonic, review Chapter 3 on Data Sufficiency.

1. In a local election, votes were cast for Mr. Dyer, Ms. Frau, and Mr. Borak in the ratio of 4:3:2. If there were no other candidates and none of the 1,800 voters cast more than one vote, how many votes did Ms. Frau receive?

- O 200
- O 300
- O 400
- O 600
- O 900

2. Does the average (arithmetic mean) of $a$, $b$, and $c$ equal $c$?

(1) $c - a = c + b$

(2) $c = 0$

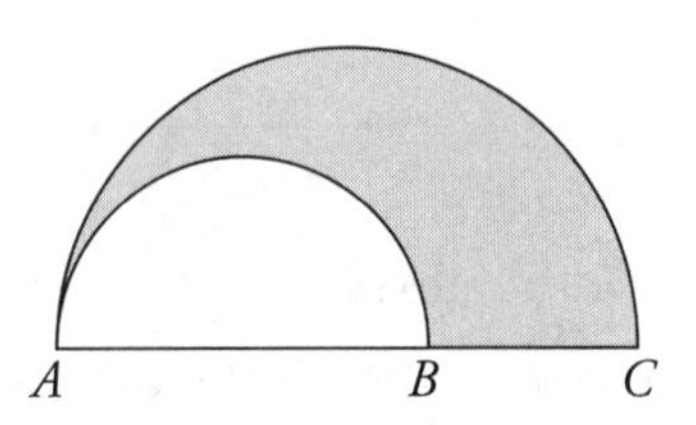


3. The figure above displays two semicircles, one with diameter $AB$ and one with diameter $AC$. If $AB$ has a length of 4 and $AC$ has a length of 6, what fraction of the larger semicircle does the shaded region represent?

- O $\frac{1}{3}$
- O $\frac{4}{9}$
- O $\frac{1}{2}$
- O $\frac{5}{9}$
- O $\frac{2}{3}$

4. If $x = 9a^2$ and $a > 0$, then $\sqrt{x} =$

- O $-3a$
- O $3a$
- O $9a$
- O $3a^2$
- O $81a^4$

5. What is the value of $x$?

(1) $x^2 - 6 = -x$

(2) $x^2 = 4$

6. A cube and a rectangular solid are equal in volume. If the lengths of the edges of the rectangular solid are 4, 8, and 16, what is the length of an edge of the cube?

   - O 4
   - O 8
   - O 12
   - O 16
   - O 64

7. Four partners initially invested $1,600 each to purchase 1,000 shares of a certain stock. If the total cost of the stock is $8,000 plus a 2 percent commission, how much would each partner have to add to cover the purchase of the stock?

   - O $100
   - O $110
   - O $220
   - O $440
   - O $880

8. A piece of paper in the shape of an isosceles right triangle is cut along a line parallel to the hypotenuse of the triangle, leaving a smaller triangular piece. If the area of the triangle was 25 square inches before the cut, what is the area of the new triangle?

   (1) The cut is made 2 inches from the hypotenuse.

   (2) There was a 40 percent decrease in the length of the hypotenuse of the triangle.

9. A survey finds that 80 percent of the apartments in City G have smoke alarms installed. Of these, 20 percent have smoke alarms that are not working. What percent of the apartments in City G were found to have working smoke alarms?

   - O 60%
   - O 64%
   - O $66\frac{2}{3}\%$
   - O 70%
   - O 72%

10. If $y \neq z$, then $\frac{xy - zx}{z - y} =$

   - O $x$
   - O 1
   - O 0
   - O $-1$
   - O $-x$

11. If the average (arithmetic mean) of 18 consecutive odd integers is 534, then the least of these integers is

   - O 517
   - O 518
   - O 519
   - O 521
   - O 525

12. If $A$, $B$, and $C$ are digits between 0 and 9, inclusive, what is the value of $B$?

(1) $\begin{array}{r} AB \\ +BA \\ \hline AAC \end{array}$

(2) $A = 1$

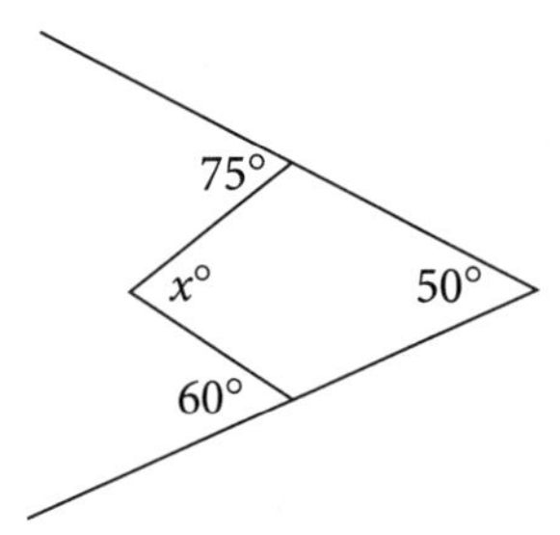


13. In the figure above, $x =$

- 85
- 90
- 95
- 120
- 140

14. If $n > 4$, which of the following is equivalent to $\frac{n - 4\sqrt{n} + 4}{\sqrt{n} - 2}$?

- $\sqrt{n}$
- $2\sqrt{n}$
- $\sqrt{n} + 2$
- $\sqrt{n} - 2$
- $n + \sqrt{n}$

15. If $x$ and $y$ are both positive, is the ratio of $x$ to $y$ greater than 5:1?

(1) The variable $x$ divided by 5 is 1 less than $y$.

(2) The ratio of $3x$ to $5y$ is greater than 2.

16. For all integers $m$ and $n$, where $m \neq n$, $m \uparrow n = \left|\frac{m^2 - n^2}{m - n}\right|$. What is the value of $-2 \uparrow 4$?

- 10
- 8
- 6
- 2
- 0

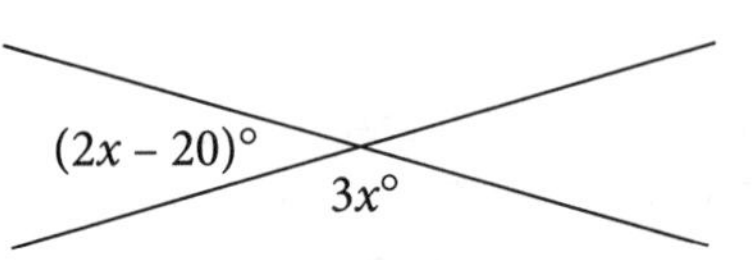


17. In the figure above, $x =$

- 40
- 60
- 80
- 100
- 120

18. In a certain law firm, there are 5 senior partners and 5 junior partners, and all senior partners receive bonuses greater than those of the junior partners. Does senior partner Johnson receive the largest bonus of the lawyers at the firm?

(1) Johnson receives a bonus greater than twice the average bonus for all the senior partners.

(2) All partners receive some bonus, and Johnson receives 5 times the average given to all the partners.

19. During a season in a certain baseball league, every team plays every other team in the league 10 times. If there are 10 teams in the league, how many games are played in the league in one season?

- O 45
- O 90
- O 450
- O 900
- O 1,000

20. A rectangle with integer side lengths has perimeter 10. What is the greatest number of these rectangles that can be cut from a piece of paper with width 24 and length 60?

- O 144
- O 180
- O 240
- O 360
- O 480

21. Julie is flipping a fair coin $x$ times. What is the value of $x$?

(1) The probability that Julie will flip exactly 2 heads is the same as the probability that she will flip exactly 3 heads.

(2) The probability that Julie will flip exactly 3 heads is the same as the probability that she will flip exactly 3 tails.

22. A factory cut its labor force by 16 percent, but then increased it by 25 percent of the new amount. What was the net percent change in the size of the workforce?

- O 5% decrease
- O No net change
- O 5% increase
- O 9% increase
- O 10% increase

23. If $3^x = 81$, then $x^3 =$

- O 12
- O 16
- O 64
- O 81
- O 128

24. A student's grade in a course is determined by 4 quizzes and 1 exam. If the exam counts twice as much as each of the quizzes, what fraction of the final grade is determined by the exam?

- O $\frac{1}{6}$
- O $\frac{1}{5}$
- O $\frac{1}{4}$
- O $\frac{1}{3}$
- O $\frac{1}{2}$

25. Guillermo can build a table in 3 hours, Terry can build an identical table in $x$ hours, and Pat can build the table in $x - 4$ hours. What is the value of $x$?

(1) Working together, Guillermo and Terry could build the table in 2 hours.

(2) Working together, Guillermo, Terry, and Pat could build the table in 1 hour.

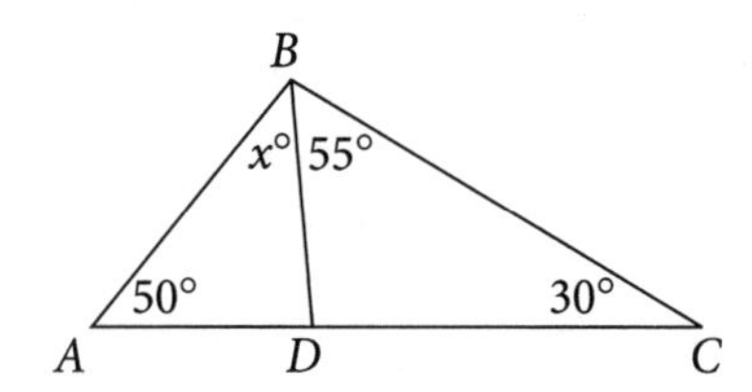


26. In $\triangle ABC$ above, $x =$

- 45
- 55
- 60
- 75
- 80

27. Points $M$ and $N$ lie on the circumference of a circle with a center at $O$. What is the diameter of circle $O$?

(1) The area of sector $MON$ is $10\pi$.

(2) The length of arc $MN$ is $4\pi$.

28. If a driver travels $m$ miles per hour for 4 hours and then travels $\frac{3}{4}m$ miles per hour every hour thereafter, how many miles will she drive in 10 hours?

- $\frac{15}{2}m$
- $8m$
- $\frac{17}{2}m$
- $10m$
- $\frac{21}{2}m$

29. Bob finishes the first half of an exam in two-thirds the time it takes him to finish the second half. If the whole exam takes him an hour, how many minutes does he spend on the first half of the exam?

- 20
- 24
- 27
- 36
- 40

| List A | 1 | 2 | 3 | 4 | 5 | $x$ |
|---|---|---|---|---|---|---|
| List B | 2 | 3 | 4 | 5 | 6 | $y$ |

30. Given the values in the table above, is the average of the values in List $A$ greater than the average of the values in List $B$?

(1) $x = 6y$

(2) $x - y > 5$

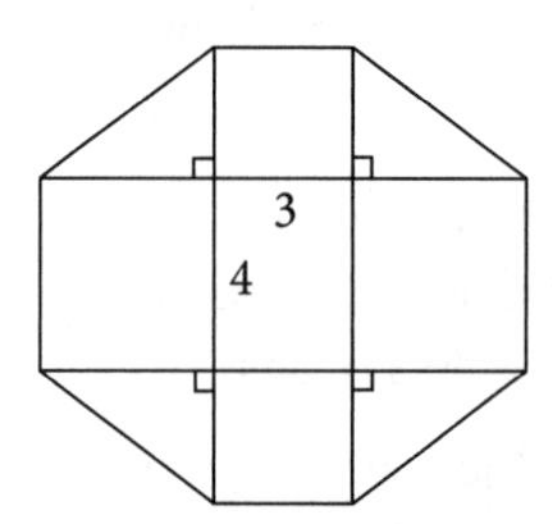


31. The figure above is composed of nine regions: four squares, four triangles, and one rectangle. If the rectangle has length 4 and width 3, what is the perimeter of the entire figure?

- 24
- 28
- 34
- 40
- 44

Answers follow on the next page. ▶ ▶ ▶

## Answer Key

### Practice Section 1

1. D
2. C
3. D
4. B
5. C
6. B
7. D
8. D
9. B
10. E
11. A
12. A
13. A
14. D
15. A
16. D
17. A
18. B
19. C
20. D
21. A
22. C
23. C
24. D
25. D
26. A
27. C
28. C
29. B
30. B
31. C

# Answers and Explanations

## Practice Section 1

**1. D**

The ratio of parts is 4:3:2, making a total of 9 parts. Since 9 parts are equal to 1,800 votes, each part represents 1,800 ÷ 9, or 200 votes. Since Ms. Frau represents 3 parts, she received a total of 3 × 200, or 600 votes.

Another way to think about it: out of every 9 votes, Ms. Frau gets 3, which is $\frac{3}{9}$, or $\frac{1}{3}$, of the total number of votes. $\frac{1}{3}$ of 1,800 is 600. You could also have solved it algebraically, by setting up a proportion, with $F$ as Ms. Frau's votes:

$$\frac{3}{9} = \frac{F}{1{,}800}$$

$$\frac{3}{9} \times 1{,}800 = F$$

$$600 = F$$

**2. C**

When will the average of *a*, *b*, and *c* equal *c*? Think of average in terms of a balance. The three numbers balance at *c*. If you remove *c* from the group, it won't change the balance in any way. Therefore, *a* and *b* must also balance at *c*, and the average of *a* and *b* must be *c* as well. Thus, the average of *a*, *b*, and *c* equals *c* only if the average of *a* and *b* is *c*.

You can cancel *c* from both sides of the equation in Statement (1): this leaves you with $-a = b$. If you then add *a* to both sides, you find that $a + b = 0$. This tells you that the average of *a* and *b* is 0, but not whether $c = 0$. You still need to know the value of *c* to answer the question. Statement (1) is insufficient. Eliminate (A) and (D).

Statement (2) tells you the value of *c*, but it says nothing about either *a* or *b*. It is insufficient, so eliminate (B). If you put the statements together, you know the value of $c = 0$, and you know that $a + b = 0$, so you know that the average of *a* and *b* equals *c*. Therefore, both statements together are sufficient. **(C)** is correct.

**3. D**

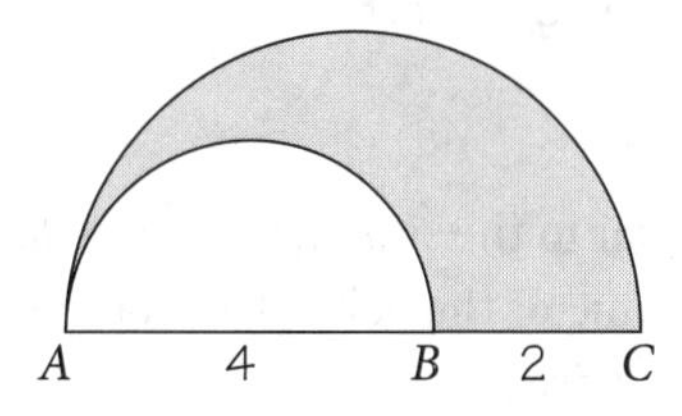


**Method I:**

The area of the shaded region equals the difference in the areas of the two semicircles; to find the fraction of the larger semicircle occupied by the shaded region, first find the area of the shaded region, then divide this by the area of the larger semicircle. The area of a semicircle is $\frac{1}{2}$ the area of the whole circle, or $\frac{1}{2}\pi r^2$. Here, the larger semicircle has a diameter of 6. Its radius is $\frac{1}{2}$ the diameter, or 3, and its area equals $\frac{1}{2}\pi r^2 = \frac{1}{2}\pi(3)^2 = \frac{9}{2}\pi$. The smaller circle has a diameter of 4 and a radius of 2, for an area of $\frac{1}{2}\pi(2)^2 = 2\pi$.

The area of the shaded region equals:

$$\frac{9\pi}{2} - 2\pi = \frac{9\pi}{2} - \frac{4\pi}{2} = \frac{5\pi}{2}$$

The fraction of the larger semicircle the shaded region occupies is:

$$\frac{\frac{5\pi}{2}}{\frac{9\pi}{2}} = \frac{5\pi}{2} \times \frac{2}{9\pi} = \frac{5}{9}$$

**Method II:**

Avoid most of this work by exploring the ratios involved here. Any two semicircles are similar. The ratio of $AB$ to $AC$ is 4 to 6 or 2 to 3. The ratio of all linear measures of the two circles (circumference, radius) will also have this ratio. The area ratio will be the **square** of this, or 4 to 9. The small semicircle has $\frac{4}{9}$ the area of the large semicircle, leaving $\frac{5}{9}$ of the area of the large semicircle for the shaded region.

**4. B**

You can find the value of $\sqrt{x}$ by substituting $9a^2$ for $x$.

$$\begin{aligned}\sqrt{x} &= \sqrt{9a^2} \\ &= \sqrt{9} \cdot \sqrt{a^2} \\ &= 3a\end{aligned}$$

Note: You could do this only because you know that $a > 0$. The radical sign ($\sqrt{\ }$) refers to the positive square root of a number.

**5. C**

In Statement (1), you can move the $x$ to the left side and find that $x^2 + x - 6 = 0$; since this is not a perfect square (it factors into the equation $(x + 3)(x - 2) = 0$), there are two solutions to the equation. Statement (1) is not sufficient. Eliminate (A) and (D).

Statement (2) provides another equation involving the square of $x$; it, too, has two solutions ($x = 2$ and $x = -2$) so is not sufficient. Eliminate (B).

Using the two statements together, you find that only one value satisfies both equations ($x$ must be 2). Both statements together are sufficient, so **(C)** is correct.

**6. B**

The volume of a rectangular solid is equal to the product $l \times w \times h$. So, the volume of this solid is $16 \times 8 \times 4$, and this is equal to the volume of the cube. The volume of a cube is the length of an edge cubed, so you can set up an equation to solve for $e$:

$$e^3 = 16 \times 8 \times 4$$

To avoid the multiplication, break the 16 down into $2 \times 8$:

$$e^3 = 2 \times 8 \times 8 \times 4$$

Now combine $2 \times 4$ to get another 8:

$$\begin{aligned}e^3 &= 8 \times 8 \times 8 \\ e &= 8\end{aligned}$$

Thus, the length of an edge of the cube is 8.

**7. D**

$$\begin{aligned}\text{The cost of stock} &= \$8{,}000 + 2\% \text{ of } \$8{,}000\\ &= \$8{,}000 + \$160\\ &= \$8{,}160\end{aligned}$$

The 4 partners have already invested \$1,600 each, that is 4 × \$1,600 = \$6,400. They need to invest \$8,160 − \$6,400 = \$1,760 more in total, and \$1,760 ÷ 4 = \$440 more per partner.

Or, since each invests an equal amount, each will ultimately invest \$8,160 ÷ 4 = \$2,040. If each partner already invested \$1,600, the amount each one still needs to invest is \$2,040 − \$1,600 = \$440. (Notice how it's a little less arithmetic to divide the whole amount into quarters first and then subtract.)

**8. D**

Make a diagram to see what you're doing. You're cutting an isosceles right triangle along a line parallel to the hypotenuse. This leaves a smaller triangle, but still an isosceles right triangle. (Since you're cutting parallel to one side, the two triangles are similar.) You know the area before the cut, so if you can find either the line ratio or the area ratio of these similar triangles, you can find the area of the smaller one.

Remember that your job isn't to solve the math, but to determine if a statement provides information sufficient to do so. Statement (1) is sufficient because it gives the distance from the hypotenuse of the old triangle to the hypotenuse of the new triangle. The question stem indicates the area of the original triangle was 25 square inches. The area of an isosceles right triangle is $\frac{1}{2} \times (\text{the length of a leg})^2$ so

$$\begin{aligned}\frac{1}{2} \times (\text{leg})^2 &= 25\\ (\text{leg})^2 &= 50\\ \text{leg} &= \sqrt{50} = 5\sqrt{2}\end{aligned}$$

The hypotenuse is $\sqrt{2} \times (\text{leg})$, so hypotenuse $= 5\sqrt{2} \cdot \sqrt{2}$ or 10. Now think of the hypotenuse as the *base* of the triangle.

$$\begin{aligned}\text{Area} &= \frac{1}{2} \times 10 \times (\text{height})\\ 25 &= \frac{1}{2} \times 10 \times (\text{height})\\ 5 &= \text{height}\end{aligned}$$

If the cut is made 2 inches from the hypotenuse, the height of the new triangle is 5 − 2, or 3. This gives you the line ratio of the similar triangles, 5:3, and that's enough to find the area ratio and the area of the smaller triangle in turn. Statement (1) is sufficient.

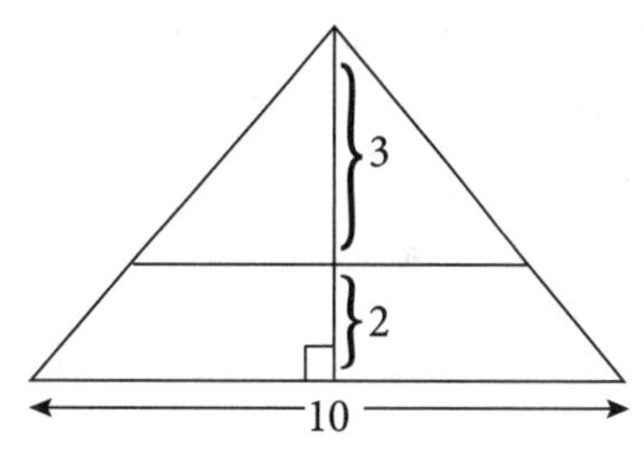


Statement (2) provides the percent reduction in the length of one side. This is enough to determine the line ratio of the triangles (100:60, or 10:6, or 5:3), so this statement is also sufficient. Each statement alone is sufficient, so **(D)** is correct.

**9. B**

If 20% of the apartments with smoke alarms were found to have smoke alarms that are not working, then the remaining 80% of the apartments with smoke alarms have smoke alarms that **are** working. Since 80% of all apartments in the city have smoke alarms, and 80% of these have working smoke alarms, 80% of 80% of all the apartments in the city have working smoke alarms. 80% of 80% equals $0.8 \times 0.8 = 0.64$ of all the apartments in the city, or 64%.

Alternatively, since you are working with percents only, try picking numbers. Let the number of apartments in City G be 100. If 80% of these have smoke alarms, then 80% of 100, or 80, apartments have smoke alarms.

If 20% of these do not work, then 80% do work. 80% of 80 is $\frac{8}{10} \times 80 = 64$ apartments. If 64 of the 100 apartments in City G have working smoke alarms, then $\frac{64}{100}$, or 64%, have working smoke alarms.

**10. E**

Whenever you are asked to simplify a fraction involving binomials, your first thought should be to factor! Since $x$ is in both terms of the numerator, you can factor out $x$ and get

$$xy - zx = x(y - z)$$

Performing this operation on the original fraction, you get the following:

$$\frac{xy - zx}{z - y} = \frac{x(y - z)}{z - y}$$

Rewriting $(z - y)$ as $-1(y - z)$, you get this:

$$= \frac{x(y - z)}{-1(y - z)}$$

Now cancel $y - z$ from the top and bottom:

$$= \frac{x}{-1} = -x$$

Note: It is important that you're told that $y \neq z$ here, otherwise you could have zero in the denominator, and the expression would be undefined.

**11. A**

The average of a group of evenly spaced numbers is equal to the middle number. Here, there is an even number of terms (18), so the average is between the two middle numbers, the 9th and 10th terms. That means the 9th consecutive odd integer here will be the first odd integer less than 534, which is 533. Once you have the 9th term, you can count backwards to find the first.

| 10th | Average | 9th | 8th | 7th |
|---|---|---|---|---|
| 535 | 534 | 533 | 531 | 529 |

| 6th | 5th | 4th | 3rd | 2nd | 1st |
|---|---|---|---|---|---|
| 527 | 525 | 523 | 521 | 519 | 517 |

### 12. A

From Statement (1), you know that a two-digit number plus another two-digit number gives a three-digit number. Therefore, the first digit of the three-digit number must be 1 (otherwise, the sum would be over 200, which is impossible for the sum of 2 two-digit numbers). So $A = 1$. Our addition now looks like this:

$$\begin{array}{r} 1B \\ +\ B1 \\ \hline 11C \end{array}$$

The only possibility for $B$ is 9; anything less would not add up to more than 100. Statement (1) is sufficient. Eliminate (B), (C), and (E).

Statement (2) only indicates the value of one of the digits; this is not enough to tell anything about either $B$ or $C$. Remember, you don't know the information from Statement (1). Statement (2) alone is insufficient. **(A)** is correct.

### 13. A

Keep in mind that the measures of the interior angles of any quadrilateral sum to 360°. The angles marked 75° and 60° are both supplementary to the two unmarked interior angles in the diagram. There are four interior angles in the quadrilateral: the two unmarked angles, the angle marked 50°, and the one marked $x$°. The angle supplementary to the 75° angle must have a measure of 180 – 75, or 105°. The angle supplementary to the 60° angle must have a measure of 180 – 60, or 120°.

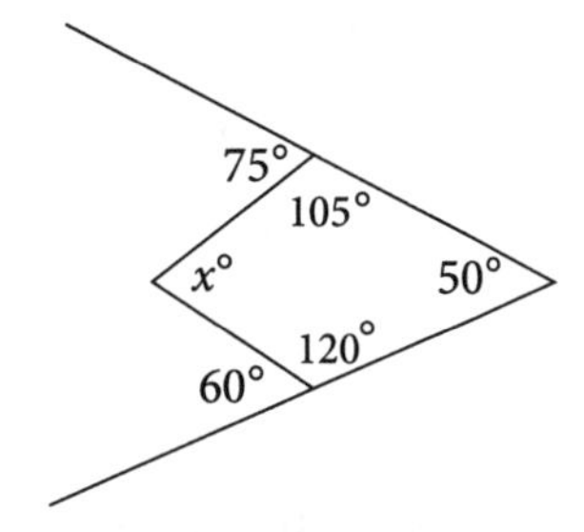


Now that you know the measures of three of the interior angles, you can set up an equation to solve for $x$:

$$x + 105 + 50 + 120 = 360$$
$$x + 275 = 360$$
$$x = 360 - 275 = 85$$

### 14. D

Get rid of the denominator by factoring it out of the numerator. $n - 4\sqrt{n} + 4$ is a difficult expression to work with. It may be easier if you let $t = \sqrt{n}$. Keep in mind that $t^2 = \sqrt{n} \times \sqrt{n} = n$.

Then, $n - 4\sqrt{n} + 4 = t^2 - 4t + 4$; this is a quadratic that you can reverse FOIL:

$$\text{Using FOIL in reverse} = (t - 2)(t - 2)$$
$$= (\sqrt{n} - 2)(\sqrt{n} - 2)$$
$$\text{So } \frac{n - 4\sqrt{n} + 4}{\sqrt{n} - 2} = \frac{(\sqrt{n} - 2)\cancel{(\sqrt{n} - 2)}}{\cancel{(\sqrt{n} - 2)}}$$
$$= \sqrt{n} - 2$$

Alternatively, you could pick a number for $n$ and try each answer choice.

**15. A**

The question asks if $\frac{x}{y} > 5$ or, alternatively, if $x > 5y$.

Statement (1) translates to $\frac{x}{5} = y - 1$. Multiplying both sides by 5 results in $x = 5y - 5$. So, $x$ is not greater than $5y$. Statement (1) is sufficient. Eliminate (B), (C), and (E).

Statement (2) translates to $\frac{3x}{5y} > 2$. Multiply both sides of the inequality by $5y$ to get $3x > 10y$, so $x > 3\frac{1}{3}y$. Thus, $x$ could be either less than or greater than $5y$. So, Statement (2) is insufficient. **(A)** is correct.

**16. D**

A fast way to solve this problem is to notice that $(m^2 - n^2)$, which is the numerator of the fraction in the expression for $m \uparrow n$, is the difference between two squares. Remember that this can be factored into the product of $(m + n)$ and $(m - n)$. So, the expression for $m \uparrow n$ can be simplified:

$$\begin{aligned} m \uparrow n &= \left|\frac{m^2 - n^2}{m - n}\right| \\ &= \left|\frac{(m+n)(m-n)}{m-n}\right| && \text{Factoring the numerator.} \\ &= |m + n| && \text{Canceling out } m - n. \end{aligned}$$

So, if you substitute –2 for $m$ and 4 for $n$ in the simplified equation, the arithmetic is much easier, and you get:

$$\begin{aligned} -2 \uparrow 4 &= |-2 + 4| \\ &= |2| \\ &= 2 \end{aligned}$$

**17. A**

The angle marked $(2x - 20)°$ and the angle marked $3x°$ together form a straight angle. This means that the sum of their degree measures must be 180°.

$$\begin{aligned} (2x - 20) + (3x) &= 180 \\ 2x - 20 + 3x &= 180 \\ 5x &= 200 \\ x &= \frac{200}{5} = 40 \end{aligned}$$

**18. B**

There isn't much to do here before you look at the statements. From Statement (1), you can deduce that Johnson must receive a larger bonus than at least some of the partners, but not necessarily bigger than all of the other partners. For instance, if Johnson and another senior partner each receive bonuses of $10,000 and the other three each receive bonuses of $1,000, then the average bonus will be $4,600. This fits the statement, but Johnson does not receive the largest bonus. The statement is not sufficient. Eliminate (A) and (D).

Statement (2) is more helpful. Johnson's bonus is 5 times the average bonus of all the other partners. The sum of all the bonuses is the average bonus times the number of bonuses. There are 10 partners, so the sum is 10 times the average. But if Johnson's bonus is 5 times the average, then Johnson has one-half of all the bonus money. Therefore, the largest bonus anyone other than Johnson could have is at most the other half of the bonus money—any more and the sum will be more than 10 times the average. But you're told that everyone gets at least some bonus, so no one partner could have the other half of the sum all to himself or herself—that would leave nothing for the other partners. Therefore, Johnson must have the largest bonus. Statement (2) is sufficient. **(B)** is correct.

**19. C**

In this ten-team league, each team plays the other nine teams 10 times each. Since $9 \times 10 = 90$, each team plays 90 games. Since there are ten different teams, and $10 \times 90 = 900$, a total of 900 games are played by the ten teams. But this counts each game twice, since it counts when Team A plays Team B as one game and when Team B plays Team A as another game. But they're the same game! In other words, each game consists of *two* teams playing each other. Therefore, you must halve the total to take into account the fact that two teams play each game: $\frac{900}{2} = 450$. So 450 games are played in total.

**20. D**

First of all, if a rectangle has perimeter 10, what could its dimensions be? Perimeter $= 2L + 2W = 2(L + W)$. The perimeter is 10, so $2(L + W) = 10$, or $L + W = 5$. Since $L$ and $W$ must be integers, there are two possibilities: $L = 4$ and $W = 1$ $(4 + 1 = 5)$, or $L = 3$ and $W = 2$ $(3 + 2 = 5)$. Consider each case separately. If $L = 4$, then how many of these rectangles would fit along the length of the larger rectangle? The length of the larger rectangle is 60, and $60 \div 4 = 15$, so 15 smaller rectangles would fit if they were lined up with their longer sides against the longer side of the large rectangle. The width of the smaller rectangles is 1, and the width of the large rectangle is 24, and $24 \div 1 = 24$, so 24 small rectangles can fit against the width of the large rectangle. The total number of small rectangles that fit inside the large rectangle is the number along the length times the number along the width: $15 \times 24 = 360$. In the second case, $L = 3$ and $W = 2$. $60 \div 3 = 20$, so 20 small rectangles fit along the length, and $24 \div 2 = 12$, so 12 small rectangles fit along the width. The total number of small rectangles is $20 \times 12$, or 240. You're asked for the greatest number, which is 360.

**21. A**

The probability of a certain result is the number of desired outcomes divided by the total number of outcomes. Order does not matter for this situation, so the combinations formula can be used to determine the number of desired results.

To evaluate Statement (1), use the combinations formula: ${}_nC_k = \frac{n!}{k!(n-k)!}$. In this problem, $n$ is the total number of flips represented by $x$, and $k$ is the given number of heads or tails. So, $\frac{n!}{3!(n-3)!} = \frac{n!}{2!(n-2)!}$.

Since these are equal and have the same numerator, work with the denominators: $3!(n-3)! = 2!(n-2)!$. Evaluate the factorials to get $6(n-3)! = 2(n-2)!$, which simplifies to $3(n-3)! = (n-2)!$. Consider how factorials work. The only difference between $(n-3)!$ and $(n-2)!$ is that $(n-3)!$ must be multiplied by the next greatest number to be the same as $(n-2)!$. For instance, 3! is $3 \times 2 \times 1$, and 4! is $4(3 \times 2 \times 1)$. Therefore, since $3(n-3)! = (n-2)!$, the next number above $(n-3)$ is 3, so $(n-3)$ is 2, and $n = 2 + 3 = 5$, which means you now know the value of $x$. Statement (1) is sufficient. Eliminate (B), (C), and (E).

While Statement (2) may look tempting, the probability of any flip being heads is the same as the probability of being tails. So, regardless of the number of flips, the two probabilities will be the same. Statement (2) is insufficient. **(A)** is correct.

**22. C**

Choose a sample value that's easy to work with; see what happens with 100 jobs. If the factory cuts its labor force by 16%, it eliminates 16% of 100 jobs, or 16 jobs, leaving a work force of 100 – 16, or 84 people. It then increases this work force by 25%, and 25% of 84 is $\frac{1}{4}$ of 84, or 21. The factory adds 21 jobs to the 84 it had, for a total of 105 jobs. Since the factory started with 100 jobs and finished with 105, it gained 5 jobs overall. This represents $\frac{5}{100}$ or a 5% increase over the original amount.

**23. C**

First, find the value of $x$ using the equation $3^x = 81$. Then find the value of $x^3$.

Express 81 as a power with a base of 3:

$$81 = 9^2 = \left(3^2\right)^2 = 3^{2\times2} = 3^4$$
$$x = 4$$
$$x^3 = 4^3$$
$$= 4 \times 4 \times 4 = 64$$

**24. D**

The grade is decided by 4 quizzes and 1 exam. Since the exam counts twice as much as each quiz, the exam equals 2 quizzes, so you can say the grade is decided by the equivalent of 4 quizzes and 2 quizzes, or 6 quizzes. The exam equals 2 quizzes, so it represents $\frac{2}{6}$, or $\frac{1}{3}$, of the grade.

**25. D**

The question sets up a combined work problem, but you're only given a numerical rate for Guillermo; Terry's and Pat's rates are given in terms of $x$, and you'll need to see if the statements give you enough information to get a value for $x$.

Statement (1) tells you the total time for Guillermo and Terry to build the table together. The combined work formula for two workers is $T = \frac{AB}{A+B}$, where $T$ is the total time and $A$ and $B$ are the individual workers' rates. Plug in what you know and simplify:

$$2 = \frac{3x}{x+3}$$
$$2(x+3) = 3x$$

At this point, you have a linear equation with one variable, which means you can solve for $x$, making Statement (1) sufficient. For the record, this simplifies to $2x + 6 = 3x$ and $x = 6$. Eliminate (B), (C), and (E).

For Statement (2), you'll need to use the formula $\frac{1}{A} + \frac{1}{B} + \frac{1}{C} = \frac{1}{T}$, where, again, $T$ is the total time and $A$, $B$, and $C$ are the workers' rates. Plug in the information that you have.

$$\frac{1}{3} + \frac{1}{x} + \frac{1}{x-4} = \frac{1}{1}$$

$$\frac{x(x-4)}{3x(x-4)} + \frac{3(x-4)}{3x(x-4)} + \frac{3x}{3x(x-4)} = \frac{1}{1}$$

$$\frac{x^2 - 4x + 3x - 12 + 3x}{3x^2 - 12x} = 1$$

$$x^2 + 2x - 12 = 3x^2 - 12x$$

$$0 = 2x^2 - 14x + 12$$

$$x^2 - 7x + 6 = 0$$

This is a quadratic equation, which means there may be two possible values for $x$. However, it's worth factoring to see what you can find out about $x$. The equation factors to $(x - 1)(x - 6) = 0$, which would mean that $x$ could be 1 or 6. But remember what you were told about the rates in the question; Terry's is $x$ and Pat's is $x - 4$. Since they represent lengths of time, they both need to be positive, and if $x = 1$, then $x - 4$ would be negative. Thus, $x = 6$, and each statement by itself is sufficient. **(D)** is correct.

**26. A**

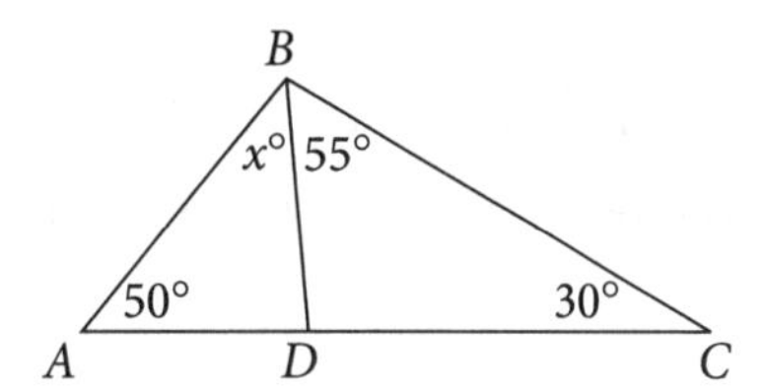


The three interior angles of $\Delta ABC$ are $\angle BAD$, with measure 50°, $\angle ACB$, with measure 30°, and $\angle ABC$, which is made up of the angle marked $x°$ and the angle with measure 55°. All these angles combined sum to 180°. Therefore:

$$50 + 30 + x + 55 = 180$$

$$135 + x = 180$$

$$x = 180 - 135$$

$$= 45$$

**27. C**

To determine the diameter of circle $O$, you'll need to determine the radius of the circle. And to do that, you'll need to find either the area or the circumference of the circle.

Statement (1) states that the area of sector $MON$ is $10\pi$, but you cannot determine the overall area of the circle from that information. It's possible that $MON$ is only a small piece of a large circle, or it could be that $MON$ makes up a large part of a smaller circle. This statement is insufficient. Eliminate (A) and (D).

Statement (2) states that the length of arc $MN$ is $4\pi$. By itself, this information cannot tell you the circumference of the entire circle. It's possible that this arc length is a small piece of a large circumference or a large piece of a smaller circumference. By itself, this statement is insufficient. Eliminate (B).

Combine the statements by setting up a proportion. The size of arc *MN* in relation to the overall circumference is the same as the area of sector *MON* in relation to the overall area: $\frac{4\pi}{2\pi r} = \frac{20\pi}{\pi r^2}$.

Cross multiply to determine that $4\pi^2 r^2 = 40\pi^2 r$. At this point, you can solve for *r*, and that is sufficient to determine that the diameter of the circle is 20. **(C)** is correct.

**28. C**

Just apply the distance formula, Distance = Rate × Time, to the two segments of the trip. In the first 4 hours, the driver drives $4m$ miles. In the next 6 hours, she drives $6 \times \frac{3}{4}m = \frac{9}{2}m$ miles. The total number of miles driven is $4m + \frac{9}{2}m$, or $\frac{17}{2}m$ miles.

**29. B**

The time it takes to complete the entire exam is the sum of the time spent on the first half of the exam and the time spent on the second half. The question states that the time spent on the first half is $\frac{2}{3}$ of the time spent on the second half. Let *S* represent the time spent on the second half; the total time spent is $\frac{2}{3}S + S$, or $\frac{5}{3}S$. You know this total time is one hour, or 60 minutes. Set up an equation to solve for *S*.

$$\frac{5}{3}S = 60$$

$$\frac{3}{5} \cdot \frac{5}{3}S = 60 \cdot \frac{3}{5}$$

$$S = 36$$

So, the second half takes 36 minutes. The first half takes $\frac{2}{3}$ of this, or 24 minutes. (You could also find the first half by subtracting 36 minutes from the total time, 60 minutes.)

**30. B**

Each value in List *B* is 1 greater than the corresponding value in List *A*, so, without *x* and *y*, the total of the values in List *B* is 5 greater than the total of the values in List *A*. So, in order for the average of List *A* to be greater than the average of List *B*, *x* must be more than 5 greater than *y*.

Statement (1) says that $x = 6y$. For numbers greater than $\frac{5}{6}$, the total of the values in List *A* will be greater than those in List *B*. However, there are no stated limitations on the values of *x* or *y*. So *x* could be less than $\frac{5}{6}$, in which case the average of List *B* would be greater. Statement (1) is insufficient. Eliminate (A) and (D).

Statement (2) can be rearranged to show that $x > y + 5$. Per the initial analysis of the question, this means that the average of List *A* is greater than that of List *B*. Statement (2) is sufficient.

**31. C**

The central rectangle shares a side with each of the four squares, and the four squares form the legs of the four right triangles. So, use the information that you're given about the rectangle. Two of its sides have a length of 4, so the two squares that share these sides must also have sides of length 4. The other two sides of the rectangle have a length of 3, so the other two squares, which share these sides, must also have sides of length 3. Each triangle shares a side with a small square and a side with a large square, so the legs of each triangle have lengths of 3 and 4, respectively.

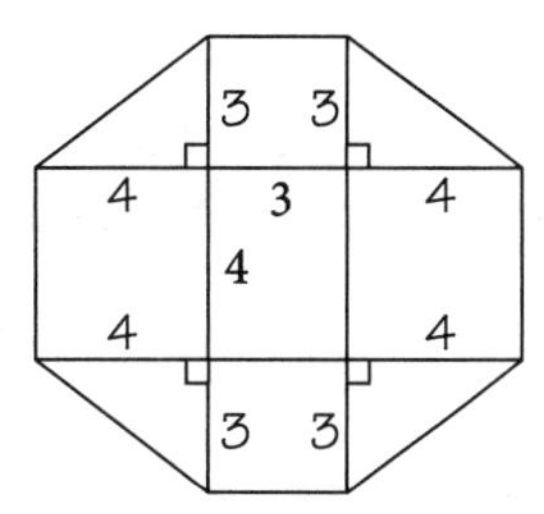


Since the legs are of length 3 and 4, the hypotenuse of each triangle must have a length of 5. (This is a Pythagorean triplet, though you could also find the hypotenuse using the Pythagorean theorem.) To get the perimeter, use the lengths of the hypotenuse and a side from each square:

$$\begin{aligned}\text{Perimeter} &= 4(5) + 2(4) + 2(3) \\ &= 20 + 8 + 6 \\ &= 34\end{aligned}$$

## Practice Section 2

62 Minutes—31 Questions

Answers and explanations are at the end of the chapter.

*Note:* Because the Data Sufficiency answer choices are always the same and should be memorized, we have omitted them here. If you need a refresher on the choices or the 12TEN mnemonic, review Chapter 3 on Data Sufficiency.

1. If the cost of $p$ plums priced at 25 cents each equals the cost of $p - 6$ nectarines priced at 28 cents each, then $p$ equals

   - 26
   - 42
   - 52
   - 56
   - 66

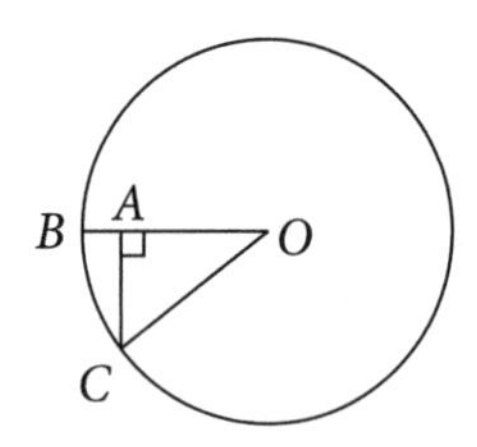


2. In the figure above, if the area of the circle with center $O$ is $100\pi$ and $CA$ has a length of 6, what is the length of $AB$?

   - 2
   - 3
   - 4
   - 5
   - 6

3. If $f(x) = -3(x - b)^2 + k$, what is the maximum value of $f(x)$?

   (1) $b = 3$

   (2) $k = 9$

4. If the ratio of integers $a$, $b$, and $c$ is 1:2:3, what is the value of $a + b + c$?

   (1) $c - a = 8$

   (2) $b - a = 4$

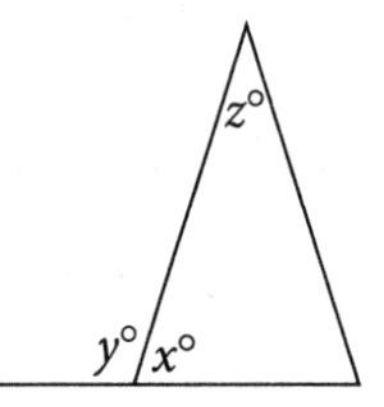


5. In the figure above, $x = 2z$ and $y = 3z$. What is the value of $z$?

   - 24
   - 30
   - 36
   - 54
   - 60

6. A car travels 60 kilometers in 1 hour before a piston breaks. Then the car travels at 30 kilometers per hour for the remaining 60 kilometers to its destination. What is its average speed in kilometers per hour for the entire trip?

   - 20
   - 40
   - 45
   - 50
   - 60

7. In a group of 60 workers, the average salary is \$80 a day per worker. If some of the workers earn \$75 a day and the rest earn \$100 a day, how many workers earn \$75 a day?

- O 12
- O 24
- O 36
- O 48
- O 54

8. Integers $x$ and $y$ are both positive, and $x > y$. How many different committees of $y$ people can be chosen from a group of $x$ people?

(1) The number of different committees of $x - y$ people that can be chosen from a group of $x$ people is 3,060.

(2) The number of different ways to arrange $y$ people in a line is 24.

9. A violinist practices 1 hour a day from Monday through Friday. How many hours must she practice on Saturday in order to have an average (arithmetic mean) of 2 hours a day for the 6-day period?

- O 5
- O 6
- O 7
- O 8
- O 12

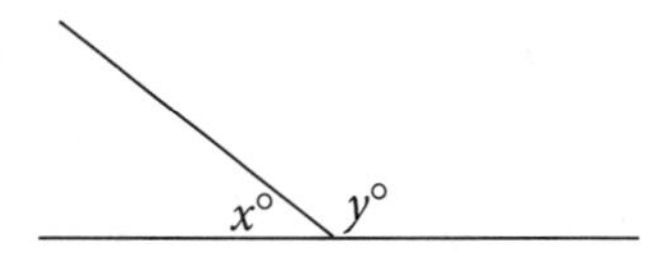


10. In the figure above, if $y = 5x$, then $x =$

- O 15
- O 30
- O 45
- O 135
- O 150

11. If $b$ is an integer, is $(a)(|a|) < 2^b$?

(1) $b < 0$

(2) $a = b$

12. If the product of two integers is an even number and the sum of the same two integers is an odd number, which of the following must be true?

- O The two integers are both odd.
- O The two integers are both even.
- O One of the two integers is odd and the other is even.
- O One of the integers is 1.
- O The two integers are consecutive.

13. How many cylindrical cans with a radius of 2 inches and a height of 6 inches can fit into a rectangular box?

(1) The volume of the box is 230 cubic inches.

(2) The length of the box is 3 inches.

14. Committee A has 7 members, and Committee B has 8 members. If 3 people serve on both committees, how many people serve on exactly one of the committees?

- O 8
- O 9
- O 10
- O 11
- O 12

15. If sheets of paper are 0.08 centimeters thick and 500 sheets cost \$3.00, how much will a stack of paper 4 meters thick cost? (1 meter = 100 centimeters)

- O \$30
- O \$45
- O \$60
- O \$72
- O \$96

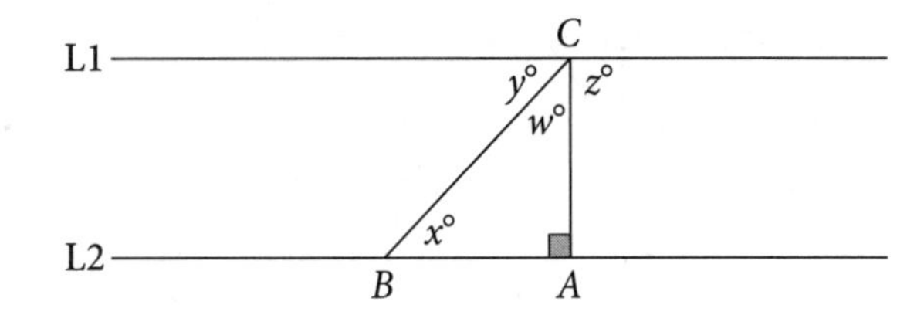


16. Does $x° = y°$?

(1) $AB = AC$

(2) $y° + w° = z°$

17. The workforce of a company is 20 percent part-time workers, with the rest of the workers full-time. At the end of the year, 30 percent of the full-time workers received bonuses. If 72 full-time workers received bonuses, how many workers does the company employ?

- 132
- 240
- 280
- 300
- 360

18. If $xyz \neq 0$, then $\frac{x^3yz^4}{xy^{-2}z^3} =$

- $x^2y^3z$
- $x^4y^{-1}z^7$
- $x^2y^{-1}z$
- $x^2y^3z^2$
- $x^2yz$

19. An optometrist charges $30 for an eye examination, frames, and glass lenses, but $42 for an eye examination, frames, and plastic lenses. If the plastic lenses cost four times as much as the glass lenses, how much do the glass lenses cost?

- $2
- $4
- $5
- $6
- $8

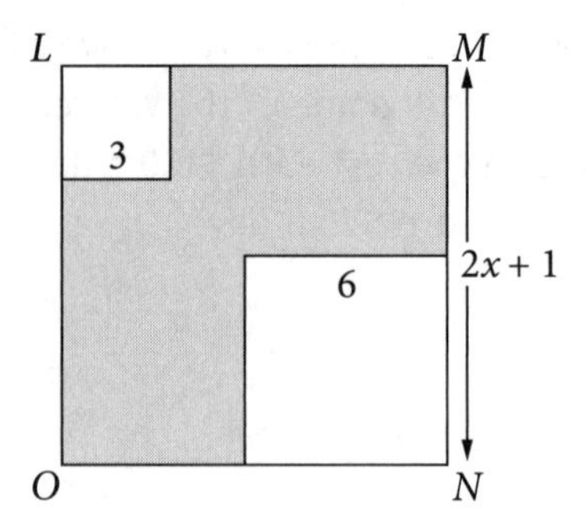


20. In the figure above, square *LMNO* has a side of length $2x + 1$, and the two smaller squares have sides of lengths 3 and 6. If the area of the shaded region is 76, what is the value of $x$?

- 5
- 6
- 7
- 11
- 14

21. If $(a,b)$ is a point on the graph of $y = -2x^2 + 2x + 24$ in the $xy$-coordinate plane, is $b < 0$?

(1) $a < 4$

(2) $a > -3$

22. A sporting goods store ordered an equal number of white and yellow tennis balls. The tennis ball company delivered 30 extra white balls, making the ratio of white balls to yellow balls 6:5. How many tennis balls did the store originally order?

- 120
- 150
- 180
- 300
- 330

23. What is the smallest integer greater than 1 that leaves a remainder of 1 when divided by any of the integers 6, 8, and 10?

   - O 21
   - O 41
   - O 121
   - O 241
   - O 481

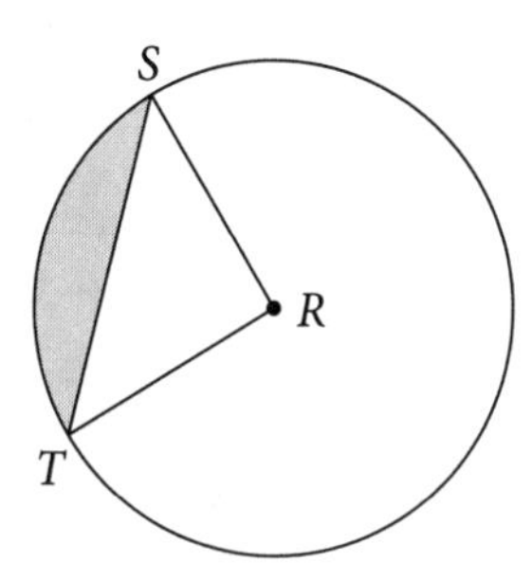


24. $R$ is the center of the above circle, and $S$ and $T$ are points on the circumference. What is the area of the shaded region?

   (1) The circumference of the circle is $24\pi$.

   (2) Minor arc $ST$ is equal to $\frac{1}{4}$ of the circumference of the circle.

25. The cube root of what positive number is equal to the square root of the square root of 81?

   - O 3
   - O 9
   - O 27
   - O 81
   - O 243

26. A bag holds 3 gold rings, 7 silver rings, and 9 bronze rings. If John picks rings from the bag, does he pick more bronze rings than silver rings?

   (1) John picks 15 rings.

   (2) John picks 3 gold rings.

27. If $m \blacktriangle n$ is defined by the equation $m \blacktriangle n = \frac{m^2 - n + 1}{mn}$ for all nonzero $m$ and $n$, then $3 \blacktriangle 1 =$

   - O $\frac{9}{4}$
   - O 3
   - O $\frac{11}{3}$
   - O 6
   - O 9

28. The length of each side of square $A$ is increased by 100 percent to make square $B$. If the length of the side of square $B$ is increased by 50 percent to make square $C$, by what percent is the area of square $C$ greater than the sum of the areas of squares $A$ and $B$?

   - O 75%
   - O 80%
   - O 100%
   - O 150%
   - O 180%

29. For all real numbers $a$ and $b$, the operation ** is defined by $a ** b = a^2 + ab$. What is the product of all possible values of $x$?

   (1) $y = x ** 8$

   (2) $3 ** y = -12$

30. The total fare for 2 adults and 3 children on an excursion boat is $14.00. If each child's fare is one-half of each adult's fare, what is the adult fare?

   - O $2.00
   - O $3.00
   - O $3.50
   - O $4.00
   - O $4.50

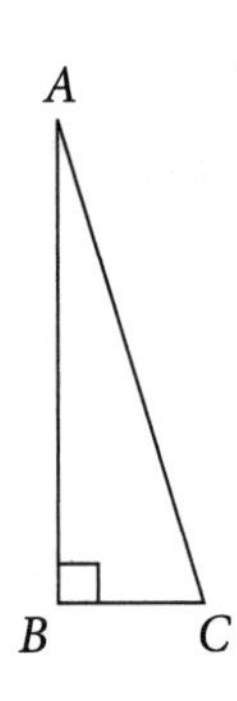


31. In the figure above, the area of $\Delta ABC$ is 6. If $BC$ is $\frac{1}{3}$ the length of $AB$, then what is the length of $AC$?

   - $\sqrt{2}$
   - 2
   - 4
   - 6
   - $2\sqrt{10}$

Answers follow on the next page. ▶ ▶ ▶

# Answer Key

## Practice Section 2

1. D
2. A
3. B
4. D
5. C
6. B
7. D
8. A
9. C
10. B
11. C
12. C
13. B
14. B
15. A
16. B
17. D
18. A
19. B
20. A
21. C
22. D
23. C
24. C
25. C
26. E
27. B
28. B
29. C
30. D
31. E

# Answers and Explanations

## Practice Section 2

### 1. D

Translate what you are given into equations, and then solve for the number of plums: $p$ plums at 25 cents each $= 25p$; $(p - 6)$ nectarines at 28 cents each $= 28(p - 6)$.

These two quantities are equal, so:

$$25p = 28(p - 6)$$

Solve for $p$.

$$\begin{aligned} 25p &= 28p - 168 \\ 168 &= 28p - 25p \\ 168 &= 3p \\ \frac{168}{3} &= p \\ 56 &= p \end{aligned}$$

### 2. A

Since you know the area of circle $O$, you can find the radius of the circle. And if you find the length of $OA$, then $AB$ is just the difference of $OB$ and $OA$.

Since the area of the circle is $100\pi = \pi r^2$, the radius must be $\sqrt{100}$, or 10. Radius $OC$, line segment $CA$, and line segment $OA$ together form a right triangle, so you can use the Pythagorean theorem to find the length of $OA$. But notice that since 10 is twice 5 and 6 is twice 3, right triangle $ACO$ has sides whose lengths are in a 3:4:5 ratio (a Pythagorean triplet).

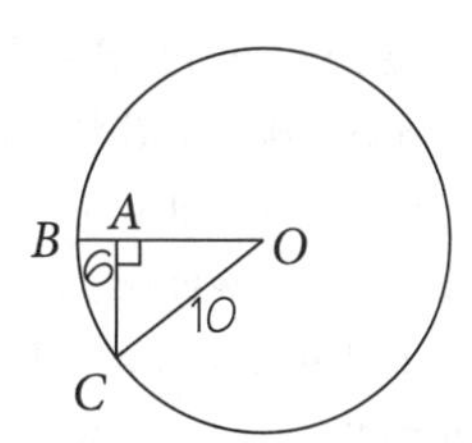


Thus, $OA$ must have a length of twice 4, or 8. $AB$ is the segment of radius $OB$ that's not a part of $OA$; its length equals the length of $OB$ minus the length of $OA$, or $10 - 8 = 2$.

### 3. B

Analyzing the given function, the term $-3(x - b)^2$ will be a negative number except for when $x = b$, in which case it will be 0. Thus, 0 is the maximum value of $-3(x - b)^2$. So, at that point, the value of $f(x)$ is $k$, which is the greatest possible value of $f(x)$ because, for any values of $x$ other than $b$, the term $-3(x - b)^2$ will be negative and $f(x)$ will be less than $k$.

From Statement (1), per the analysis, knowing $b$ will not determine the maximum value of $f(x)$. Statement (1) is insufficient. Eliminate (A) and (D).

Statement (2) provides the value of $k$, which, per the analysis, is the maximum value of $f(x)$. So, Statement (2) is sufficient. **(B)** is correct.

**4. D**

Since you know the ratio, finding the value of any of the integers will tell you the value of all of them, from which you can find the sum. Statement (1) tells you the difference of two integers. You know the ratio of $a$ to $c$, so, given their difference, you can find their actual values. Since $c = 3a$, you can rewrite the expression $c - a = 8$ as $3a - a = 8$. Thus, you can find $a$. Statement (1) is sufficient. Eliminate (B), (C), and (E).

Similarly, Statement (2) gives you another difference; you can find the actual values from this, too. Each statement alone is sufficient. **(D)** is correct.

**5. C**

Since the angle marked $x°$ and the angle marked $y°$ together form a straight angle, their measures must sum to 180°.

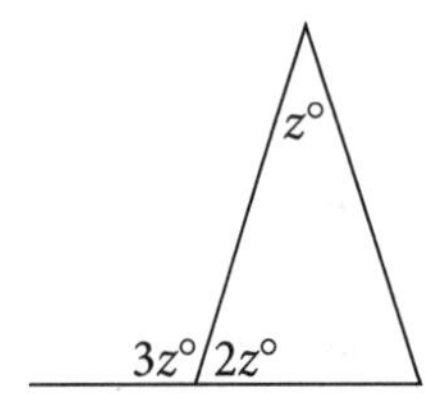


Substitute $2z$ for $x$ and $3z$ for $y$, and solve for $z$.

$$x + y = 180$$
$$2z + 3z = 180$$
$$5z = 180$$
$$z = \frac{1}{5} \cdot 180 = 36$$

**6. B**

The average speed equals the total distance the car travels divided by the total time. You're told the car goes 60 kilometers in an hour before its piston breaks, and then travels another 60 kilometers at 30 kilometers per hour. The second part of the trip must have taken 2 hours (if you go 30 kilometers in 1 hour, then you'll go twice as far, 60 kilometers, in twice as much time, 2 hours). So, the car travels a total of 60 + 60, or 120 kilometers, and covers this distance in 1 + 2, or 3 hours. Its average speed equals 120 kilometers divided by 3 hours, or 40 kilometers per hour.

Notice that the average speed over the entire trip is not simply the average of the two speeds. (That would be the average of 60 and 30, which is 45.) This is because the car spent different amounts of time traveling at these two different speeds. Be wary of problems that ask for an average rate over a trip that encompasses different rates.

**7. D**

If the average salary of the 60 workers is \$80, the total amount received by the workers is $60 \times \$80$, or \$4,800. This equals the total income from the \$75 workers plus the total income from the \$100 workers. Let $x$ represent the number of \$75 workers.

Since you know there are 60 workers altogether, and everyone earns either \$75 or \$100, then $60 - x$ must earn \$100. You can set up an equation for the total amount received by the workers by multiplying the salary by the number of workers receiving that salary and adding:

$$75x + 100(60 - x) = 4{,}800$$

Solve this equation to find $x$, the number of workers earning \$75.

$$75x + 6{,}000 - 100x = 4{,}800$$
$$-25x = -1{,}200$$
$$25x = 1{,}200$$
$$x = 48$$

There are 48 workers earning \$75.

**8. A**

Since the question involves committees, the order in which the people are chosen does not matter, so this is a combinations question. The formula for combinations is ${}_rC_k = \frac{r!}{k!(r-k)!}$, where $r$ is the number of total items and $k$ is the number of items being chosen. Ideally, knowing the values of $r$ and $k$ would be sufficient.

Statement (1) gives the number of committees of $x - y$ members that can be formed. The formula for this is $\frac{x!}{(x-y)!(x-(x-y))!} = \frac{x!}{(x-y)!(y)!}$. This is exactly the same as the formula for the number of committees that can be formed by selecting $y$ people. Therefore, Statement (1) is sufficient. Eliminate (B), (C), and (E).

Statement (2) allows you to calculate the value of $y$ using permutations. Since $4! = 4 \times 3 \times 2 \times 1 = 24$, $y = 4$. However, the value of $x$ is still unknown, so Statement (2) is insufficient. **(A)** is correct.

**9. C**

To average 2 hours a day over 6 days, the violinist must practice $2 \times 6$, or 12 hours. From Monday through Friday, she practices 5 hours, 1 hour each day. To total 12 hours, she must practice $12 - 5 = 7$ hours, on Saturday.

**10. B**

Together, the angle marked $x°$ and the angle marked $y°$ form a straight angle, so $x + y$ equals 180. You're also told that $y = 5x$.

x°
5x°

Substitute $5x$ for $y$:

$$x + y = 180$$
$$x + 5x = 180$$
$$6x = 180$$
$$x = 30$$

**11. C**

Thoroughly analyzing the possibilities for the given inequality will greatly simplify evaluating the statements. Since $b$ is an integer, it can be positive, negative, or zero. If $b > 0$, then $2^b \geq 2$. If $b = 0$, then $2^b = 1$. Recall that a negative exponent is equivalent to the same value as a positive exponent in the denominator of a fraction with a numerator of 1. If $b < 0$, then the greatest possible value of $2^b$ is $\frac{1}{2}$ when $b = -1$. As $b$ gets more negative, the value of $2^b$ becomes a smaller and smaller fraction, so $0 < 2^b < \frac{1}{2}$. Examining $a$, if $a < 0$, then $(a)(|a|)$ is negative. If $a = 0$, then $(a)(|a|) = 0$. Finally, if $a > 0$, then $(a)(|a|) > 0$.

Statement (1) states that $b$ is negative, but does not provide any information about $a$. Thus, Statement (1) is insufficient. Eliminate (A) and (D).

Statement (2) states that $a = b$. If both are 0 or negative, then the answer is yes. Evaluate some positive numbers. If $a = b = 1$, then $(a)(|a|) < 2^b$, so the answer is still yes. However, if $a = b = 3$, then $(3)(3) = 9$, but $2^3 = 8$, so the answer is no. Statement (2) is also insufficient. Eliminate (B).

When combined, the statements tell you that both $a$ and $b$ are negative. From the analysis of Statement (2), you know that the answer is yes. So, taken together, the statements are sufficient. **(C)** is correct.

**12. C**

If two numbers have an even product, at least one of the numbers is even, so you can eliminate (A). If both numbers were even, their sum would be even, but you know the sum of these numbers is odd, so you can eliminate (B). If one number is odd and the other is even, their product is even and their sum is odd. **(C)** gives you what you're looking for. (D) and (E) both can be true, but they're not necessarily true.

**13. B**

The volume of a can is not relevant here; what is relevant is realizing that to find the number of cans that can fit in the box, you need the actual dimensions of the box. Statement (1) doesn't give you the dimensions, only the volume; this is insufficient. Eliminate (A) and (D).

Statement (2) gives the length; this would ordinarily be insufficient, except that since the length of the box is smaller than either the diameter or the height of the can, you can determine that *none* of the cans can fit into the box; it is too narrow. Statement (2) is sufficient. **(B)** is correct.

**14. B**

Of the 7 people on Committee A, 3 of them are also on Committee B, leaving $7 - 3 = 4$ people who are only on Committee A. Similarly, there are 8 people on Committee B; 3 of them are on both committees, leaving $8 - 3 = 5$ people only on Committee B. There are 4 people only on A, and 5 people only on B, making $4 + 5 = 9$ people on only one committee.

**15. A**

First, you have to find the number of sheets of paper in the pile and then calculate the cost from that. If you have trouble working with very small numbers (or very large numbers) and can't quite figure out how to calculate the number of sheets, you may want to try it with some easier numbers to see which operation you need. Suppose you've got sheets of paper 1 meter thick and need to stack enough for 4 meters. To calculate the number of sheets, you divide 1 into 4, dividing the thickness for each sheet into the total thickness, and you end up with the number of sheets: 4.

$$\frac{\text{Total thickness}}{\text{Thickness per sheet}} = \text{Number of sheets}$$

Here, of course, you use the same technique. Divide the thickness per sheet into the total thickness. First, change the meters to centimeters (you could change the thickness per sheet into meters, but you've got enough zeros as it is). There are 100 centimeters in a meter, so in 4 meters there are $4 \times 100 = 400$ centimeters. Now you can divide:

$$\frac{400}{0.08} = \frac{40{,}000}{8} = 5{,}000$$

So, you have 5,000 sheets. If 500 sheets cost \$3, then 5,000 sheets will cost ten times as much, or \$30.

**16. B**

The question simply asks if $x° = y°$. There could be many ways to establish this, so keep an open mind as you evaluate the statements. Note, however, that if L1 and L2 were parallel, $x$ and $y$ would be corresponding acute angles created by a transversal, and thus equal.

Statement (1) establishes that triangle *ABC* is isosceles, and since it's a right triangle, that means that $x°$ and $w°$ both equal 45. But that doesn't tell you anything about $y°$, so there's no way to know if it's equal to $x°$; this statement is insufficient. Eliminate (A) and (D).

Statement (2) tells you that $y° + w° = z°$. These three angles make a straight line, which means that $y° + w° + z° = 180$. Substitute $y° + w°$ for $z°$ in the second equation to get $z° + z° = 180$, or $z° = 90$. Since line segment *AC* is thus perpendicular to both L1 and L2, L1 and L2 must be parallel. And, as you already established, if they're parallel, then $x° = y°$; this statement is sufficient. **(B)** is correct.

**17. D**

You're only given one figure for any group of workers: 72 for the number of full-time workers who received bonuses. You can find the total number of workers if you know what percent of the total number of workers these 72 represent. 20% of the workers are part-time, so 80% of the workers are full-time. Furthermore, 30% of the full-time workers received bonuses, and this amounts to 72 workers.

If $E$ is the total number of workers employed by the company, then 80% of $E =$ the number of full-time workers, so:

$$30\% \text{ of } 80\% \text{ of } E = 72$$

$$\frac{3}{10} \times \frac{8}{10} \times E = 72$$

$$\frac{24}{100} \times E = 72$$

$$E = 72 \times \frac{100}{24}$$

$$= 300$$

The company employs 300 workers.

**18. A**

First, break up the expression to separate the variables, transforming the fraction into a product of three simpler fractions:

$$\frac{x^3yz^4}{xy^{-2}z^3} = \left(\frac{x^3}{x}\right)\left(\frac{y}{y^{-2}}\right)\left(\frac{z^4}{z^3}\right)$$

Now carry out each division by keeping the base and subtracting the exponents.

$$\frac{x^3}{x} = x^{3-1} = x^2$$

$$\frac{y}{y^{-2}} = y^{1-(-2)} = y^{1+2} = y^3$$

$$\frac{z^4}{z^3} = z^{4-3} = z^1 = z$$

The answer is the product of these three expressions, or $x^2y^3z$.

**19. B**

In each case, the examination and the frames are the same; the difference in cost must be due to a difference in the costs of the lenses. This is \$42 − \$30 = \$12. You can set up two equations to solve for the cost of the glass lenses: $p = 4g$ and $p - g = 12$. Next, substitute $4g$ for $p$ in the second equation: $4g - g = 12$, or $3g = 12$, so $g = \$4$.

**20. A**

The shaded area and the two small squares all combine to form the large square, *LMNO*. Therefore, the area of square *LMNO* equals the sum of the shaded area and the area of the two small squares. You know the shaded area; you can find the areas of the two small squares since you're given side lengths for each square. The smallest square has a side of length 3; its area is $3^2$, or 9. The other small square has a side of length 6; its area is $6^2$, or 36. The area of square *LMNO*, then, is $9 + 36 + 76 = 121$.

Since square *LMNO* has an area of 121, then each side has a length of $\sqrt{121}$, or 11. Since you have an expression for the length of a side of the large square in terms of $x$, you can set up an equation and solve for $x$:

$$2x + 1 = 11$$

$$2x = 10$$

$$x = 5$$

**21. C**

This is a quadratic equation, so it'll form a parabola when graphed. Before you evaluate the statements, set the quadratic equation equal to 0 and factor it to find the intercepts:

$$-2x^2 + 2x + 24 = 0$$

$$x^2 - x - 12 = 0$$

$$(x - 4)(x + 3) = 0$$

So, the $x$-intercepts are at $x = 4$ and $x = -3$. Since the coefficient of the squared term in the original equation is negative, the parabola will open downward. Therefore, any point on the parabola with an $x$ value between the two intercepts will have a positive $y$ value (because it will fall above the $x$-axis), and any point with an $x$ value outside the two intercepts will have a negative $y$ value (because it will fall below the $x$-axis).

Statement (1) establishes that $a$ is less than 4. All points with a positive $y$ value have an $x$ value of less than 4, but not all points that have an $x$ value of less than 4 will have a positive $y$ value, since those with an $x$ value less than $-3$ have a negative $y$ value. So, Statement (1) allows for some yes answers and some no answers, which means it's insufficient. Eliminate (A) and (D).

Using the same logic, you can determine that Statement (2) allows for points with both positive and negative $y$ values, so it's insufficient as well. Eliminate (B).

Combined, however, the statements tell you that the $x$-coordinate of $(a,b)$ is between the $x$-intercepts of the parabola, which means that $b$ must be positive. The question asks if $b$ is negative; thus, the two statements combined are sufficient to answer the question with a definitive no. **(C)** is correct.

**22. D**

You can solve this algebraically. Let the number of yellow balls received be $x$. Then the number of white balls received is 30 more than this, or $x + 30$.

$$\frac{\text{\# of white balls}}{\text{\# of yellow balls}} = \frac{6}{5} = \frac{x+30}{x}$$

$$\text{Cross multiply: } 6x = 5(x + 30)$$

$$\text{Solve for } x\text{: } 6x = 5x + 150$$

$$x = 150$$

Since the number of white balls ordered equals the number of yellow balls ordered, the total number of balls ordered is $2x$, which is $2 \times 150$, or 300.

You could also solve this more intuitively.

The store originally ordered an equal number of white and yellow balls; they ended up with a white to yellow ratio of 6:5. This means for every 5 yellow balls, they got 6 white balls, or they got $\frac{1}{5}$ more white balls than yellow balls. The difference between the number of white balls and the number of yellow balls is just the 30 extra white balls they got. So 30 balls represents $\frac{1}{5}$ of the number of yellow balls. Then, the number of yellow balls is $5 \times 30$, or 150. Since they ordered the same number of white balls as yellow balls, they also ordered 150 white balls, for a total order of $150 + 150$, or 300 balls.

**23. C**

You're asked for the smallest positive integer that leaves a remainder of 1 when divided by 6, 8, or 10. In other words, if you find the smallest integer that is a common multiple of these three numbers, you can add 1 to that number to get the answer. Subtracting 1 from each of the answer choices gives you 20, 40, 120, 240, and 480. Your best tactic is to work from the smallest up until you get your answer. All are multiples of 10, but 20 is not a multiple of 6 or 8, and 40 is not a multiple of 6; 120 is a multiple of 6 ($6 \times 20$), 8 ($8 \times 15$), and 10 ($10 \times 12$). One more than 120 is 121. Answer choice **(C)**, 121, is thus the smallest number to leave a remainder of 1.

An alternative approach to finding the least common multiple is to look at their prime factors:

$$6 = 2 \times 3$$
$$8 = 2 \times 2 \times 2$$
$$10 = 2 \times 5$$

So, a common multiple must have three factors of 2, one factor of 3, and one factor of 5.

$$2 \times 2 \times 2 \times 3 \times 5 = 120; 120 + 1 = 121$$

**24. C**

The triangle in this circle has one vertex at the center of the circle and two on its circumference. Thus, sides *RT* and *RS* are radii of the circle. These radii also define a sector of the circle. So, the area of the shaded region will be the area of that sector minus the area of the triangle. To find the area of the sector, you'd need the area of the circle and the measure of the central angle that creates the sector. To find the area of the triangle, you'd need its base and height. Check out the statements to see if they provide enough information to determine those.

Statement (1) gives the circumference of the circle. Since $C = 2\pi r$, this would allow you to figure out the radius of the circle and thus its area. But without the central angle, you can't find the area of the sector. Eliminate (A) and (D).

Statement (2) tells you something about the length of minor arc *ST*. Central angles are proportional to the arcs they create, so if that arc is $\frac{1}{4}$ of the circumference, central angle *SRT* is also $\frac{1}{4}$ of the circle, or 90°. Sectors are also proportional to the central angle, so sector *SRT* is equal to $\frac{1}{4}$ of the area of the circle. Additionally, since the central angle is 90°, triangle *SRT* is a right triangle, so you'd be able to find its area with the length of the two legs, *RS* and *RT*. Even though this statement tells you a lot, you still need the radius of the circle to find its area and the area of the triangle. So, it's insufficient as well. Eliminate (B).

Now, consider the statements together. You determined that Statement (1) allows you to figure out the radius of the circle, and Statement (2) gives you everything you need to find the areas of the sector and the triangle except for the radius of the circle. Thus, together, they're sufficient. **(C)** is correct.

**25. C**

This problem rewards careful translation. The square root of 81 is 9, and the square root *of the square root* of 81 is $\sqrt{9} = 3$. The question asks for the positive number whose cube root is 3. That's $3^3 = 27$.

**26. E**

Statement (1) states that John picks 15 rings. He could pick more bronze rings than silver rings, but he could also pick all 3 gold rings, all 7 silver rings, and only 5 bronze rings. This is not sufficient. Eliminate (A) and (D).

Statement (2) states that John picks 3 gold rings. This, by itself, tells you nothing about the number of silver or bronze rings, so it's not sufficient. Eliminate (B).

Using the statements together, you know that $15 - 3 = 12$ of the rings are either silver or bronze, but you still don't know which is greater. Both statements are insufficient. **(E)** is correct.

**27. B**

Here you have a symbolism problem involving a symbol (▲) that doesn't really exist in mathematics. All you need to do is follow the directions given in the definition of this symbol. To find the value of 3 ▲ 1, simply plug 3 and 1 into the formula given for $m$ ▲ $n$, substituting 3 for $m$ and 1 for $n$. Then the equation becomes:

$$\begin{aligned} 3 \blacktriangle 1 &= \frac{(3)^2 - (1) + 1}{(3)(1)} \\ &= \frac{9 - 1 + 1}{3} \\ &= \frac{9}{3} \\ &= 3 \end{aligned}$$

**28. B**

The best way to solve this problem is to pick a value for the length of a side of square $A$. You want numbers that are easy to work with, so pick 10 for the length of each side of square $A$. The length of each side of square $B$ is 100% greater, or twice as great as a side of square $A$. So, the length of a side of square $B$ is $2 \times 10$, or 20. The length of each side of square $C$ is 50% greater, or 1.5 times as great as a side of square $B$, or $1.5 \times 20 = 30$.

The area of square $A$ is $10^2$, or 100. The area of square $B$ is $20^2$, or 400. The sum of the areas of squares $A$ and $B$ is $100 + 400 = 500$. The area of square $C$ is $30^2$, or 900. The area of square $C$ is greater than the sum of the areas of squares $A$ and $B$ by $900 - 500$, or 400. The percent that the area of square $C$ is greater than the sum of the areas of squares $A$ and $B$ is $\frac{400}{500} \times 100\%$, or 80%.

**29. C**

The variable $x$ is not mentioned in the stem, so you'll need to look at the statements.

Statement (1) translates to $y = x^2 + 8x$. Lacking a value for $y$, you cannot determine any value for $x$. Thus, Statement (1) is insufficient. Eliminate (A) and (D).

Statement (2) translates to $-12 = 3^2 + 3y$, which does not even mention $x$. So, Statement (2) is also insufficient. Eliminate (B).

Consider the two statements together. Plugging $x$ ** 8 in for $y$ in the second equation results in $3^2 + (3)(x^2 + 8x) = 9 + 3x^2 + 24x = -12$. This can be rearranged as the quadratic $3x^2 + 24x + 21 = 0$. This further simplifies to $x^2 + 8x + 7 = 0$. This factors to $(x + 7)(x + 1) = 0$, from which the values of $x$ and their product can be derived. So, taken together, the statements are sufficient. **(C)** is correct.

**30. D**

If each adult's fare is twice as much as each child's fare, then 2 adults' fares are equivalent to 4 children's fares. This, added to the 3 children's fares, gives you a total of $4 + 3 = 7$ children's fares. This equals \$14. If 7 children's fares cost \$14, then the cost of each child's fare is $\frac{14}{7}$, or \$2. The adult fare costs twice as much, or \$4.

**31. E**

First, solve for the length of *BC*, the shortest side. You can then find the length of *AB* and the length of *AC* using the Pythagorean theorem.

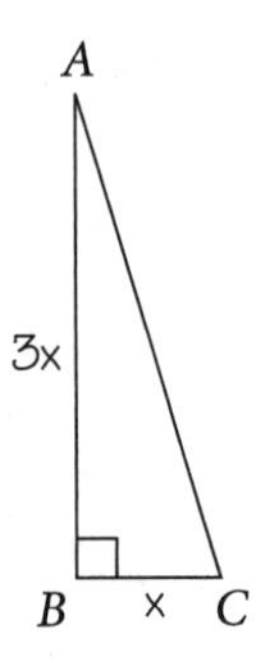


The area of any right triangle equals one-half the product of the legs. If *BC* has a length of $x$, then *AB* has a length of $3x$. (If *BC* is one-third the length of *AB*, then *AB* is three times the length of *BC*.) The area of the triangle is one-half their product, or $\frac{1}{2}(x)(3x)$. This equals 6.

$$\frac{1}{2}(x)(3x) = 6$$
$$3x^2 = 12$$
$$x^2 = 4$$
$$x = 2$$

*BC* has a length of 2. So *AB*, which is $3x$, is 6. Now use the Pythagorean theorem to find *AC*:

$$AC^2 = AB^2 + BC^2$$
$$AC^2 = 6^2 + 2^2$$
$$AC^2 = 36 + 4$$
$$AC = \sqrt{40} = \sqrt{4 \cdot 10} = \sqrt{4}\sqrt{10} = 2\sqrt{10}$$

PART FOUR

# Guide to GMAT Math

CHAPTER 9

# Math Reference

The math on the GMAT covers a lot of ground—from number properties and arithmetic, to algebra and symbol problems, to geometry and statistics.

In this chapter, we've highlighted the most important math concepts on the GMAT and divided them into four main sections:

1. Arithmetic and Number Properties
2. Algebra
3. Formulas, Statistics, and Data Analysis
4. Geometry

Use the contents of this chapter as a resource to help you brush up on math concepts that you might have forgotten or learn new concepts that you are seeing for the first time.

## Arithmetic and Number Properties

### Arithmetic Terms

**Consecutive numbers:** Numbers of a certain type, following one another without interruption. Numbers may be consecutive in ascending or descending direction. The GMAT prefers to test consecutive integers (e.g., −2, −1, 0, 1, 2, 3 . . .), but you may encounter other types of consecutive numbers. For example:

−4, −2, 0, 2, 4, 6, . . . is a series of consecutive even numbers.

−3, 0, 3, 6, 9, . . . is a series of consecutive multiples of 3.

2, 3, 5, 7, 11, . . . is a series of consecutive prime numbers.

**Cube:** A number raised to the third power. For example $4^3 = (4)(4)(4) = 64$, and 64 is the cube of 4.

**Decimal:** A fraction written in decimal system format. For example, 0.6 is a decimal. To convert a fraction to a decimal, divide the numerator by the denominator.

**Decimal system:** A numbering system based on the powers of 10. The decimal system is the only numbering system used on the GMAT. Each figure, or digit, in a decimal number occupies a particular position, from which it derives its place value.

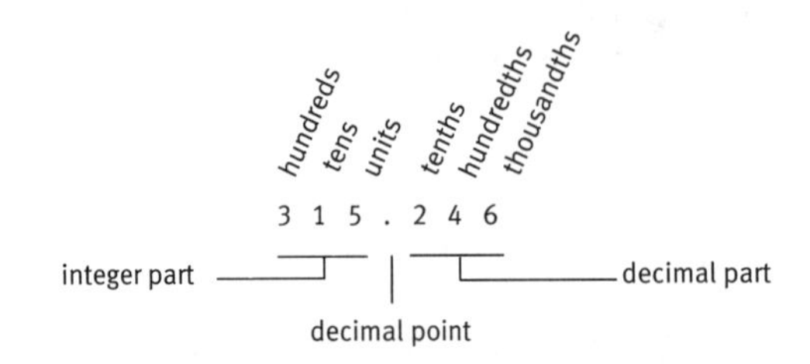


**Denominator:** The quantity in the bottom of a fraction, representing the whole.

**Difference:** The result of subtraction.

**Digit:** One of the numerals 0, 1, 2, 3, 4, 5, 6, 7, 8, or 9. A number can have several digits. For example, the number 542 has three digits: a 5, a 4, and a 2. The number 321,321,000 has nine digits, but only four distinct (different) digits: 3, 2, 1, and 0.

**Element:** One of the members of a set.

**Exponent:** The number that denotes the power to which another number or variable is raised. The exponent is typically written as a superscript to a number. For example, $5^3$ equals $(5)(5)(5)$. The exponent is also occasionally referred to as a "power." For example, $5^3$ can be described as "5 to the third power." The product, 125, is "the third power of 5."

**Fraction:** The division of a part by a whole. $\frac{\text{Part}}{\text{Whole}} = \text{Fraction}$. For example, $\frac{3}{5}$ is a fraction.

**Integer:** A number without fractional or decimal parts, including negative whole numbers and zero. All integers are multiples of 1. The following are examples of integers: $-5, -4, -3, -2, -1, 0, 1, 2, 3, 4, 5$.

**Number line:** A straight line, extending infinitely in either direction, on which numbers are represented as points. The number line below shows the integers from $-3$ to 4. Decimals and fractions can also be depicted on a number line, as can irrational numbers, such as $\sqrt{2}$.

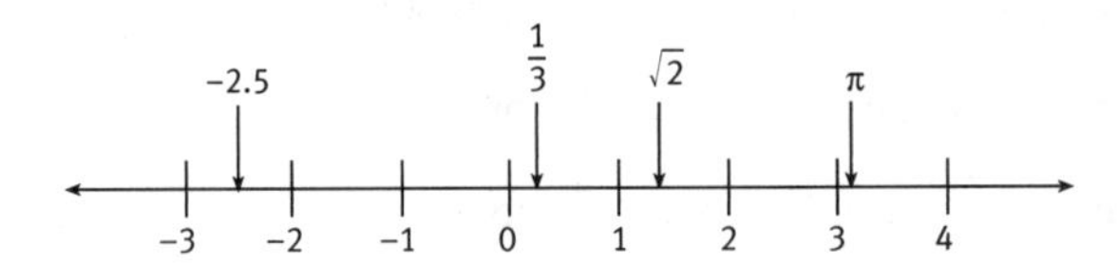


The values of numbers get larger as you move to the right along the number line. Numbers to the right of zero are *positive*; numbers to the left of zero are *negative*. **Zero is neither positive nor negative.** Any positive number is larger than any negative number. For example, $-300 < 4$.

**Numerator:** The quantity in the top of the fraction, representing the part.

**Operation:** A function or process performed on one or more numbers. The four basic arithmetic operations are addition, subtraction, multiplication, and division.

**Part:** A specified number of the equal sections that comprise a whole.

**Product:** The result of multiplication.

**Set:** A well-defined collection of items, typically numbers, objects, or events. The bracket symbols { } are normally used to define sets of numbers. For example, {2, 4, 6, 8} is a set of numbers.

**Square:** The product of a number multiplied by itself. A squared number has been raised to the second power. For example, $4^2 = (4)(4) = 16$, and 16 is the square of 4.

**Sum:** The result of addition.

**Whole:** A quantity that is regarded as a complete unit.

## Math Symbols

| | |
|---|---|
| $=$ | is equal to |
| $\neq$ | is not equal to |
| $<$ | is less than |
| $>$ | is greater than |
| $\leq$ | is less than or equal to |
| $\geq$ | is greater than or equal to |
| $\div$ | divided by |
| $\pi$ | pi (the ratio of the circumference of a circle to the diameter) |
| $\pm$ | plus or minus |
| $\sqrt{\ }$ | square root |
| $\angle$ | angle |

## Order of Operations (PEMDAS)

There are certain mathematical laws governing the results of the four basic operations: addition, subtraction, multiplication, and division. Although you won't need to know the names of these laws for the GMAT, you'll benefit from understanding them.

### PEMDAS

A string of operations must be performed in the proper order. The acronym PEMDAS stands for the correct order of operations:

Parentheses
Exponents

Multiplication } simultaneously from left to right
Division }

Addition } simultaneously from left to right
Subtraction }

If you have trouble remembering PEMDAS, you can think of the mnemonic "Please Excuse My Dear Aunt Sally."

**Example:** $66(3 - 2) \div 11$

If you were to perform all the operations sequentially from left to right, without using PEMDAS, you would arrive at an answer of $\frac{196}{11}$. But if you perform the operation within the parentheses first, you get $66(1) \div 11 = 66 \div 11 = 6$, which is the correct answer.

**Example:**

$$30 - 5(4) + \frac{(7-3)^2}{8}$$
$$= 30 - 5(4) + \frac{4^2}{8}$$
$$= 30 - 5(4) + \frac{16}{8}$$
$$= 30 - 20 + 2$$
$$= 10 + 2$$
$$= 12$$

## Adding and Subtracting

Numbers can be treated as though they have two parts: a positive or negative sign and a number. Numbers without any sign are understood to be positive.

*To add two numbers that have the same sign*, add the number parts and keep the sign. Example: To add $(-6) + (-3)$, add 6 and 3 and then attach the negative sign from the original numbers to the sum: $(-6) + (-3) = -9$.

*To add two numbers that have different signs*, find the difference between the number parts and keep the sign of the number whose number part is larger. Example: To add $(-7) + (+4)$, subtract 4 from 7 to get 3. Because $7 > 4$ (the number part of $-7$ is greater than the number part of 4), the final sum will be negative: $(-7) + (+4) = -3$.

*Subtraction is the opposite of addition.* You can rephrase any subtraction problem as an addition problem by changing the operation sign from a minus to a plus and switching the sign on the second number. Example: $8 - 5 = 8 + (-5)$. There's no real advantage to rephrasing if you are subtracting a smaller positive number from a larger positive number. But the concept comes in very handy when you are subtracting a negative number from any other number, a positive number from a negative number, or a larger positive number from a smaller positive number.

*To subtract a negative number*, rephrase as an addition problem and follow the rules for addition of signed numbers. For instance, $9 - (-10) = 9 + 10 = 19$.

*To subtract a positive number from a negative number, or from a smaller positive number,* change the sign of the number that you are subtracting from positive to negative and follow the rules for addition of signed numbers. For example, $(-4) - 1 = (-4) + (-1) = -5$.

## Commutative Laws of Addition and Multiplication

Addition and multiplication are both commutative; switching the order of any two numbers being added or multiplied together does not affect the result.

**Examples:**

$$5+8=8+5$$
$$(2)(3)(6)=(6)(3)(2)$$
$$a+b=b+a$$
$$ab=ba$$

Division and subtraction are not commutative; switching the order of the numbers changes the result. For instance, $3-2\neq 2-3$; the left side yields a difference of 1, while the right side yields a difference of $-1$. Similarly, $\frac{6}{2}\neq\frac{2}{6}$; the left side equals 3, while the right side equals $\frac{1}{3}$.

## Associative Laws of Addition and Multiplication

Addition and multiplication are also associative; regrouping the numbers does not affect the result.

**Example:**

$$(3+5)+8=3+(5+8) \qquad (a+b)+c=a+(b+c)$$
$$8+8=3+13 \qquad (ab)c=a(bc)$$
$$16=16$$

## The Distributive Law

In multiplication, the distributive law of multiplication allows you to "distribute" a factor over numbers that are added or subtracted. You do this by multiplying that factor by each number in the group.

**Example:**

$$4(3+7)=(4)(3)+(4)(7) \qquad a(b+c)=ab+ac$$
$$4(10)=12+28$$
$$40=40$$

The law works for the numerator in division as well.

$$\frac{a+b}{c}=\frac{a}{c}+\frac{b}{c}$$

However, when the sum or difference is in the denominator—that is, when you're dividing by a sum or difference—no distribution is possible.

$\frac{9}{4+5}$ is *not* equal to $\frac{9}{4}+\frac{9}{5}$.

## Multiplication and Division of Positive and Negative Numbers

Multiplying or dividing two numbers with the same sign gives a positive result.

**Examples:** $(-4)(-7) = +28$

$(-50) \div (-5) = +10$

Multiplying or dividing two numbers with different signs gives a negative result.

**Examples:** $(-2)(+3) = -6$

$8 \div (-4) = -2$

## Properties of Even and Odd Numbers

*Even* numbers are integers that are evenly divisible by 2; *odd* numbers are integers that are not evenly divisible by 2. Integers whose last digit is 0, 2, 4, 6, or 8 are even; integers whose last digit is 1, 3, 5, 7, or 9 are odd. The terms *odd* and *even* apply only to integers, but they may be used for either positive or negative integers. 0 is considered even.

### Rules for Odds and Evens

Odd + Odd = Even

Even + Even = Even

Odd + Even = Odd

Odd × Odd = Odd

Even × Even = Even

Odd × Even = Even

Note that multiplying any even number by *any* integer always produces another even number.

It may be easier to pick numbers in problems that ask you to decide whether some unknown will be odd or even.

**Example:** Is the sum of two odd numbers odd or even?

Pick any two odd numbers, for example, 3 and 5. $3 + 5 = 8$. Since the sum of the two odd numbers that you picked is an even number, 8, it's safe to say that the sum of any two odd numbers is even.

Picking numbers will work in any odds/evens problem, no matter how complicated. The only time you have to be careful is when division is involved, especially if the problem is in Data Sufficiency format; different numbers may yield different results.

**Example:** Integer $x$ is evenly divisible by 2. Is $\frac{x}{2}$ even?

By definition, any multiple of 2 is even, so integer $x$ is even. And $\frac{x}{2}$ must be an integer. But is $\frac{x}{2}$ even or odd? In this case, picking two different even numbers for $x$ can yield two different results. If you let $x = 4$, then $\frac{x}{2} = \frac{4}{2} = 2$, which is even. But if you let $x = 6$, then $\frac{x}{2} = \frac{6}{2} = 3$, which is odd. So, $\frac{x}{2}$ could be even or odd—and you wouldn't know that if you picked only one number.

## Absolute Value

The *absolute value* of a number is the value of a number without its sign. It is written as two vertical lines, one on either side of the number and its sign.

**Example:** $|-3| = |+3| = 3$

The absolute value of a number can be thought of as the number's distance from zero on the number line. Since both 3 and $-3$ are 3 units from 0, each has an absolute value of 3. If you are told that $|x| = 5$, $x$ could equal 5 or $-5$.

## Properties of Zero

Adding zero to or subtracting zero from a number does not change the number.

$$x + 0 = x$$
$$0 + x = x$$
$$x - 0 = x$$

**Examples:**

$5 + 0 = 5$
$0 + (-3) = -3$
$4 - 0 = 4$

Notice, however, that subtracting a number from zero changes the number's sign. It's easy to see why if you rephrase the problem as an addition problem.

**Example:** Subtract 5 from 0.

$0 - 5 = -5$. That's because $0 - 5 = 0 + (-5)$, and according to the rules for addition with signed numbers, $0 + (-5) = -5$.

The product of zero and any number is zero.

**Examples:**

$(0)(z) = 0$
$(z)(0) = 0$
$(0)(12) = 0$

Division by zero is undefined. For GMAT purposes, that translates as "it can't be done." Since fractions are essentially division (that is, $\frac{1}{4}$ means $1 \div 4$), any fraction with zero in the denominator is also undefined. So, when you are given a fraction that has an algebraic expression in the denominator, be sure that the expression cannot equal zero.

## Properties of 1 and $-1$

Multiplying or dividing a number by 1 does not change the number.

$$(a)(1) = a$$
$$(1)(a) = a$$
$$a \div 1 = a$$

**Examples:**

$$(4)(1) = 4$$
$$(1)(-5) = -5$$
$$(-7) \div 1 = -7$$

Multiplying or dividing a nonzero number by $-1$ changes the sign of the number.

$$(a)(-1) = -a$$
$$(-1)(a) = -a$$
$$a \div (-1) = -a$$

**Examples:**

$$(6)(-1) = -6$$
$$(-3)(-1) = 3$$
$$(-8) \div (-1) = 8$$

## Factors, Multiples, and Remainders

### Multiples and Divisibility

A *multiple* is the product of a specified number and an integer. For example, 3, 12, and 90 are all multiples of 3, because $3 = (3)(1)$; $12 = (3)(4)$; and $90 = (3)(30)$. The number 4 is not a multiple of 3, because there is no integer that can be multiplied by 3 and yield 4.

The concepts of multiples and factors are tied together by the idea of divisibility. A number is said to be evenly *divisible* by another number if the result of the division is an integer with no remainder. A number that is evenly divisible by a second number is also a multiple of the second number.

For example, $52 \div 4 = 13$, which is an integer. So, 52 is evenly divisible by 4, and it's also a multiple of 4.

On some GMAT math problems, you will find yourself trying to assess whether one number is evenly divisible by another. You can use several simple rules to save time:

- An integer is divisible by 2 if its last digit is divisible by 2.
- An integer is divisible by 3 if its digits add up to a multiple of 3.
- An integer is divisible by 4 if its last two digits are a multiple of 4.
- An integer is divisible by 5 if its last digit is 0 or 5.
- An integer is divisible by 6 if it is divisible by 2 and 3.
- An integer is divisible by 9 if its digits add up to a multiple of 9.

**Example:** 6,930 is a multiple of 2, since 0 is even.

. . . a multiple of 3, since $6 + 9 + 3 + 0 = 18$, which is a multiple of 3.

. . . not a multiple of 4, since 30 is not a multiple of 4.

. . . a multiple of 5, since it ends in 0.

. . . a multiple of 6, since it is a multiple of 2 and 3.

. . . a multiple of 9, since $6 + 9 + 3 + 0 = 18$, a multiple of 9.

## Factors and Primes

The *factors*, or *divisors*, of an integer are the positive integers by which it is evenly divisible (leaving no remainder).

**Example:** What are the factors of 36?

36 has nine factors: 1, 2, 3, 4, 6, 9, 12, 18, and 36. You can group these factors in pairs: $(1)(36) = (2)(18) = (3)(12) = (4)(9) = (6)(6)$.

The *greatest common factor*, or greatest common divisor, of a pair of integers is the largest factor that they share.

To find the greatest common factor, break down both integers into their prime factorizations and multiply all the prime factors they have in common: $36 = (2)(2)(3)(3)$ and $48 = (2)(2)(2)(2)(3)$. What they have in common is two 2s and one 3, so the GCF is $(2)(2)(3) = 12$.

A *prime number* is an integer greater than 1 that has only two factors: itself and 1. The number 1 is not considered a prime, because it is divisible only by itself. The number 2 is the smallest prime number and the only even prime. (Any other even number must have 2 as a factor and therefore cannot be prime.)

## Prime Factors

The *prime factorization* of a number is the expression of the number as the product of its prime factors (the factors that are prime numbers).

There are two common ways to determine a number's prime factorization. The rules given above for determining divisibility by certain numbers come in handy in both methods.

**Method #1:** Work your way up through the prime numbers, starting with 2. (You'll save time in this process, especially when you're starting with a large number, by knowing the first ten prime numbers by heart: 2, 3, 5, 7, 11, 13, 17, 19, 23, and 29.)

**Example:** What is the prime factorization of 210?

$$210 = (2)(105)$$

Since 105 is odd, it can't contain another factor of 2. The next smallest prime number is 3. The digits of 105 add up to 6, which is a multiple of 3, so 3 is a factor of 105.

$$210 = (2)(3)(35)$$

The digits of 35 add up to 8, which is not a multiple of 3. But 35 ends in 5, so it is a multiple of the next largest prime number, 5.

$$210 = (2)(3)(5)(7)$$

Since 7 is a prime number, this equation expresses the complete prime factorization of 210.

**Method #2:** Figure out one pair of factors, and then determine their factors, continuing the process until you're left with only prime numbers. Those primes will be the prime factorization.

**Example:** What is the prime factorization of 1,050?

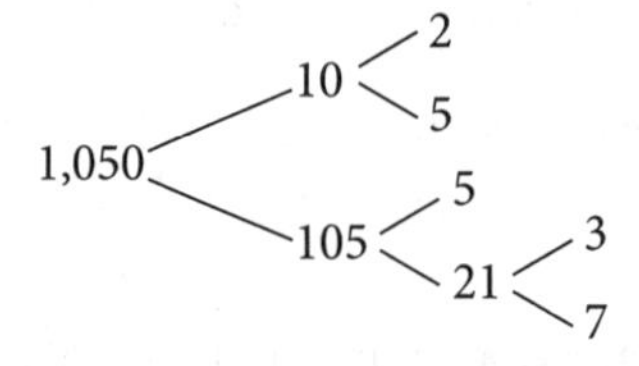


The discrete prime factors of 1,050 are therefore 2, 3, 5, and 7, with the prime number 5 occurring twice in the prime factorization. It is common to write out the prime factorization by putting the prime numbers in increasing order. Here, that would be (2)(3)(5)(5)(7). The prime factorization can also be expressed in exponential form: $(2)(3)(5^2)(7)$.

## The Least Common Multiple

The *least common multiple* of two or more integers is the smallest number that is a multiple of each of the integers. Here's one quick way to find it:

1. Determine the prime factorization of each integer.
2. Write out each prime number the maximum number of times that it appears in any one of the prime factorizations.
3. Multiply those prime numbers together to get the least common multiple of the original integers.

**Example:** What is the least common multiple of 6 and 8?

Start by finding the prime factors of 6 and 8.

$$6 = (2)(3)$$
$$8 = (2)(2)(2)$$

The factor 2 appears three times in the prime factorization of 8, while 3 appears as only a single factor of 6. So, the least common multiple of 6 and 8 will be (2)(2)(2)(3), or 24.

Note that the least common multiple of two integers is smaller than their product if they have any factors in common. For instance, the product of 6 and 8 is 48, but their least common multiple is only 24.

Although you won't see the term *least common multiple* very often on the GMAT, you'll find the concept useful whenever you're adding or subtracting fractions with different denominators.

### Remainders

The *remainder* is what is "left over" in a division problem. A remainder is always smaller than the number you are dividing by. For instance, 17 divided by 3 is 5, with a remainder of 2. Likewise, 12 divided by 6 is 2, with a remainder of 0 (since 12 is evenly divisible by 6).

GMAT writers often disguise remainder problems. For instance, a problem might state that the slats of a fence are painted in three colors, which appear in a fixed order, such as red, yellow, and blue. You would then be asked something like, "If the first slat is red, what color is the 301st slat?" Since 3 goes into 300 evenly, the whole pattern must finish on the 300th slat and start all over again on the 301st. Therefore, the 301st would be red.

## Exponents and Roots

### Rules of Operations with Exponents

To multiply two powers with the same base, keep the base and add the exponents together.

**Example:** $2^2 \times 2^3 = (2 \times 2)(2 \times 2 \times 2) = 2^5$

or

$2^2 \times 2^3 = 2^{2+3} = 2^5$

To divide two powers with the same base, keep the base and subtract the exponent of the denominator from the exponent of the numerator.

**Example:** $4^5 \div 4^2 = \frac{(4)(4)(4)(4)(4)}{(4)(4)} = 4^3$

or

$4^5 \div 4^2 = 4^{5-2} = 4^3$

To raise a power to another power, multiply the exponents.

**Example:** $\left(3^2\right)^4 = (3 \times 3)^4$

or

$\left(3^2\right)^4 = (3 \times 3)(3 \times 3)(3 \times 3)(3 \times 3)$

or

$\left(3^2\right)^4 = 3^{2\times4} = 3^8$

### Commonly Tested Properties of Powers

Many Data Sufficiency problems test your understanding of what happens when negative numbers and fractions are raised to a power.

Raising a fraction between zero and one to a power produces a smaller result.

**Example:** $\left(\frac{1}{2}\right)^2 = \left(\frac{1}{2}\right)\left(\frac{1}{2}\right) = \frac{1}{4}$

Raising a negative number to an even power produces a positive result.

**Example:** $(-2)^2 = 4$

Raising a negative number to an odd power gives a negative result.

**Example:** $(-2)^3 = -8$

## Powers of 10

When 10 is raised to an exponent that is a positive integer, that exponent tells how many zeros the number would contain if it were written out.

**Example:** Write $10^6$ in ordinary notation.

The exponent 6 indicates that you will need six zeros after the 1: 1,000,000. That's because $10^6$ means six factors of 10, that is, $(10)(10)(10)(10)(10)(10)$.

To multiply a number by a power of 10, move the decimal point the same number of places to the right as the exponent (or as the number of zeros in that power of 10).

**Example:** Multiply 0.029 by $10^3$.

The exponent is 3, so move the decimal point three places to the right.

$$(0.029)10^3 = 0029. = 29$$

If you had been told to multiply 0.029 by 1,000, you could have counted the number of zeros in 1,000 and done exactly the same thing.

Sometimes you'll have to add zeros as placeholders.

**Example:** Multiply 0.029 by $10^6$.

Add zeros until you can move the decimal point six places to the right:

$$0.029 \times 10^6 = 0029000. = 29{,}000$$

To divide by a power of 10, move the decimal point the corresponding number of places to the left, inserting zeros as placeholders if necessary.

**Example:** Divide 416.03 by 10,000.

There are four zeros in 10,000, but only three places to the left of the decimal point. You'll have to insert another zero:

$$416.03 \div 10{,}000 = .041603 = 0.041603$$

By convention, one zero is usually written to the left of the decimal point on the GMAT. It's a placeholder and doesn't change the value of the number.

## Scientific Notation

Very large numbers (and very small decimals) take up a lot of space and are difficult to work with. So, in some scientific texts, they are expressed in a shorter, more convenient form, called *scientific notation*.

For example, 123,000,000,000 would be written in scientific notation as $(1.23)(10^{11})$, and 0.000000003 would be written as $(3.0)(10^{-9})$. (If you're already familiar with the concept of negative exponents, you'll know that multiplying by $10^{-9}$ is equivalent to dividing by $10^9$.)

To express a number in scientific notation, rewrite it as a product of two factors. The first factor must be greater than or equal to 1 but less than 10. The second factor must be a power of 10.

To translate a number from scientific notation to ordinary notation, use the rules for multiplying and dividing by powers of 10.

**Example:** $5.6 \times 10^6 = 5{,}600{,}000$, or 5.6 million

## Rules of Operations with Roots and Radicals

A square root of any nonnegative number $x$ is a number that, when multiplied by itself, yields $x$. Every positive number has two square roots, one positive and one negative. For instance, the positive square root of 25 is 5, because $5^2 = 25$. The negative square root of 25 is $-5$, because $(-5)^2$ also equals 25.

By convention, the radical symbol $\sqrt{\ }$ stands for the positive square root only. Therefore, $\sqrt{9} = 3$ only, even though both $3^2$ and $(-3)^2$ equal 9. This has important implications in Data Sufficiency.

**Example:** What is the value of $x$?

(1) $x = \sqrt{16}$

(2) $x^2 = 16$

The first statement is sufficient, since there is only one possible value for $\sqrt{16}$, positive 4. The second statement is insufficient since $x$ could be 4 or $-4$.

When applying the four basic arithmetic operations, radicals (roots written with the radical symbol) are treated in much the same way as variables.

### Addition and Subtraction of Radicals

Only like radicals can be added to or subtracted from one another.

**Example:**

$$\begin{aligned} &2\sqrt{3} + 4\sqrt{2} - \sqrt{2} - 3\sqrt{3} \\ &= \left(4\sqrt{2} - \sqrt{2}\right) + \left(2\sqrt{3} - 3\sqrt{3}\right) \\ &= 3\sqrt{2} + \left(-\sqrt{3}\right) \\ &= 3\sqrt{2} - \sqrt{3} \end{aligned}$$

This expression cannot be simplified any further.

### Multiplication and Division of Radicals

To multiply or divide one radical by another, multiply or divide the numbers outside the radical signs, then the numbers inside the radical signs.

**Example:** $(6\sqrt{3})2\sqrt{5} = (6)(2)(\sqrt{3})(\sqrt{5}) = 12\sqrt{15}$

**Example:** $12\sqrt{15} \div 2\sqrt{5} = \left(\frac{12}{2}\right)\left(\frac{\sqrt{15}}{\sqrt{5}}\right) = 6\sqrt{\frac{15}{5}} = 6\sqrt{3}$

### Simplifying Radicals

If the number inside the radical is a multiple of a perfect square, the expression can be simplified by factoring out the perfect square.

**Example:** $\sqrt{72} = (\sqrt{36})\sqrt{2} = 6\sqrt{2}$

## Fractions

The simplest way to understand the meaning of a fraction is to picture the denominator as the number of equal parts into which a whole unit is divided. The numerator represents a certain number of those equal parts.

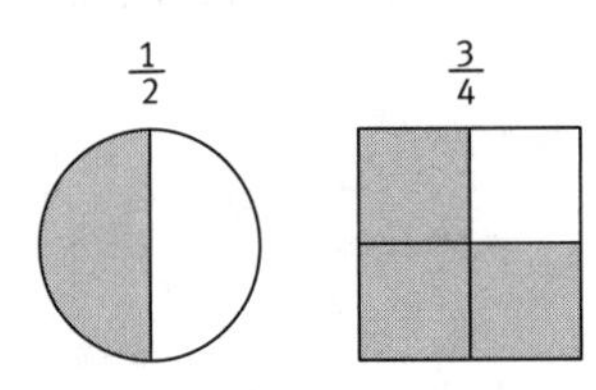


On the left, the shaded portion is one of two equal parts that make up the whole. On the right, the shaded portion is three of four equal parts that make up the whole.

The fraction bar is interchangeable with a division sign. You can divide the numerator of a fraction by the denominator to get an equivalent decimal. However, the numerator and denominator must each be treated as a single quantity.

**Example:** Evaluate $\frac{5+2}{7-3}$.

You can't just rewrite the fraction as $5 + 2 \div 7 - 3$, because the numerator and the denominator are each considered distinct quantities. Instead, you would rewrite the fraction as $(5 + 2) \div (7 - 3)$. The order of operations (remember PEMDAS?) tells you that operations in parentheses must be performed first. That gives you $7 \div 4$. Your final answer would be $\frac{7}{4}$, $1\frac{3}{4}$, or 1.75, depending on the form of the answer choices.

## Equivalent Fractions

Since multiplying or dividing a number by 1 does not change the number, multiplying the numerator and denominator of a fraction by the same nonzero number doesn't change the value of the fraction—it's the same as multiplying the entire fraction by 1.

**Example:** Change $\frac{1}{2}$ into an equivalent fraction with a denominator of 4.

To change the denominator from 2 to 4, you'll have to multiply it by 2. But to keep the value of the fraction the same, you'll also have to multiply the numerator by 2.

$$\frac{1}{2} = \frac{1}{2}\left(\frac{2}{2}\right) = \frac{2}{4}$$

Similarly, dividing the numerator and denominator by the same nonzero number leaves the value of the fraction unchanged.

**Example:** Change $\frac{16}{20}$ into an equivalent fraction with a denominator of 10.

To change the denominator from 20 to 10, you'll have to divide it by 2. But to keep the value of the fraction the same, you'll have to divide the numerator by the same number.

$$\frac{16}{20} = \frac{16 \div 2}{20 \div 2} = \frac{8}{10}$$

## Reducing (Canceling)

Most fractions on the GMAT are in lowest terms. That means that the numerator and denominator have no common factor greater than 1.

For example, the final answer of $\frac{8}{10}$ obtained in the previous example was not in lowest terms, because both 8 and 10 are divisible by 2. In contrast, the fraction $\frac{7}{10}$ is in lowest terms, because there is no factor greater than 1 that 7 and 10 have in common. To convert a fraction to its lowest terms, use a method called reducing, or canceling. To reduce, simply divide any common factors out of both the numerator and the denominator.

**Example:** Reduce $\frac{15}{35}$ to lowest terms.

$\frac{15}{35} = \frac{15 \div 5}{35 \div 5} = \frac{3}{7}$ (because a 5 cancels out, top and bottom)

The fastest way to reduce a fraction that has very large numbers in both the numerator and denominator is to find the greatest common factor and divide it out of both the top and the bottom.

**Example:** Reduce $\frac{1{,}040}{1{,}080}$ to lowest terms.

$$\frac{1{,}040}{1{,}080} = \frac{104}{108} = \frac{52}{54} = \frac{26}{27}$$

## Adding and Subtracting Fractions

You cannot add or subtract fractions unless they have the same denominator. If they don't, you'll have to convert each fraction to an equivalent fraction with the least common denominator. Then add or subtract the numerators (not the denominators!) and, if necessary, reduce the resulting fraction to its lowest terms.

Given two fractions with different denominators, the least common denominator is the least common multiple of the two denominators, that is, the smallest number that is evenly divisible by both denominators.

**Example:** What is the least common denominator of $\frac{2}{15}$ and $\frac{3}{10}$?

The least common denominator of the two fractions will be the least common multiple of 15 and 10.

Because $15 = (5)(3)$ and $10 = (5)(2)$, the least common multiple of the two numbers is $(5)(3)(2)$, or 30. That makes 30 the least common denominator of $\frac{2}{15}$ and $\frac{3}{10}$.

**Example:** $\frac{2}{15} + \frac{3}{10} = ?$

As you saw in the previous example, the least common denominator of the two fractions is 30. Change each fraction to an equivalent fraction with a denominator of 30.

$$\frac{2}{15}\left(\frac{2}{2}\right) = \frac{4}{30}$$
$$\frac{3}{10}\left(\frac{3}{3}\right) = \frac{9}{30}$$

Then add:

$$\frac{4}{30} + \frac{9}{30} = \frac{13}{30}$$

Since 13 and 30 have no common factor greater than 1, the fraction $\frac{13}{30}$ is in lowest terms. You can't reduce it further.

## Multiplying Fractions

To multiply fractions, multiply the numerators and multiply the denominators.

$$\frac{5}{7}\left(\frac{3}{4}\right) = \frac{15}{28}$$

Multiplying numerator by numerator and denominator by denominator is simple. But it's easy to make careless errors if you have to multiply a string of fractions or work with large numbers. You can minimize those errors by reducing before you multiply.

**Example:** Multiply $\left(\frac{10}{9}\right)\left(\frac{3}{4}\right)\left(\frac{8}{15}\right)$.

First, cancel a 5 out of the 10 and the 15, a 3 out of the 3 and the 9, and a 4 out of the 8 and the 4:

$$\left(\frac{\overset{2}{\cancel{10}}}{\underset{3}{\cancel{9}}}\right)\left(\frac{\overset{1}{\cancel{3}}}{\underset{1}{\cancel{4}}}\right)\left(\frac{\overset{2}{\cancel{8}}}{\underset{3}{\cancel{15}}}\right)$$

Then, multiply numerators together and denominators together:

$$\left(\frac{2}{3}\right)\left(\frac{1}{1}\right)\left(\frac{2}{3}\right)=\frac{4}{9}$$

## Reciprocals

To get the reciprocal of a common fraction, turn the fraction upside-down so that the numerator becomes the denominator, and vice versa. If a fraction has a numerator of 1, the fraction's reciprocal will be equivalent to an integer.

**Example:** What is the reciprocal of $\frac{1}{25}$?

Inverting the fraction gives you the reciprocal, $\frac{25}{1}$. But dividing a number by 1 doesn't change the value of the number.

Since $\frac{25}{1}=25$, the reciprocal of $\frac{1}{25}$ equals 25.

## Dividing Common Fractions

To divide fractions, multiply by the reciprocal of the number or fraction that follows the division sign.

$$\frac{1}{2}\div\frac{3}{5}=\frac{1}{2}\left(\frac{5}{3}\right)=\frac{5}{6}$$

(The operation of division produces the same result as multiplication by the inverse.)

**Example:** $\frac{4}{3}\div\frac{4}{9}=\frac{4}{3}\left(\frac{9}{4}\right)=\frac{36}{12}=3$

## Comparing Positive Fractions

Given two positive fractions with the same denominator, the fraction with the larger numerator will have the larger value.

**Example:** Which is greater, $\frac{3}{8}$ or $\frac{5}{8}$?

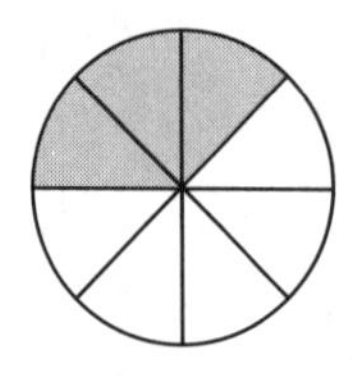

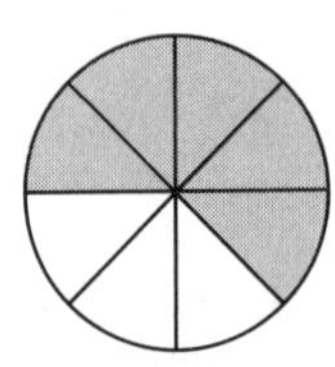

$$\frac{3}{8} < \frac{5}{8}$$

But if you're given two positive fractions with the same numerator but different denominators, the fraction with the smaller denominator will have the larger value.

**Example:** Which is greater, $\frac{3}{4}$ or $\frac{3}{8}$?

The diagrams below show two wholes of equal size. The one on the left is divided into 4 equal parts, 3 of which are shaded. The one on the right is divided into 8 equal parts, 3 of which are shaded.

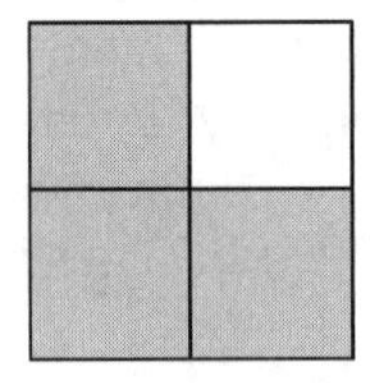

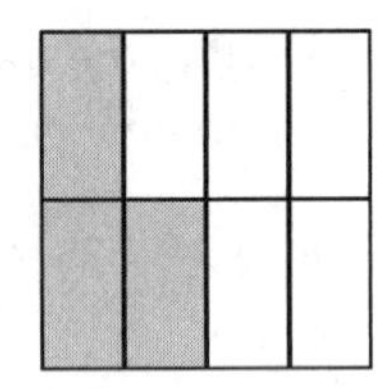

$\frac{3}{4}$ is clearly greater than $\frac{3}{8}$.

If neither the numerators nor the denominators are the same, you have three options. You can turn both fractions into their decimal equivalents. Alternatively, you can express both fractions in terms of some common denominator and then see which new equivalent fraction has the largest numerator. Yet another approach is to cross multiply the numerator of each fraction by the denominator of the other. If you write the products next to the numerators, the greater result will wind up next to the greater fraction.

**Example:** Which is greater, $\frac{5}{6}$ or $\frac{7}{9}$?

$$\overset{45}{\frac{5}{6}} \times \overset{42}{\frac{7}{9}}$$

Since $45 > 42$, $\frac{5}{6} > \frac{7}{9}$.

## Mixed Numbers and Improper Fractions

A *mixed number* consists of an integer and a fraction.

An *improper fraction* is a fraction whose numerator is greater than its denominator. To convert an improper fraction to a mixed number, divide the numerator by the denominator. The number of "whole" times that the denominator goes into the numerator will be the integer portion of the improper fraction; the remainder will be the numerator of the fractional portion.

**Example:** Convert $\frac{23}{4}$ to a mixed number.

Dividing 23 by 4 gives you 5 with a remainder of 3, so $\frac{23}{4} = 5\frac{3}{4}$.

To change a mixed number to a fraction, multiply the integer portion of the mixed number by the denominator and add the numerator. This new number is your numerator. The denominator will not change.

**Example:** Convert $2\frac{3}{7}$ to a fraction.

$$2\frac{3}{7} = \frac{7(2)+3}{7} = \frac{17}{7}$$

## Properties of Fractions Between −1 and +1

The reciprocal of a fraction between 0 and 1 is greater than both the original fraction and 1.

**Example:** The reciprocal of $\frac{2}{3}$ is $\frac{3}{2}$, which is greater than both 1 and $\frac{2}{3}$.

The reciprocal of a fraction between −1 and 0 is less than both the original fraction and −1.

**Example:** The reciprocal of $\frac{-2}{3}$ is $\frac{-3}{2}$, or $-1\frac{1}{2}$, which is less than both −1 and $\frac{-2}{3}$.

The square of a fraction between 0 and 1 is less than the original fraction.

**Example:** $\left(\frac{1}{2}\right)^2 = \left(\frac{1}{2}\right)\left(\frac{1}{2}\right) = \frac{1}{4}$

But the square of any fraction between 0 and −1 is greater than the original fraction, because multiplying two negative numbers gives you a positive product, and any positive number is greater than any negative number.

**Example:** $\left(-\frac{1}{2}\right)^2 = \left(-\frac{1}{2}\right)\left(-\frac{1}{2}\right) = \frac{1}{4}$

Multiplying any positive number by a fraction between 0 and 1 gives a product smaller than the original number.

**Example:** $6\left(\frac{1}{4}\right) = \frac{6}{4} = \frac{3}{2}$

Multiplying any negative number by a fraction between 0 and 1 gives a product greater than the original number.

**Example:** $(-3)\left(\frac{1}{2}\right) = \frac{-3}{2}$

## Decimals

### Converting Decimals

It's easy to convert decimals to common fractions, and vice versa. Any decimal number is equivalent to some common fraction with a power of 10 in the denominator.

To convert a decimal between 0 and 1 to a fraction, determine the place value of the last nonzero digit and set this as the denominator. Then, use all the digits of the decimal number as the numerator, ignoring the decimal point. Finally, if necessary, reduce the fraction to its lowest terms.

**Example:** Convert 0.875 to a fraction in lowest terms.

The last nonzero digit is the 5, which is in the thousandths place. So, the denominator of the common fraction will be 1,000. The numerator will be 875: $\frac{875}{1{,}000}$.

(You can ignore the zero to the left of the decimal point since there are no nonzero digits to its left; it's just a "placeholder.")

Both 875 and 1,000 contain a factor of 25. Canceling it out leaves you with $\frac{35}{40}$. Reducing that further by a factor of 5 gives you $\frac{7}{8}$, which is in lowest terms.

To convert a fraction to a decimal, simply divide the numerator by the denominator.

**Example:** What is the decimal equivalent of $\frac{4}{5}$?

$$4 \div 5 = 0.8$$

### Comparing Decimals

Knowing place values allows you to assess the relative values of decimals.

**Example:** Which is greater, 0.254 or 0.3?

Of course, 254 is greater than 3. But $0.3 = \frac{3}{10}$, which is equivalent to $\frac{300}{1{,}000}$, while 0.254 is equivalent to only $\frac{254}{1{,}000}$. Since $\frac{300}{1{,}000} > \frac{254}{1{,}000}$, 0.3 is greater than 0.254.

Here's the simplest way to compare decimals: add zeros after the last digit to the right of the decimal point in each decimal fraction until all the decimals you're comparing have the same number of digits. Essentially, what you're doing is giving all the fractions the same denominator so that you can just compare their numerators.

**Example:** Arrange in order from smallest to largest: 0.7, 0.77, 0.07, 0.707, and 0.077.

The numbers 0.707 and 0.077 end at the third place to the right of the decimal point—the thousandths place. Add zeros after the last digit to the right of the decimal point in each of the other numbers until you reach the thousandths place:

$$0.7 = 0.700 = \frac{700}{1{,}000}$$
$$0.77 = 0.770 = \frac{770}{1{,}000}$$
$$0.07 = 0.070 = \frac{70}{1{,}000}$$
$$0.707 = \frac{707}{1{,}000}$$
$$0.077 = \frac{77}{1{,}000}$$

$$\frac{70}{1{,}000} < \frac{77}{1{,}000} < \frac{700}{1{,}000} < \frac{707}{1{,}000} < \frac{770}{1{,}000}$$

Therefore, $0.07 < 0.077 < 0.7 < 0.707 < 0.77$.

## Estimation and Rounding on the GMAT

You should be familiar and comfortable with the practice of "rounding off" numbers. To round off a number to a particular place, look at the digit immediately to the right of that place. If the digit is 0, 1, 2, 3, or 4, don't change the digit that is in the place to which you are rounding. If it is 5, 6, 7, 8, or 9, change the digit in the place to which you are rounding to the next higher digit. Replace all digits to the right of the place to which you are rounding with zeros.

For example, to round off 235 to the tens place, look at the units place. Since it is occupied by a 5, you'll round the 3 in the tens place up to a 4, giving you 240. If you had been rounding off 234, you would have rounded down to the existing 3 in the tens place; that would have given you 230.

**Example:** Round off 675,978 to the hundreds place.

The 7 in the tens place means that you will have to round the hundreds place up. Since there is a 9 in the hundreds place, you'll have to change the thousands place as well. Rounding 675,978 to the hundreds place gives you 676,000.

Rounding off large numbers before calculation will allow you quickly to estimate the correct answer.

Estimating can save you valuable time on many GMAT problems. But before you estimate, check the answer choices to see how close they are. If they are relatively close together, you'll have to be more accurate than if they are farther apart.

## Percents

The word *percent* means "hundredths," and the percent sign, %, means $\frac{1}{100}$. For example, 25% means $25\left(\frac{1}{100}\right) = \frac{25}{100}$. (Like the division sign, the percent sign evolved from the fractional relationship; the slanted bar in a percent sign represents a fraction bar.)

Percents measure a part-to-whole relationship with an assumed whole equal to 100. The percent relationship can be expressed as $\frac{\text{Part}}{\text{Whole}} \times 100\%$. For example, if $\frac{1}{4}$ of a rectangle is shaded, the percent of the rectangle that is shaded is $\frac{1}{4}(100\%) = 25\%$.

Like fractions, percents express the relationship between a specified part and a whole. In fact, by plugging the part and whole from the shaded rectangle problem into the fraction and decimal versions of the part-whole equation, you can verify that 25%, $\frac{25}{100}$, and 0.25 are simply different names for the same part-whole relationship.

### Translating English to Math in Part-Whole Problems

On the GMAT, many fractions and percents appear in word problems. You'll solve the problems by plugging the numbers you're given into some variation of one of the three basic formulas:

$$\frac{\text{Part}}{\text{Whole}} = \textit{Fraction}$$

$$\frac{\text{Part}}{\text{Whole}} = \textit{Decimal}$$

$$\frac{\text{Part}}{\text{Whole}}(100) = \textit{Percent}$$

To avoid careless errors, look for the key words *is* and *of*. *Is* (or *are*) often introduces the part, while *of* almost invariably introduces the whole.

### Properties of 100%

Since the percent sign means $\frac{1}{100}$, 100% means $\frac{100}{100}$, or one whole. The key to solving some GMAT percent problems is to recognize that all the parts add up to one whole: 100%.

**Example:** All 1,000 registered voters in Smithtown are Democrats, Republicans, or independents. If 75 percent of the registered voters are Democrats, and 5 percent are independents, how many are Republicans?

First, calculate that 75% + 5%, or 80%, of the 1,000 registered voters are either Democrats or independents. The three party affiliations together must account for 100% of the voters; thus, the percentage of Republicans must be 100% – 80%, or 20%. Therefore, the number of Republicans must be 20% of 1,000, which is 20%(1,000), or 200.

Multiplying or dividing a number by 100% is just like multiplying or dividing by 1; it doesn't change the value of the original number.

## Converting Percents

To change a fraction to its percent equivalent, multiply by 100%.

**Example:** What is the percent equivalent of $\frac{5}{8}$?

$$\frac{5}{8}(100\%) = \frac{500}{8}\% = 62\frac{1}{2}\%$$

To change a decimal number to a percent, you can use the rules for multiplying by powers of 10. Move the decimal point two places to the right and insert a percent sign.

**Example:** What is the percent equivalent of 0.17?

$$0.17 = 0.17\,(100\%) = 17\%$$

To change a percent to its fractional equivalent, divide by 100%.

**Example:** What is the common fraction equivalent of 32 percent?

$$32\% = \frac{32\%}{100\%} = \frac{8}{25}$$

To convert a percent to its decimal equivalent, use the rules for dividing by powers of 10—just move the decimal point two places to the left.

**Example:** What is the decimal equivalent of 32 percent?

$$32\% = \frac{32\%}{100\%} = \frac{32}{100} = 0.32$$

When you divide a percent by another percent, the percent sign "drops out," just as you would cancel out a common factor.

**Example:** $\frac{100\%}{5\%} = \frac{100}{5} = 20$

Translation: There are 20 groups of 5% in 100%.

When you divide a percent by a regular number (not by another percent), the percent sign remains.

**Example:** $\frac{100\%}{5} = 20\%$

Translation: One-fifth of 100% is 20%.

## Common Percent Equivalents

As you can see, changing percents to fractions, or vice versa, is pretty straightforward. But it does take a second or two that you might spend more profitably doing other computations or setting up another GMAT math problem. Familiarity with the following common equivalents will save you time.

| | |
|---|---|
| $\frac{1}{20} = 5\%$ | $\frac{1}{2} = 50\%$ |
| $\frac{1}{12} = 8\frac{1}{3}\%$ | $\frac{3}{5} = 60\%$ |
| $\frac{1}{10} = 10\%$ | $\frac{5}{8} = 62\frac{1}{2}\%$ |
| $\frac{1}{8} = 12\frac{1}{2}\%$ | $\frac{2}{3} = 66\frac{2}{3}\%$ |
| $\frac{1}{6} = 16\frac{2}{3}\%$ | $\frac{7}{10} = 70\%$ |
| $\frac{1}{5} = 20\%$ | $\frac{3}{4} = 75\%$ |
| $\frac{1}{4} = 25\%$ | $\frac{4}{5} = 80\%$ |
| $\frac{3}{10} = 30\%$ | $\frac{5}{6} = 83\frac{1}{3}\%$ |
| $\frac{1}{3} = 33\frac{1}{3}\%$ | $\frac{7}{8} = 87\frac{1}{2}\%$ |
| $\frac{3}{8} = 37\frac{1}{2}\%$ | $\frac{9}{10} = 90\%$ |
| $\frac{2}{5} = 40\%$ | $\frac{11}{12} = 91\frac{2}{3}\%$ |

## Using the Percent Formula to Solve Percent Problems

You can solve most percent problems by plugging the given data into the percent formula:

$$\frac{\text{Part}}{\text{Whole}}(100\%) = \text{Percent}$$

Most percent problems give you two of the three variables and ask for the third.

**Example:** Ben spends \$30 of his annual gardening budget on seed. If his total annual gardening budget is \$150, what percentage of his budget does he spend on seed?

This problem specifies the whole (\$150) and the part (\$30) and asks for the percentage. Plugging those numbers into the percent formula gives you this:

$$\text{Percent} = \frac{30}{150}(100\%) = \frac{1}{5}(100\%) = 20\%$$

Ben spends 20% of his annual gardening budget on seed.

## Percent Increase and Decrease

When the GMAT tests percent increase or decrease, use the formulas:

$$\text{Percent increase} = \frac{\text{Increase (100\%)}}{\text{Original}} \text{ or Percent decrease} = \frac{\text{Decrease (100\%)}}{\text{Original}}$$

To find the increase or decrease, just take the difference between the original and the new. Note that the "original" is the base from which change occurs. It may or may not be the first number mentioned in the problem.

**Example:** Two years ago, 450 seniors graduated from Inman High School. Last year, 600 seniors graduated. By what percentage did the number of graduating seniors increase?

The original is the figure from the earlier time (two years ago): 450. The increase is 600 − 450, or 150. So, the percentage increase is $\frac{150}{450}(100\%) = 33\frac{1}{3}\%$.

**Example:** If the price of a $120 dress is increased by 25 percent, what is the new selling price?

To find the new whole, you'll first have to find the amount of increase. The original whole is $120, and the percent increase is 25%. Plug these values into the formula:

$$\frac{\text{Increase}}{120}(100\%) = 25\%$$

$$\frac{\text{Increase}}{120} = \frac{25}{100}$$

$$\frac{\text{Increase}}{120} = \frac{1}{4}$$

$$\text{Increase} = \frac{120}{4}$$

$$\text{Increase} = 30$$

The amount of increase is $30, so the new selling price is $120 + $30, or $150.

### Multistep Percent Problems

On some difficult problems, you'll be asked to find more than one percent, or to find a percent of a percent. Be careful: you can't add percents of different wholes.

**Example:** The price of an antique is reduced by 20 percent, and then the new price is reduced by 10 percent. If the antique originally cost \$200, what is its final price?

The most common mistake in this kind of problem is to reduce the original price by a total of 20% + 10%, or 30%. That would make the final price 70% of the original, or 70%(\$200) = \$140. This is not the correct answer. In this example, the second (10%) price reduction is taken off of the first sale price—the new whole, not the original whole.

To get the correct answer, first find the new whole. You can find it by calculating either \$200 – (20% of \$200) or 80%(\$200). Either way, you will find that the first sale price is \$160. That price then has to be reduced by 10%. Either calculate \$160 – (10%(\$160)) or 90%(\$160). In either case, the final price of the antique is \$144.

### Picking Numbers with Percents

Certain types of percent problems lend themselves readily to the alternative technique of picking numbers. These include problems in which no actual values are mentioned, just percents. If you assign values to the percents you are working with, you'll find the problem less abstract.

You should almost always pick 100 in percent problems, because it's relatively easy to find percentages of 100.

**Example:** The price of a share of Company A's stock fell by 20 percent two weeks ago and by another 25 percent last week to its current price. By what percent of the current price does the share price need to rise in order to return to its original price?

- O 45%
- O 55%
- O $66\frac{2}{3}\%$
- O 75%
- O 82%

Pick a value for the original price of the stock. Since it is a percent question, picking \$100 will make the math easy. The first change in the price of the stock was by 20% of \$100, or \$20, making the new price \$100 – \$20 = \$80. The price then fell by another 25%.

25% is the same as $\frac{1}{4}$, and $\frac{1}{4}$ of \$80 is \$20. Therefore, the current price is \$80 – \$20 = \$60. To return to its original price, the stock needs to rise from \$60 to \$100, that is, by \$100 – \$60 = \$40. Then \$40 is what percent of the current price, \$60?

$$\frac{40}{60}(100\%) = \frac{2}{3}(100\%) = 66\frac{2}{3}\%$$

## Percent Word Problems

Percent problems are often presented as word problems. You have already seen how to identify the percent, the part, and the whole in simple percent word problems. Here are some other terms that you are likely to encounter in more complicated percent word problems:

*Profit* made on an item is the seller's price minus the costs to the seller. If a seller buys an item for \$10 and sells it for \$12, he or she has made \$2 profit. The percent of the selling price that is profit is $\frac{\text{Profit}}{\text{Original selling price}}(100\%) = \frac{\$2}{\$12}(100\%) = 16\frac{2}{3}\%$.

A *discount* on an item is the original price minus the reduced price. If an item that usually sells for \$20 is sold for \$15, the discount is \$5. Discount is often represented as a percentage of the original price. In this case, the percentage discount $= \frac{\text{Discount}}{\text{Original price}}(100\%) = \frac{\$5}{\$20}(100\%) = 25\%$.

The *sale price* is the final price after the discount.

Occasionally, percent problems will involve *interest*. Interest is given as a percent per unit of time, such as 5% per month. The sum of money invested is the *principal*. The most common type of interest you will see is *simple interest*. In simple interest, the interest payments received are kept separate from the principal.

**Example:** If an investor invests \$100 at 20 percent simple annual interest, how much does he have at the end of 3 years?

The principal of \$100 yields 20% interest every year. Because 20% of \$100 is \$20, after three years the investor will have $3 \times \$20$, or \$60, plus the principal, for a total of \$160.

In *compound interest*, the money earned as interest is reinvested. The principal grows after every interest payment is received.

**Example:** If an investor invests \$100 at 20 percent compounded annually, how much does she have at the end of 3 years?

The first year, the investor earns 20% of $\$100 = \$20$. So, after one year, she has $\$100 + \$20 = \$120$.

The second year, the investor earns 20% of $\$120 = \$24$. So, after two years, she has $\$120 + \$24 = \$144$.

The third year, the investor earns 20% of $\$144 = \$28.80$. So, after three years, she has $\$144 + \$28.80 = \$172.80$.

### Percents and Data Sufficiency

Data Sufficiency questions (covered in Chapter 3) test your knowledge of percents in a different way. The crux of these problems, as a rule, is finding all the pieces of the percent formula. You can use the percent formula to pinpoint exactly what you need to achieve sufficiency.

**Example:** By what percent did the price of Stock X increase?

(1) The price after the increase was $12.

(2) The stock increased in price by $1.50.

To prove sufficiency, you would have to be capable of filling in all parts of the equation. Statement (1) informs you of the price after the increase. This does not give you either the amount of increase or the original price, so it is not sufficient. Statement (2) informs you of the increase in price, but not the original price, so it, too, is not sufficient. Combining the statements, however, gives you the increase in price, $1.50, and the original price, $12.00 − $1.50 = $10.50. So the correct answer is **(C)**: neither statement by itself is sufficient, but both statements together are sufficient.

## Ratios

A ratio is the proportional relationship between two quantities. The ratio, or relationship, between two numbers, for example, 10 and 15, may be expressed with a colon between the two numbers (10:15), in words ("the ratio of 10 to 15"), or as a common fraction $\left(\frac{10}{15}\right)$.

To translate a ratio in words to numbers separated by a colon, replace *to* with a colon.

To translate a ratio in words to a fractional ratio, use whatever follows the word *of* as the numerator and whatever follows the word *to* as the denominator. For example, if you had to express the ratio of glazed doughnuts *to* chocolate doughnuts in a box of doughnuts that contained 5 glazed and 7 chocolate doughnuts, you would do so as $\frac{5}{7}$. Note that the fraction $\frac{5}{7}$ does not mean that $\frac{5}{7}$ of all the doughnuts are glazed doughnuts. There are 5 + 7, or 12 doughnuts all together, so of the doughnuts, $\frac{5}{12}$ are glazed. The $\frac{5}{7}$ ratio indicates the proportion of glazed to chocolate doughnuts. For every 5 glazed doughnuts, there are 7 chocolate doughnuts.

Treating ratios as fractions usually makes computation easier. Like fractions, ratios often require division. And, like fractions, ratios can be reduced to lowest terms.

**Example:** Joe is 16 years old, and Mary is 12 years old. Express the ratio of Joe's age to Mary's age in lowest terms.

The ratio of Joe's age to Mary's age is $\frac{16}{12} = \frac{4}{3}$, or 4:3.

### Part:Whole Ratios

In a part:whole ratio, the "whole" is the entire set (for instance, all the workers in a factory), while the "part" is a certain subset of the whole (for instance, all the union workers in the factory).

In GMAT ratio question stems, the word *fraction* generally indicates a part:whole ratio. "What fraction of the workers are union members?" means "What is the ratio of the number of union workers to the total number of workers?"

**Example:** The sophomore class at Milford Academy consists of 15 honor roll students and 20 students who did not make the honor roll. What fraction of the sophomore class is not on the honor roll?

The following three statements are equivalent:

(1) $\frac{4}{7}$ of the sophomores are not on the honor roll.

(2) 4 out of every 7 sophomores are not on the honor roll.

(3) The ratio of non-honor-roll sophomores to total sophomores is 4:7.

## Ratio vs. Actual Number

Ratios are usually reduced to their simplest form (that is, to lowest terms). If the ratio of waitstaff to kitchen staff in a restaurant is 5:3, you cannot necessarily infer that there are exactly five waitstaff and three kitchen employees.

To determine specific values, you need additional information beyond just the simple ratio. For example, assume that the only employees in the restaurant are waitstaff and kitchen staff, and suppose you know that there are 32 total employees in the restaurant. If the waitstaff-to-kitchen-staff ratio is 5 to 3, then the ratio of waitstaff to the total number of employees is $5:(5 + 3)$, which is 5:8. You can set up an equation as $\frac{5}{8} = \frac{\text{\# of waitstaff in restaurant}}{32}$. Solving, you will find that the number of waitstaff members in the restaurant is 20.

**Example:** The ratio of domestic sales revenues to foreign sales revenues of a certain product is 3:5. What fraction of the total sales revenues comes from domestic sales?

At first, this question may look more complicated than the previous example. You have to convert from a part:part ratio to a part:whole ratio (the ratio of domestic sales revenues to total sales revenues). And you're not given actual dollar figures for domestic or foreign sales. But since all sales are either foreign or domestic, "total sales revenues" must be the sum of the revenues from domestic and foreign sales. You can convert the given ratio to a part:whole ratio, because the sum of the parts equals the whole.

Although it's impossible to determine dollar amounts for the domestic, foreign, or total sales revenues from the given information, the 3:5 ratio tells you that of every \$8 in sales revenues, \$3 come from domestic sales and \$5 from foreign sales. Therefore, the ratio of domestic sales revenues to total sales revenues is 3:8, or $\frac{3}{8}$.

You can convert a part:part ratio to a part:whole ratio (or vice versa) only if there are no missing parts and no overlap among the parts; that is, if the whole is equal to the sum of the parts.

This concept is often tested in Data Sufficiency.

**Example:** In a certain bag, what is the ratio of the number of red marbles to the total number of marbles?

(1) The ratio of the number of red marbles to the number of blue marbles in the bag is 3:5.

(2) There are only red and blue marbles in the bag.

In this case, Statement (1), by itself, is insufficient. You cannot convert a part-to-part ratio (red marbles to blue marbles) to a part-to-whole ratio (red marbles to all marbles) because you don't know whether there are any other colored marbles in the bag. Only when you combine the two statements do you have enough information to answer the question, so the correct answer is **(C)**: neither statement by itself is sufficient, but both statements together are sufficient.

**Example:** Of the 25 people in Fran's apartment building, what is the ratio of people who use the roof to total residents?

(1) There are 9 residents who use the roof for tanning and 8 residents who use the roof for gardening.

(2) The roof is only used by tanners and gardeners.

In this question, you do not know if there is any overlap between tanners and gardeners. How many, if any, residents do both? Since that cannot be determined, the correct answer is **(E)**: neither statement by itself is sufficient, and the statements together are insufficient.

## Ratios of More Than Two Terms

Most of the ratios that you'll see on the GMAT have two terms, but it is possible to set up ratios with more than two terms. These ratios express more relationships, and therefore convey more information, than two-term ratios. However, most of the principles discussed so far with respect to two-term ratios are just as applicable to ratios of more than two terms.

**Example:** The ratio of $x$ to $y$ is 5:4. The ratio of $y$ to $z$ is 1:2. What is the ratio of $x$ to $z$?

You want the $y$'s in the two ratios to equal each other, because then you can combine the $x:y$ ratio and the $y:z$ ratio to form the $x:y:z$ ratio that you need to answer this question. To make the $y$'s equal, you can multiply the second ratio by 4. When you do so, you must perform the multiplication on both components of the ratio. Since a ratio is a constant proportion, it can be multiplied or divided by any number without losing its meaning, as long as the multiplication and division are applied to all the components of the ratio. In this case, the new ratio for $y$ to $z$ is 4:8. You can combine this with the first ratio to find a new $x$ to $y$ to $z$ ratio of 5:4:8. Therefore, the ratio of $x$ to $z$ is 5:8.

# Algebra

## Algebraic Terms

**Variable:** A letter or symbol representing an unknown quantity.

**Constant (term):** A number not multiplied by any variable(s).

**Term:** A numerical constant; also, the product of a numerical constant and one or more variables.

**Coefficient:** The numerical constant by which one or more variables are multiplied. The coefficient of $3x^2$ is 3. A variable (or product of variables) without a numerical coefficient, such as $z$ or $xy^3$, is understood to have a coefficient of 1.

**Algebraic expression:** An expression containing one or more variables, one or more constants, and possibly one or more operation symbols. In the case of the expression $x$, there is an implied coefficient of 1. An expression does not contain an equal sign. For example, $x$, $3x^2 + 2x$, and $\frac{7x+1}{3x^2-14}$ are all algebraic expressions.

**Monomial:** An algebraic expression with only one term. To simplify monomials, multiply or divide the coefficients and the variables separately: $2a \times 3a = (2 \times 3)(a \times a) = 6a^2$.

**Polynomial:** The general name for an algebraic expression with more than one term.

**Binomial:** A polynomial with exactly two terms.

**Algebraic equation:** Two algebraic expressions separated by an equal sign or one algebraic expression separated from a number by an equal sign.

## Basic Operations

### Combining Like Terms

The process of simplifying an expression by adding together or subtracting terms that have the same variable factors is called *combining like terms.*

**Example:** Simplify the expression $2x - 5y - x + 7y$.

$$2x - 5y - x + 7y = (2x - x) + (7y - 5y) = x + 2y$$

Notice that the commutative, associative, and distributive laws that govern arithmetic operations with ordinary numbers also apply to algebraic terms and polynomials.

### Adding and Subtracting Polynomials

To *add or subtract polynomials,* combine like terms.

$$(3x^2 + 5x + 7) - (x^2 + 12) = (3x^2 - x^2) + 5x + (7 - 12) = 2x^2 + 5x - 5$$

### Factoring Algebraic Expressions

Factoring a polynomial means expressing it as a product of two or more simpler expressions. Common factors can be factored out by using the distributive law.

**Example:** Factor the expression $2a + 6ac$.

The greatest common factor of $2a + 6ac$ is $2a$. Using the distributive law, you can factor out $2a$ so that the expression becomes $2a(1 + 3c)$.

**Example:** All three terms in the polynomial $3x^3 + 12x^2 - 6x$ contain a factor of $3x$. Pulling out the common factor yields $3x(x^2 + 4x - 2)$.

## Advanced Operations

### Substitution

Substitution, a process of plugging values into equations, is used to evaluate an algebraic expression or to express it in terms of other variables.

Replace every variable in the expression with the number or quantity you are told is its equivalent. Then carry out the designated operations, remembering to follow the order of operations (PEMDAS).

**Example:** Express $\frac{a-b^2}{b-a}$ in terms of $x$ if $a = 2x$ and $b = 3$.

Replace every $a$ with $2x$ and every $b$ with 3:

$$\frac{a-b^2}{b-a} = \frac{2x-9}{3-2x}$$

Without more information, you can't simplify or evaluate this expression further.

### Solving Equations

When you manipulate any equation, *always do the same thing on both sides of the equal sign.* Otherwise, the two sides of the equation will no longer be equal.

To solve an algebraic equation without exponents for a particular variable, you have to manipulate the equation until that variable is on one side of the equal sign, with all numbers or other variables on the other side. You can perform addition, subtraction, or multiplication; you can also perform division, as long as the quantity by which you are dividing does not equal zero.

Typically, at each step of the process, you'll try to isolate the variable by using the reverse of whatever operation has been applied to the variable. For example, in solving the equation $n + 6 = 10$ for $n$, you have to get rid of the 6 that has been added to the $n$. You do that by subtracting 6 from both sides of the equation: $n + 6 - 6 = 10 - 6$, so $n = 4$.

**Example:** If $4x - 7 = 2x + 5$, what is the value of $x$?

Start by adding 7 to both sides. This gives $4x = 2x + 12$. Now subtract $2x$ from both sides. This yields $2x = 12$. Finally, divide both sides by 2. The result is $x = 6$.

## Inequalities

There are two differences between solving an inequality (such as $2x < 5$) and solving an equation (such as $2x - 5 = 0$).

First, the solution to an inequality is almost always a range of possible values, rather than a single value. You can see the range easily by expressing it visually on a number line.

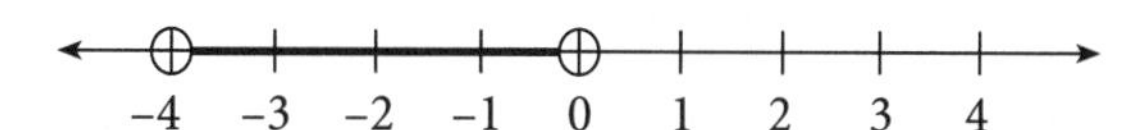


The shaded portion of the number line above shows the set of all numbers between −4 and 0 excluding the endpoints −4 and 0; this range would be expressed algebraically by the inequality $-4 < x < 0$.

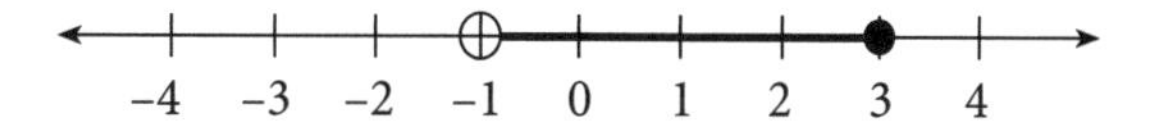


The shaded portion of the number line above shows the set of all numbers greater than −1, up to and including 3; this range would be expressed algebraically by the inequality $-1 < x \leq 3$.

The other difference when solving an inequality—and the only thing you really have to remember—is that if you multiply or divide the inequality by a negative number, you have to reverse the direction of the inequality. For example, when you multiply both sides of the inequality $-3x < 2$ by −1, you get $3x > -2$.

**Example:** Solve for $x$: $3 - \frac{x}{4} \geq 2$

Multiply both sides of the inequality by 4: $12 - x \geq 8$

Subtract 12 from both sides: $-x \geq -4$

Multiply (or divide) both sides by −1 and change the direction of the inequality sign: $x \leq 4$

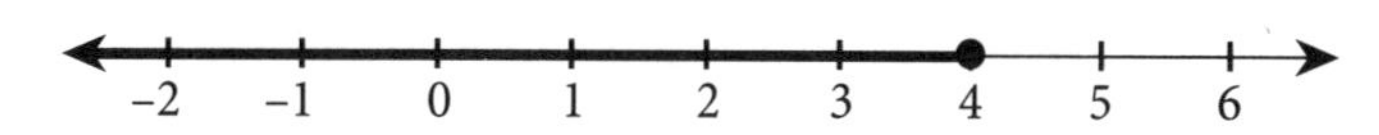


As you can see from the number line, the range of values that satisfies this inequality includes 4 and all numbers less than 4.

### Solving for One Unknown in Terms of Another

In general, in order to solve for the value of an unknown, you need as many distinct equations as you have variables. If there are two variables, for instance, you need two distinct equations.

However, some GMAT problems do not require you to solve for the numerical value of an unknown. Instead, you are asked to solve for one variable in terms of the other(s). To do so, isolate the desired variable on one side of the equation and move all the constants and other variables to the other side.

**Example:** In the formula $z = \frac{xy}{a + yb}$, solve for $y$ in terms of $x$, $z$, $a$, and $b$.

Clear the denominator by multiplying both sides by $a + yb$: $(a + yb)z = xy$

Remove parentheses by distributing: $az + ybz = xy$

Put all terms containing $y$ on one side and all other terms on the other side: $az = xy - ybz$

Factor out the common factor, $y$: $az = y(x - bz)$

Divide by the coefficient of $y$ to get $y$ alone: $\frac{az}{x - bz} = y$

## Simultaneous Equations

You've already discovered that you need as many different equations as you have variables to solve for the actual value of a variable. When a single equation contains more than one variable, you can only solve for one variable in terms of the others.

This has important implications for Data Sufficiency. For sufficiency, you usually must have at least as many equations as you have variables.

On the GMAT, you will often have to solve two simultaneous equations, that is, equations that give you different information about the same two variables. There are two methods for solving simultaneous equations.

### Method 1—Substitution

Step 1: Solve one equation for one variable in terms of the second.

Step 2: Substitute the result back into the other equation and solve.

**Example:** If $x - 15 = 2y$ and $6y + 2x = -10$, what is the value of $y$?

Solve the first equation for $x$ by adding 15 to both sides.

$$x = 2y + 15$$

Substitute $2y + 15$ for $x$ in the second equation:

$$\begin{aligned} 6y + 2(2y + 15) &= -10 \\ 6y + 4y + 30 &= -10 \\ 10y &= -40 \\ y &= -4 \end{aligned}$$

### Method 2—Adding to Cancel

Combine the equations in such a way that one of the variables cancels out. To solve the two equations $4x + 3y = 8$ and $x + y = 3$, multiply both sides of the second equation by $-3$ to get $-3x - 3y = -9$. Now add the two equations; the $3y$ and the $-3y$ cancel out, leaving: $x = -1$.

Before you use either method, make sure you really do have two distinct equations. For example, $2x + 3y = 8$ and $4x + 6y = 16$ are really the same equation in different forms; multiply the first equation by 2, and you'll get the second.

Whichever method you use, you can check the result by plugging both values back into both equations and making sure they work.

**Example:** If $m = 4n + 2$, and $3m + 2n = 16$, find the values of $m$ and $n$.

Since the first equation already expresses $m$ in terms of $n$, this problem is best approached by substitution.

Substitute $4n + 2$ for $m$ into $3m + 2n = 16$, and solve for $n$.

$$\begin{aligned} 3(4n+2)+2n &= 16 \\ 12n+6+2n &= 16 \\ 14n &= 10 \\ n &= \frac{5}{7} \end{aligned}$$

Now solve either equation for $m$ by plugging in $\frac{5}{7}$ for $n$.

$$\begin{aligned} m &= 4n+2 \\ m &= 4\left(\frac{5}{7}\right)+2 \\ m &= \frac{20}{7}+2 \\ m &= \frac{20}{7}+\frac{14}{7} \\ m &= \frac{34}{7} \end{aligned}$$

So, $m = \frac{34}{7}$ and $n = \frac{5}{7}$.

**Example:** If $3x + 3y = 18$ and $x - y = 10$, find the values of $x$ and $y$.

You could solve this problem by the substitution method. But look what happens if you multiply the second equation by 3 and add it to the first:

$$\begin{aligned} 3x+3y &= 18 \\ +\ (3x-3y &= 30) \\ \hline 6x &= 48 \end{aligned}$$

If $6x = 48$, then $x = 8$. Now you can just plug 8 into either equation in place of $x$ and solve for $y$. Your calculations will be simpler if you use the second equation: $8 - y = 10$; $-y = 2$; $y = -2$.

## Simultaneous Equations in Data Sufficiency

Data Sufficiency questions will sometimes test your understanding of how many equations you need to solve for a variable.

**Example:** What is the value of $x$?

(1) $x - 6y = 24$

(2) $4x + 2y = 16$

Neither statement alone is sufficient, since each equation allows you only to solve for $x$ in terms of *another variable*. However, both statements together give two different equations with two unknowns—enough information to find the value of $x$. So the correct answer is **(C)**: neither statement by itself is sufficient, but both statements together are sufficient.

**Example:** What is the value of $x + y$?

(1) $x + 4y = -12$

(2) $5x + 5y = 18$

To answer this question, you don't need the value of either variable by itself, but their sum. The second statement gives you enough information. If you divided both sides by 5, you could find the value of $x + y$. The correct answer then is **(B)**: Statement (1) by itself is not sufficient, but Statement (2) by itself *is* sufficient.

## Symbolism

Don't panic if you see strange symbols like *, ☆, and ♦ in a GMAT problem.

Problems of this type usually require nothing more than substitution. Read the question stem carefully for a definition of the symbols and for any examples of how to use them. Then, just follow the given model, substituting the numbers that are in the question stem.

**Example:** An operation symbolized by ★ is defined by the equation $x ★ y = x - \frac{1}{y}$. What is the value of $2 ★ 7$?

The ★ symbol is defined as a two-stage operation performed on two quantities, which are symbolized in the equation as $x$ and $y$. The two steps are (1) find the reciprocal of the second quantity and (2) subtract the reciprocal from the first quantity. To find the value of $2 ★ 7$, substitute the numbers 2 and 7 into the equation, replacing the $x$ (the first quantity given in the equation) with the 2 (the first number given) and the $y$ (the second quantity given in the equation) with the 7 (the second number given). The reciprocal of 7 is $\frac{1}{7}$, and subtracting $\frac{1}{7}$ from 2 gives you

$$2 - \frac{1}{7} = \frac{14}{7} - \frac{1}{7} = \frac{13}{7}$$

When a symbolism problem involves only one quantity, the operations are usually a little more complicated. Nonetheless, you can follow the same steps to find the correct answer.

**Example:** Let $x*$ be defined by the equation: $x* = \frac{x^2}{1-x^2}$. Evaluate $\left(\frac{1}{2}\right)^*$.

$$\left(\frac{1}{2}\right)^* = \frac{\left(\frac{1}{2}\right)^2}{1-\left(\frac{1}{2}\right)^2} = \frac{\frac{1}{4}}{1-\frac{1}{4}} = \frac{\frac{1}{4}}{\frac{3}{4}} = \frac{1}{4} \times \frac{4}{3} = \frac{1}{3}$$

Every once in a while, you'll see a symbolism problem that doesn't even include an equation. The definitions in this type of problem usually test your understanding of number properties.

**Example:** ✻$x$ is defined as the largest even number that is less than the negative square root of $x$. What is the value of ✻81?

- O −82
- O −80
- O −10
- O −8
- O 8

Plug in 81 for $x$ and work backward logically. The negative square root of 81 is −9 because $(-9)(-9) = 81$. The largest even number that is less than −9 is −10. (The number part of −8 is smaller than the number part of −9; however, you're dealing with negative numbers, so you have to look for the even number that would be just to the *left* of −9 along the number line.) Thus, the correct choice is **(C)**, −10.

### Sequences

Sequences are lists of numbers. The value of a number in a sequence is related to its position in the list. Sequences are often represented on the GMAT as follows:

$$s_1, s_2, s_3, \ldots s_n, \ldots$$

The subscript part of each number gives you the position of each element in the series. For example, $s_1$ is the first number in the list, $s_2$ is the second number in the list, and so on.

You may be given a formula that defines each element. For example, if you are told that $s_n = 2n + 1$, then the sequence would be $(2 \times 1) + 1, (2 \times 2) + 1, (2 \times 3) + 1, \ldots$, or $3, 5, 7, \ldots$

## Polynomials and Quadratics

### The FOIL Method

When two binomials are multiplied, each term is multiplied by each term in the other binomial. This process is often called the FOIL method, because it involves adding the products of the First, Outer, Inner, and Last terms. Using the FOIL method to multiply out $(x + 5)(x - 2)$, the product of the first terms is $x^2$, the product of the outer terms is $-2x$, the product of the inner terms is $5x$, and the product of the last terms is $-10$. When simplified, the answer is $x^2 + 3x - 10$.

### Factoring the Product of Binomials

Many of the polynomials that you'll see on the GMAT can be factored into a product of two binomials by using the FOIL method backwards.

**Example:** Factor the polynomial $x^2 - 3x + 2$.

You can factor this into two binomials, each containing an $x$ term. Start by writing down what you know:

$$x^2 - 3x + 2 = (x \quad)(x \quad)$$

You'll need to fill in the missing term in each binomial factor. The product of the two missing terms will be the last term in the original polynomial: 2. The sum of the two missing terms will be the coefficient of the second term of the polynomial: $-3$. Find the factors of 2 that add up to $-3$. Since $(-1) + (-2) = -3$, you can fill the empty spaces with $-1$ and $-2$.

Thus, $x^2 - 3x + 2 = (x - 1)(x - 2)$.

Note: Whenever you factor a polynomial, you can check your answer by using FOIL to multiply the factors and obtain the original polynomial.

### Factoring the Difference of Two Squares

A common factorable expression on the GMAT is the difference of two squares (for example, $a^2 - b^2$). Once you recognize a polynomial as the difference of two squares, you'll be able to factor it automatically, since any polynomial of the form $a^2 - b^2$ can be factored into a product of the form $(a + b)(a - b)$.

**Example:** Factor the expression $9x^2 - 1$.

$9x^2 = (3x)^2$ and $1 = 1^2$, so $9x^2 - 1$ is the difference of two squares.

Therefore, $9x^2 - 1 = (3x + 1)(3x - 1)$.

### Factoring Polynomials of the Form $a^2 + 2ab + b^2$

Any polynomial of this form is the square of a binomial expression, as you can see by using the FOIL method to multiply $(a + b)(a + b)$ or $(a - b)(a - b)$.

To factor a polynomial of this form, check the sign in front of the $2ab$ term. If it's a *plus* sign, the polynomial is equal to $(a + b)^2$. If it's a *minus* sign, the polynomial is equal to $(a - b)^2$.

**Example:** Factor the polynomial $x^2 + 6x + 9$.

$x^2$ and 9 are both perfect squares, and $6x$ is $2(3x)$, which is twice the product of $x$ and 3, so this polynomial is of the form $a^2 + 2ab + b^2$ with $a = x$ and $b = 3$. Since there is a plus sign in front of the $6x$, $x^2 + 6x + 9 = (x + 3)^2$.

## Quadratic Equations

A quadratic equation is an equation of the form $ax^2 + bx + c = 0$. Many quadratic equations have two solutions. In other words, the equation will be true for two different values of $x$.

When you see a quadratic equation on the GMAT, you'll generally be able to solve it by factoring the algebraic expression, setting each of the factors equal to zero, and solving the resulting equations.

**Example:** $x^2 - 3x + 2 = 0$. Solve for $x$.

To find the solutions, or roots, start by factoring $x^2 - 3x + 2 = 0$ into $(x - 2)(x - 1) = 0$.

The product of two quantities equals zero only if one (or both) of the quantities equals zero. So, if you set each of the factors equal to zero, you will be able to solve the resulting equations for the solutions of the original quadratic equation. Setting the two binomials equal to zero gives you

$$x - 2 = 0 \quad \text{or} \quad x - 1 = 0$$

That means that $x$ can equal 2 or 1. As a check, you can plug each of those values in turn into $x^2 - 3x + 2 = 0$, and you'll see that either value makes the equation work.

## Linear Equations in the Coordinate Plane

In coordinate geometry, the locations of points in a plane are indicated by ordered pairs of real numbers.

### Important Terms and Concepts

**Plane:** A flat surface that extends indefinitely in any direction.

**$x$-axis and $y$-axis:** The horizontal ($x$) and vertical ($y$) lines that intersect perpendicularly to indicate location on a coordinate plane. Each axis is a number line.

**Ordered pair:** Two numbers or quantities separated by a comma and enclosed in parentheses. An example is (8,7). All the ordered pairs that you'll see in GMAT coordinate geometry problems will be in the form $(x,y)$, where the first quantity, $x$, tells you how far the point is to the left or right of the $y$-axis, and the second quantity, $y$, tells you how far the point is above or below the $x$-axis.

**Coordinates:** The numbers that designate distance from an axis in coordinate geometry. The first number is the $x$-coordinate; the second is the $y$-coordinate. In the ordered pair (8,7), 8 is the $x$-coordinate and 7 is the $y$-coordinate.

**Origin:** The point where the $x$- and $y$-axes intersect; its coordinates are (0,0).

### Plotting Points

Here's what a coordinate plane looks like:

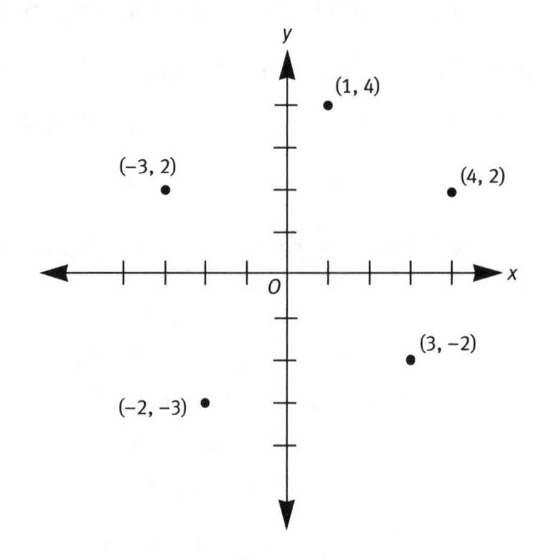


Any point in a coordinate plane can be identified by an ordered pair consisting of its $x$-coordinate and its $y$-coordinate. Every point that lies on the $x$-axis has a $y$-coordinate of 0, and every point that lies on the $y$-axis has an $x$-coordinate of 0.

When you start at the origin and move:

| | |
|---|---|
| to the right | $x$ is positive |
| to the left | $x$ is negative |
| up | $y$ is positive |
| down | $y$ is negative |

Therefore, the coordinate plane can be divided into four quadrants, as shown below.

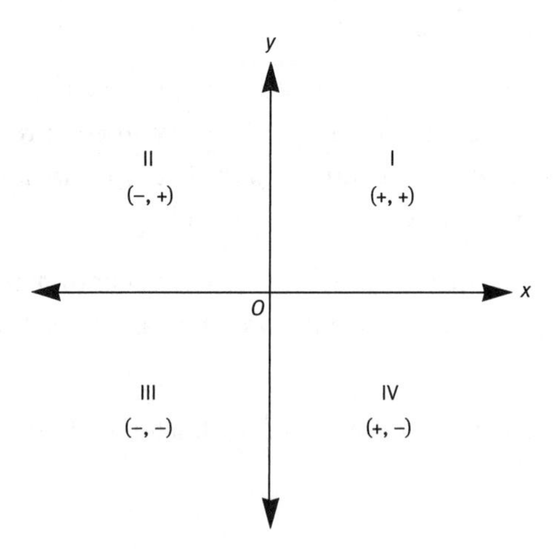

## Equations of Lines

Straight lines can be described by linear equations.

The *slope-intercept form* of a line is given by

$$y = mx + b,$$

where $m$ is the slope $\left(\frac{\Delta y}{\Delta x}\right)$ and $b$ is the point where the line intercepts the $y$-axis.

Lines that are parallel to the $x$-axis have a slope of zero and therefore have the equation $y = b$. Lines that are parallel to the $y$-axis have the equation $x = a$, where $a$ is the $x$-intercept of that line.

If you're comfortable with linear equations, you'll sometimes want to use them to find the slope of a line or the coordinates of a point on a line. However, many such questions can be answered without determining or manipulating equations. Check the answer choices to see if you can eliminate any by common sense.

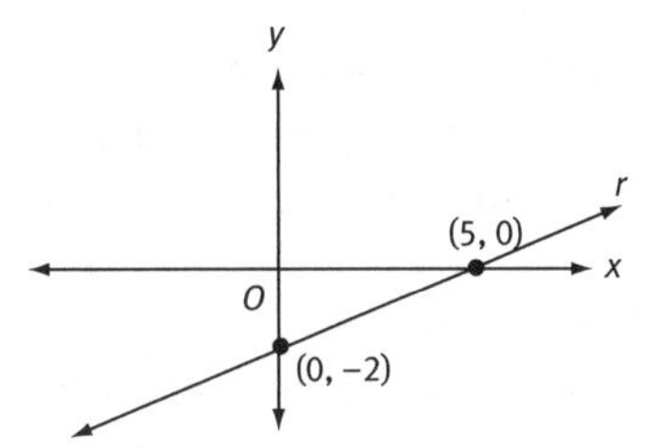


**Example:** Line $r$ is a straight line as shown above. Which of the following points lies on line $r$?

- O (6,6)
- O (7,3)
- O (8,2)
- O (9,3)
- O (10,2)

Line $r$ intercepts the $y$-axis at $(0,-2)$, so you can plug $-2$ in for $b$ in the slope-intercept form of a linear equation. Line $r$ has a rise ($\Delta y$) of 2 and a run ($\Delta x$) of 5, so its slope is $\frac{2}{5}$. That makes the slope-intercept form $y = \frac{2}{5}x - 2$.

The easiest way to proceed from here is to substitute the coordinates of each answer choice into the equation in place of $x$ and $y$; only the coordinates that satisfy the equation can lie on the line. Choice **(E)** is the best answer to start with, because 10 is the only $x$-coordinate that will not create a fraction on the right side of the equal sign. Plugging in (10,2) for $x$ and $y$ in the slope-intercept equation gives you $2 = \frac{2}{5}(10) - 2$, which simplifies to $2 = 4 - 2$.

That's true, so the correct answer choice is **(E)**.

## Alternative Strategies for Multiple-Choice Algebra

### Backsolving

On GMAT Problem Solving questions, you may find it easier to attack algebra problems by backsolving.

To backsolve, substitute each answer choice into the equation until you find the one that satisfies the equation.

**Example:** If $x^2 + 10x + 25 = 0$, what is the value of $x$?

- O 25
- O 10
- O 5
- O −5
- O −10

The textbook approach to solve this problem would be to recognize the polynomial expression as the square of the binomial $(x + 5)$ and set $x + 5 = 0$. That's the fastest way to arrive at the correct answer of −5.

But you could also plug each answer choice into the equation until you find the one that makes the equation true. Backsolving can be pretty quick if the correct answer is the first choice you plug in, but here, you have to get all the way down to choice **(D)** before you find that $(-5)^2 + 10(-5) + 25 = 0$.

**Example:** If $\frac{5x}{3} + 9 = \frac{x}{6} + 18$, then $x =$

- O 12
- O 8
- O 6
- O 5
- O 4

To avoid having to try all five answer choices, look at the equation and decide which choice(s), if plugged in for $x$, would make your calculations easiest. Since $x$ is in the numerators of the two fractions in this equation, and the denominators are 3 and 6, try plugging in a choice that is divisible by both 3 and 6. Choices (A) and (C) are divisible by both numbers, so start with one of them.

Choice (A):

$$20 + 9 = 2 + 18$$
$$29 \neq 20$$

This is not true, so $x$ cannot equal 12.

Choice (C):

$$10 + 9 = 1 + 18$$
$$19 = 19$$

This is correct, so $x$ must equal 6. Therefore, choice **(C)** is correct.

Backsolving may not be the fastest method for a multiple-choice algebra problem, but it's useful if you don't think you'll be able to solve the problem in the conventional way.

### Picking Numbers

On other types of multiple-choice algebra problems, especially where the answer choices consist of variables or algebraic expressions, you may want to pick numbers to make the problem less abstract. Evaluate the answer choices and the information in the question stem by picking a number and substituting it for the variable wherever the variable appears.

**Example:** If $a > 1$, the ratio of $2a + 6$ to $a^2 + 2a - 3$ is

- O $2a$
- O $a + 3$
- O $\frac{2}{a-1}$
- O $\frac{2a}{3(3-a)}$
- O $\frac{a-1}{2}$

You can simplify the process by replacing the variable $a$ with a number in each algebraic expression. Since $a$ has to be greater than 1, why not pick 2? Then the expression $2a + 6$ becomes $2(2) + 6$, or 10. The expression $a^2 + 2a - 3$ becomes $2^2 + 2(2) - 3 = 4 + 4 - 3 = 5$.

Now the question reads, "The ratio of 10 to 5 is what?" That's easy enough to answer: 10:5 is the same as $\frac{10}{5}$, or 2. Now you can just eliminate any answer choice that doesn't give a result of 2 when you substitute 2 for $a$. Choice (A) gives you 2(2), or 4, so discard it. Choice (B) results in 5—also not what you want. Choice (C) yields $\frac{2}{1}$ or 2. That looks good, but you can't stop here.

If another answer choice gives you a result of 2, you will have to pick another number for $a$ and reevaluate the expressions in the question stem and the choices that worked when you let $a = 2$.

Choice (D) gives you $\frac{2(2)}{3(3-2)}$ or $\frac{4}{3}$, so eliminate choice (D).

Choice (E) gives you $\frac{2-1}{2}$ or $\frac{1}{2}$, so discard choice (E).

Fortunately, in this case, only choice **(C)** works out to 2, so it is the correct answer. But remember: when picking numbers, always check every answer choice to make sure you haven't chosen a number that works for more than one answer choice.

## Using Picking Numbers to Solve for One Unknown in Terms of Another

It is also possible to solve for one unknown in terms of another by picking numbers. If the first number you pick doesn't lead to a single correct answer, be prepared to either pick a new number (and spend more time on the problem) or settle for guessing strategically among the answers that you haven't eliminated.

**Example:** If $\frac{x^2-16}{x^2+6x+8}=y$ and $x>-2$, which of the following is an expression for $x$ in terms of $y$?

- $\frac{1+y}{2-y}$
- $\frac{2y+4}{1-y}$
- $\frac{4y-4}{y+1}$
- $\frac{2y-4}{2+y}$
- $\frac{y+4}{y+1}$

Pick a value for $x$ that will simplify your calculations. If you let $x$ equal 4, then $x^2-16=4^2-16=0$, and so the entire fraction on the left side of the equation is equal to zero.

Now, substitute 0 for $y$ in each answer choice in turn. Each choice is an expression for $x$ in terms of $y$, and since $y=0$ when $x=4$, the correct answer will have to give a value of 4 when $y=0$. Just remember to evaluate all the answer choices, because you might find more than one that gives a result of 4.

Substituting 0 for $y$ in choices (A), (C), and (D) yields $\frac{1}{2}$, $\frac{-4}{1}$, and $\frac{-4}{2}$, respectively, so none of those choices can be right. But both (B) and (E) give results of 4 when you make the substitution; choosing between them will require picking another number.

Again, pick a number that will make calculations easy. If $x=0$, then $y=\frac{x^2-16}{x^2+6x+8}=\frac{0-16}{0+0+8}=\frac{-16}{8}=-2$.

Therefore, $y=-2$ when $x=0$. You don't have to try the new value of $y$ in all the answer choices, just in (B) and (E). When you substitute $-2$ for $y$ in choice (B), you get 0. That's what you're looking for, but again, you have to make sure it doesn't work in choice (E). Plugging $-2$ in for $y$ in (E) yields $-2$ for $x$, so **(B)** is correct.

# Formulas, Statistics, and Data Analysis

## Rates

A rate is a special type of ratio. Instead of relating a part to the whole, or to another part, a rate relates one kind of quantity to a completely different kind. When talking about rates, it is common to use the word *per*, as in "miles per hour," "cost per item," etc. Since *per* means "for one" or "for each," you express the rates as ratios reduced to a denominator of 1.

### Speed

The most commonly tested rate on the GMAT is speed. This is usually expressed in miles or kilometers per hour. The relationship between speed, distance, and time is given by the formula $\text{Speed} = \frac{\text{Distance}}{\text{Time}}$, which can be rewritten two ways: $\text{Time} = \frac{\text{Distance}}{\text{Speed}}$ and $\text{Distance} = (\text{Speed})(\text{Time})$.

Any time you can find two out of the three elements in this equation, you can find the third.

For example, if a car travels 300 miles in 5 hours, it has averaged $\frac{300 \text{ miles}}{5 \text{ hours}} = 60$ miles per hour. (Note that speeds are usually expressed as averages because they are not necessarily constant. For instance, in the previous example, the car traveled 300 miles in 5 hours. It moved at an "average speed" of 60 miles per hour, but probably not at a constant speed of 60 miles per hour.)

Likewise, a rearranged version of the formula can be used to solve for missing speed or time.

**Example:** How far do you drive if you travel for 5 hours at 60 miles per hour?

$$\text{Distance} = (\text{Speed})(\text{Time})$$
$$\text{Distance} = (60 \text{ mph})(5 \text{ hours})$$
$$\text{Distance} = 300 \text{ miles}$$

**Example:** How much time does it take to drive 300 miles at 60 miles per hour?

$$\text{Time} = \frac{\text{Distance}}{\text{Speed}}$$
$$\text{Time} = \frac{300 \text{ miles}}{60 \text{ mph}}$$
$$\text{Time} = 5 \text{ hours}$$

### Other Rates

Speed is not the only rate that appears on the GMAT. For instance, you might get a word problem involving liters per minute or cost per unit. All rate problems, however, can be solved using the speed formula and its variants by conceiving of "speed" as "rate," and "distance" as "quantity."

**Example:** How many hours will it take to fill a 500-liter tank at a rate of 2 liters per minute?

Plug the numbers into the rate formula:

$$\text{Time} = \frac{\text{Quantity}}{\text{Rate}}$$
$$\text{Time} = \frac{500 \text{ liters}}{2 \text{ liters per minute}}$$
$$\text{Time} = 250 \text{ minutes}$$

Now convert 250 minutes to hours:

250 minutes $\div$ 60 minutes per hour $= 4\frac{1}{6}$ hours to fill the tank. (As you can see from this problem, GMAT Problem Solving questions test your ability to convert minutes into hours, and vice versa. Pay close attention to what units the answer choice must use.)

In some cases, you should use proportions to answer rate questions.

**Example:** If 350 widgets cost $20, how much will 1,400 widgets cost at the same rate?

Set up a proportion:

$$\frac{\text{Number of widgets}}{\text{Cost}} = \frac{350 \text{ widgets}}{\$20} = \frac{1{,}400 \text{ widgets}}{\$x}$$

Solving, you will find that $x = 80$.

So, 1,400 widgets will cost $80 at that rate.

## Combined Rate Problems

Rates can be added.

**Example:** Nelson can mow 200 square meters of lawn per hour. John can mow 100 square meters of lawn per hour. Working simultaneously but independently, how many hours will it take Nelson and John to mow 1,800 square meters of lawn?

Add Nelson's rate to John's rate to find the combined rate.

200 meters per hour + 100 meters per hour = 300 meters per hour.

Divide the total lawn area, 1,800 square meters, by the combined rate, 300 square meters per hour, to find the number of required hours, 6.

## Work Problems (Given Hours per Unit of Work)

The work formula can be used to find out how long it takes a number of people working together to complete a task. Imagine there are three people. The first takes $a$ units of time to complete the job, the second takes $b$ units of time to complete the job, and the third takes $c$ units of time. If the time it takes all three working together to complete the job is $T$, then $\frac{1}{a} + \frac{1}{b} + \frac{1}{c} = \frac{1}{T}$.

**Example:** John can weed the garden in 3 hours. If Mary can weed the garden in 2 hours, how long will it take them to weed the garden at this rate, working independently?

Set John's time per unit of work as $a$ and Mary's time per unit of work as $b$. (There is no need for the variable $c$, since there are only two people.) Plugging in, you find that

$$\frac{1}{3}+\frac{1}{2}=\frac{1}{T}$$
$$\frac{2}{6}+\frac{3}{6}=\frac{1}{T}$$
$$\frac{5}{6}=\frac{1}{T}$$
$$T=\frac{6}{5}\text{ hours}$$

## Work Formula

You can use the above equation, $\frac{1}{a}+\frac{1}{b}=\frac{1}{T}$, to derive the work formula, a convenient formula to use on Test Day.

$$\frac{1}{a}+\frac{1}{b}=\frac{1}{T}$$
$$(ab)\left(\frac{1}{a}+\frac{1}{b}\right)=\left(\frac{1}{T}\right)(ab)$$
$$\frac{ab}{a}+\frac{ab}{b}=\frac{ab}{T}$$
$$b+a=\frac{ab}{T}$$
$$T(b+a)=\left(\frac{ab}{T}\right)T$$
$$T(b+a)=ab$$
$$T=\frac{ab}{a+b}$$

This last equation is the *work formula.*

Here, $a =$ the amount of time is takes person $a$ to complete the job and $b =$ the amount of time it takes person $b$ to complete the job.

**Example:** John takes 3 hours to weed the garden, and Mary takes 2 hours to weed the same garden. How long will it take them to weed the garden together?

$$\text{Work formula}=\frac{a\times b}{a+b}=\frac{3\times 2}{3+2}=\frac{6}{5}\text{ hours}$$

## Average Formula

The average of a group of numbers is defined as the sum of the terms divided by the number of terms.

$$\text{Average} = \frac{\text{Sum of terms}}{\text{Number of terms}}$$

This equation can be rewritten two ways:

$$\text{Number of terms} = \frac{\text{Sum of terms}}{\text{Average}}$$

$$\text{Sum of terms} = (\text{Number of terms})(\text{Average})$$

Thus, any time you have two out of the three values (average, sum of terms, number of terms), you can find the third.

**Example:** Henry buys three items costing \$2.00, \$1.75, and \$1.05. What is the average price (arithmetic mean) of the three items? (Don't let the phrase *arithmetic mean* throw you; it's just another term for *average*.)

$$\text{Average} = \frac{\text{Sum of terms}}{\text{Number of terms}}$$

$$\text{Average} = \frac{\$2.0 + \$1.75 + \$1.05}{3}$$

$$\text{Average} = \frac{\$4.80}{3}$$

$$\text{Average} = \$1.60$$

**Example:** June pays an average price of \$14.50 for 6 articles of clothing. What is the total price of all 6 articles?

$$\text{Sum of terms} = (\text{Average})(\text{Number of terms})$$

$$\text{Total price} = (\$14.50)(6)$$

$$\text{Total price} = \$87.00$$

**Example:** The total weight of the licorice sticks in a jar is 30 ounces. If the average weight of each licorice stick is 2 ounces, how many licorice sticks are there in the jar?

$$\text{Number of terms} = \frac{\text{Sum of terms}}{\text{Average}}$$

$$\text{Number of sticks} = \frac{30 \text{ ounces}}{2 \text{ ounces}}$$

$$\text{Number of sticks} = 15$$

### Using the Average to Find a Missing Number

If you're given the average, the total number of terms, and all but one of the actual numbers, you can find the missing number.

**Example:** The average annual rainfall in Boynton for 1976–1979 was 26 inches per year. Boynton received 24 inches of rain in 1976, 30 inches in 1977, and 19 inches in 1978. How many inches of rainfall did Boynton receive in 1979?

You know that total rainfall equals 24 + 30 + 19 + (number of inches of rain in 1979).

You know that the average rainfall was 26 inches per year.

You know that there were 4 years.

So, plug these numbers into any of the three expressions of the average formula to find that Sum of terms = (Average)(Number of terms).

$$\begin{aligned} 24+30+19+\text{inches in 1979} &= (26)(4) \\ 73+\text{inches in 1979} &= (26)(4) \\ 73+\text{inches in 1979} &= 104 \\ \text{inches in 1979} &= 31 \end{aligned}$$

### Another Way to Find a Missing Number: The Concept of "Balanced Value"

Another way to find a missing number is to understand that the *sum of the differences between each term and the mean of the set must equal zero.* Plugging in the numbers from the previous problem, for example, you find that

$$\begin{aligned} (24-26)+(30-26)+(19-26)+(\text{inches in 1979}-26) &= 0 \\ (-2)+(4)+(-7)+(\text{inches in 1979}-26) &= 0 \\ -5+(\text{inches in 1979}-26) &= 0 \\ \text{inches in 1979} &= 31 \end{aligned}$$

It may be easier to comprehend why this is true by visualizing a balancing, or weighting, process. The combined distances of the numbers above the average from the mean must be balanced with the combined distances of the numbers below the average from the mean.

**Example:** The average of 63, 64, 85, and $x$ is 80. What is the value of $x$?

Think of each value in terms of its position relative to the average, 80.

63 is 17 less than 80.

64 is 16 less than 80.

85 is 5 greater than 80.

So, these three terms are a total of 17 + 16 − 5, or 28, less than the average. Therefore, $x$ must be 28 greater than the average to restore the balance at 80. So, $x = 28 + 80 = 108$.

### Average of Consecutive, Evenly Spaced Numbers

When consecutive numbers are evenly spaced, the average is the middle value. For example, the average of consecutive integers 6, 7, and 8 is 7.

If there is an even number of evenly spaced numbers, there is no single middle value. In that case, the average is midway between (that is, the average of) the middle two values. For example, the average of 5, 10, 15, and 20 is 12.5, midway between the middle values 10 and 15.

Note that not all consecutive numbers are evenly spaced. For instance, consecutive prime numbers arranged in increasing order are not evenly spaced. But you can use the handy technique of finding the middle value whenever you have consecutive integers, consecutive odd or even numbers, consecutive multiples of an integer, or any other consecutive numbers that are evenly spaced.

### Combining Averages

When there is an equal number of terms in each set, and *only when there is an equal number of terms in each set,* you can average averages.

For example, suppose there are two bowlers, and you must find their average score per game. One has an average score per game of 100, and the other has an average score per game of 200. If both bowlers bowled the same number of games, you can average their averages to find their combined average. Suppose they both bowled 4 games. Their combined average will be equally influenced by both bowlers. Hence, their combined average will be the average of 100 and 200. You can find this quickly by remembering that the quantity above the average and the quantity below the average must be equal. Therefore, the average will be halfway between 100 and 200, which is 150. Or, you could solve using the average formula:

$$\text{Average} = \frac{\text{Sum of terms}}{\text{Number of terms}} = \frac{4(100) + 4(200)}{8} = 150$$

However, if the bowler with the average score of 100 had bowled 4 games, and the bowler with the 200 average had bowled 16 games, the combined average would be weighted further toward 200 than toward 100, to reflect the greater influence of the 200 bowler than the 100 bowler upon the total. This is known as a *weighted average.*

Again, you can solve this by using the concept of a balanced average or by using the average formula.

Since the bowler bowling an average score of 200 bowled $\frac{4}{5}$ of the games, the combined average will be $\frac{4}{5}$ of the distance along the number line between 100 and 200, which is 180. Or, you can plug the numbers into the average formula to find that

$$\text{Average} = \frac{\text{Sum of terms}}{\text{Number of terms}}$$

$$\text{Average} = \frac{4(100) + 16(200)}{20}$$

$$\text{Average} = \frac{400 + 3{,}200}{20}$$

$$\text{Average} = 180$$

### Averages and Data Sufficiency

For Data Sufficiency average questions, you will have to scan the statements for any two elements of the average formula, from which you will know that you can find the third.

**Example:** If the receipts for a matinee performance at the Granada Theater totaled \$2,400, how many tickets were sold for that performance?

(1) The average price of a ticket sold was \$7.50.

(2) All tickets sold cost either \$10.00 or \$6.00.

Use the average formula: $\text{Average} = \frac{\text{Sum of terms}}{\text{Number of terms}}$. In this case, you already know the sum of terms (total receipts = \$2,400). All that you need to find the number of terms (number of tickets sold) is the other part of the equation: the average price of a ticket sold. Statement (1) gives you this information, so it is sufficient. Since you don't know how many \$10.00 versus \$6.00 tickets were sold, Statement (2) does not give you the number of tickets sold and so is not sufficient. So the correct answer is **(A)**: Statement (1) by itself is sufficient, and Statement (2) by itself is *not* sufficient.

## Median, Mode, and Range

**Median:** The middle term in a group of terms that are arranged in numerical order. To find the median of a group of terms, first arrange the terms in numerical order. If there is an odd number of terms in the group, then the median is the middle term.

**Example:** Bob's test scores in Spanish are 84, 81, 88, 70, and 87. What is his median score?

In increasing order, his scores are 70, 81, 84, 87, and 88. The median test score is the middle one: 84.

If there is an even number of terms in the group, the median is the average of the two middle terms.

**Example:** John's test scores in biology are 92, 98, 82, 94, 85, and 97. What is his median score?

In numerical order, his scores are 82, 85, 92, 94, 97, and 98. The median test score is the average of the two middle terms, or $\frac{92+94}{2} = 93$.

The median of a group of numbers is often different from its average.

**Example:** Caitlin's test scores in math are 92, 96, 90, 85, and 82. Find the difference between Caitlin's median score and the average (arithmetic mean) of her scores.

In ascending order, Caitlin's scores are 82, 85, 90, 92, and 96. The median score is the middle one: 90. Her average score is $\frac{82+85+90+92+96}{5} = \frac{445}{5} = 89$.

As you can see, Caitlin's median score and average score are not the same. The difference between them is 90 – 89, or 1.

**Mode:** The term that appears most frequently in a set.

**Example:** The daily temperatures in City Q for one week were 25°, 33°, 26°, 25°, 27°, 31°, and 22°. What was the mode of the daily temperatures in City Q for that week?

Each of the temperatures occurs once on the list except for 25°, which occurs twice. Since 25° appears more frequently than any other temperature, it is the mode.

A set may have more than one mode if two or more terms appear an equal number of times within the set and each appears more times than any other term.

**Example:** The table below represents the score distribution for a class of 20 students on a recent chemistry test. Which score, or scores, are the mode?

| Score | # of Students Receiving That Score |
|---|---|
| 100 | 2 |
| 91 | 1 |
| 87 | 5 |
| 86 | 2 |
| 85 | 1 |
| 84 | 5 |
| 80 | 1 |
| 78 | 2 |
| 56 | 1 |

The largest number in the second column is 5, which occurs twice. Therefore, there were two mode scores on this test: 87 and 84. Equal numbers of students received those scores, and more students received those scores than any other score.

If every element in the set occurs an equal number of times, then the set has no mode.

## Combinations and Permutations

A combination question asks you how many unordered subgroups can be formed from a larger group.

Some combination questions on the GMAT can be solved without any computation just by counting or listing possible combinations.

**Example:** Allen, Betty, and Claire must wash the dishes. They decide to work in shifts of two people. How many shifts will it take before all possible combinations have been used?

It is possible, and not time-consuming, to solve this problem by writing a list. Call Allen *A*, Betty *B*, and Claire *C*. There are three possible combinations (*AB*, *AC*, *BC*).

## The Combination Formula

Some combination questions use numbers that make quick, non-computational solving difficult. In these cases, use the combination formula $\frac{n!}{k!(n-k)!}$, where $n$ is the number of items in the group as a whole, and $k$ is the number of items in each subgroup formed. The ! symbol means factorial (for example, $5! = (5)(4)(3)(2)(1) = 120$).

**Example:** The 4 finalists in a spelling contest win commemorative plaques. If there are 7 entrants in the spelling contest, how many possible groups of winners are there?

Plug the numbers into the combination formula, such that $n$ is 7 (the number in the large group) and $k$ is 4 (the number of people in each subgroup formed).

$$\frac{7!}{4!(7-4)!}$$

$$\frac{7!}{4!3!}$$

At this stage, it is helpful to reduce these terms. Since 7 factorial contains all the factors of 4 factorial, you can write 7! as $(7)(6)(5)(4!)$ and then cancel the 4! in the numerator and denominator.

$$\frac{(7)(6)(5)}{(3)(2)(1)} = ?$$

You can reduce further by crossing off the 6 in the numerator and the $(3)(2)$ in the denominator.

$$\frac{(7)(5)}{1} = 35$$

There are 35 potential groups of spelling contest finalists.

When you are asked to find potential combinations from multiple groups, multiply the potential combinations from each group.

**Example:** How many groups can be formed consisting of 2 people from Room A and 3 people from Room B if there are 5 people in Room A and 6 people in Room B?

Insert the appropriate numbers into the combination formula for each room and then multiply the results. For Room A, the number of combinations of 2 in a set of 5 is $\frac{n!}{k!(n-k)!} = \frac{5!}{2!3!} = \frac{(5)(4)(3)(2)(1)}{(2)(1)(3)(2)(1)}$. Reducing this, you get $\frac{(5)(4)}{(2)} = 10$. For Room B, the number of combinations of 3 in a set of 6 is $\frac{n!}{k!(n-k)!} = \frac{6!}{3!3!} = \frac{(6)(5)(4)(3)(2)(1)}{(3)(2)(1)(3)(2)(1)}$. Reducing this, you get $\frac{(6)(5)(4)}{(3)(2)} = 20$. Multiply these to find that there are $(10)(20) = 200$ possible groups consisting of 2 people from Room A and 3 people from Room B.

Sometimes the GMAT will ask you to find the number of possible subgroups when choosing one item from a set. In this case, the number of possible subgroups will always equal the number of items in the set.

**Example:** Restaurant A has 5 appetizers, 20 main courses, and 4 desserts. If a meal consists of 1 appetizer, 1 main course, and 1 dessert, how many different meals can be ordered at Restaurant A?

The number of possible outcomes from each set is the number of items in the set. So, there are 5 possible appetizers, 20 possible main courses, and 4 possible desserts. The number of different meals that can be ordered is $(5)(20)(4) = 400$.

### Permutation

Within any group of items or people, there are multiple arrangements, or *permutations*, possible. For instance, within a group of three items (for example: *A*, *B*, *C*), there are six permutations (*ABC*, *ACB*, *BAC*, *BCA*, *CAB*, and *CBA*).

Permutations differ from combinations in that permutations are ordered. By definition, each combination larger than 1 has multiple permutations. On the GMAT, a question asking "How many ways/arrangements/orders/schedules are possible?" generally indicates a permutation problem.

To find permutations, think of each place that needs to be filled in a particular arrangement as a blank space. The first place can be filled with any of the items in the larger group. The second place can be filled with any of the items in the larger group except for the one used to fill the first place. The third place can be filled with any of the items in the group except for the two used to fill the first two places, etc.

**Example:** In a spelling contest, the winner will receive a gold medal, the second-place finisher will receive a silver medal, the third-place finisher will receive a bronze medal, and the fourth-place finisher will receive a blue ribbon. If there are 7 entrants in the contest, how many different arrangements of award winners are there?

The gold medal can be won by any of 7 people. The silver medal can be won by any of the remaining 6 people. The bronze medal can be won by any of the remaining 5 people. And the blue ribbon can be won by any of the remaining 4 people. Thus, the number of possible arrangements is $(7)(6)(5)(4) = 840$.

## Probability

*Probability* is the numerical representation of the likelihood of an event or combination of events. This is expressed as a ratio of the number of desired outcomes to the total number of possible outcomes. Probability is usually expressed as a fraction (for example, "the probability of Event A occurring is $\frac{1}{3}$"), but it can also be expressed in words ("the probability of Event A occurring is 1 in 3"). The probability of any event occurring cannot exceed 1 (a probability of 1 represents a 100% chance of an event occurring), and it cannot be less than 0 (a probability of 0 represents a 0% chance of an event occurring).

**Example:** If you flip a fair coin, what is the probability that it will fall with the heads side facing up?

The probability of the coin landing heads up is $\frac{1}{2}$, since there is one outcome you are interested in (landing heads up) and two possible outcomes (heads up or tails up).

**Example:** What is the probability of rolling a 5 or a 6 on a six-sided die numbered 1 through 6?

The probability of rolling a 5 or a 6 on a six-sided die numbered 1 through 6 is $\frac{2}{6} = \frac{1}{3}$, since there are 2 desired outcomes (rolling a 5 or a 6) and 6 possible outcomes (rolling a 1, 2, 3, 4, 5, or 6).

The sum of all possible outcomes, desired or otherwise, must equal 1. In other words, if there is a 25% chance that Event A will occur, then there is a 75% chance that it will not occur. So, to find the probability that an event does *not* occur, subtract the probability that it *does* occur from 1. In the previous example, the probability of not throwing a 5 or a 6 on the die is $1 - \frac{1}{3} = \frac{2}{3}$.

When events are independent, that is, the events do not depend on the other event or events, the probability that several events all occur is the product of the probability of each event occurring individually.

**Example:** A fair coin is flipped twice. What is the probability of its landing with the heads side facing up on both flips?

Multiply the probability for each flip: $\left(\frac{1}{2}\right)\left(\frac{1}{2}\right) = \frac{1}{4}$.

## Probability of Dependent Events

In some situations, the probability of a later event occurring varies according to the results of an earlier event. In this case, the probability fraction for the later event must be adjusted accordingly.

**Example:** A bag contains 10 marbles, 4 of which are blue and 6 of which are red. If 2 marbles are removed without replacement, what is the probability that both marbles removed are red?

The probability that the first marble removed will be red is $\frac{6}{10} = \frac{3}{5}$. The probability that the second marble removed will be red will not be the same, however. There will be fewer marbles overall, so the denominator will be one less. There will also be one fewer red marble. (Note that since the question asks about the probability of picking two red marbles, you are only interested in choosing a second marble if the first was red. Don't concern yourself with situations in which a blue marble is chosen first.) If the first marble removed is red, the probability that the second marble removed will also be red is $\frac{5}{9}$.

So, the probability that both marbles removed will be red is $\left(\frac{3}{5}\right)\left(\frac{5}{9}\right) = \frac{15}{45} = \frac{1}{3}$.

## Dealing with Word Problems

The key to solving word problems is translation: turning English into math. Rather than having an equation set up for you, *you* have to decide what arithmetic or algebraic operations to perform on which numbers.

For example, suppose the core of a problem involves working with the equation $3j = s - 4$.

In a word problem, this might be presented as "If John had three times as many macaroons as he has now, he would have four fewer macaroons than Susan would."

Your job is to translate the problem from English into math. A phrase like "three times as many as John has" can be translated as $3j$; the phrase "four fewer than Susan" can be translated as "$s - 4$."

Many people dislike word problems. But on the GMAT, the math involved is often easier than in other math problems. Once you've translated the language, most word problems boil down to rather simple mathematical concepts and processes—probably because the test makers figure that the extra step of translation makes the problem difficult enough.

Here's a general approach to any word problem:

1. Read through the whole question once, without lingering over details, to get a sense of the overall problem.
2. Identify and label the variables or unknowns in a way that makes it easy to remember what they stand for.
3. Translate the problem into one or more equations, sentence by sentence. Be careful of the order in which you translate the terms. For example, consider the phrase "5 less than $4x$ equals 9." The *correct* way to translate it is "$4x - 5 = 9$." But many students make the mistake of writing the terms in the order in which they appear in words: "$5 - 4x = 9$."
4. Solve the equation(s).
5. Check your work, if time permits.

### Translation Table

This table contains common phrases used in GMAT math problems. The left column lists words and phrases that occur frequently; the right column lists the corresponding algebraic symbols.

| | |
|---|---|
| Equals, is, was, will be, has, costs, adds up to, is the same as | $=$ |
| Times, of, multiplied by, product of, twice, double, half, triple | $\times$ |
| Divided by, per, out of, each, ratio of _ to _ | $\div$ |
| Plus, added to, sum, combined, and, total | $+$ |
| Minus, subtracted from, less than, decreased by, difference between | $-$ |
| What, how much, how many, a number | Variable ($x$, $n$, etc.) |

**Example:** Beatrice has three dollars more than twice the number of dollars Allan has.

Translate into $B = 3 + 2A$.

## For Word Problems:

### Add...

- when you are given the amounts of individual quantities and asked to find the total.

**Example:** If the sales tax on a $12.00 lunch is $1.20, what is the total amount of the check?

$$\$12.00 + \$1.20 = \$13.20$$

- when you are given an original amount and an increase, and then asked to find the new amount.

**Example:** The bus fare used to be 55 cents. If the fare increased by 35 cents, what is the new fare?

$$55 \text{ cents} + 35 \text{ cents} = 90 \text{ cents}$$

### Subtract...

- when you are given the total and one part of the total, and you want to find the remaining part or parts.

**Example:** If 32 out of 50 children are girls, what is the number of boys?

$$50 \text{ children} - 32 \text{ girls} = 18 \text{ boys}$$

- when you are given two numbers and asked *how much more* or *how much less* one number is than the other. The amount is called the **difference**.

**Example:** How much larger than 30 is 38?

$$38(\text{larger}) - 30(\text{smaller}) = 8$$

### Multiply...

- when you are given an amount for *one* item and asked for the total amount of *many* of these items.

**Example:** If 1 book costs $6.50, what is the cost of 12 copies of the same book?

$$12(\$6.50) = \$78.00$$

### Divide...

- when you are given a total amount for *many* items and asked for the amount for *one* item.

**Example:** If 5 pounds of apples cost $6.75, what is the price of 1 pound of apples?

$$\$6.75 \div 5 = \$1.35$$

- when you are given the size of one group and the total size for many such identical groups and asked how many of the small groups fit into the larger one.

**Example:** How many groups of 30 students can be formed from a total of 240 students?

$$240 \div 30 = 8 \text{ groups of 30 students}$$

**SPECIAL WORD PROBLEMS TIP #1**

Don't try to combine several sentences into one equation; each sentence usually translates into a separate equation.

**SPECIAL WORD PROBLEMS TIP #2**

Pay attention to what the question asks for and make a note to yourself if it is not one of the unknowns in the equation(s). Otherwise, you may stop working on the problem too early.

## Logic Problems

You won't always have to set up an equation to solve a word problem. Some of the word problems you'll encounter on the GMAT won't fall into recognizable textbook categories. Many of these problems are designed to test your analytical and deductive logic. You can solve them with common sense and a little basic arithmetic. Ask yourself how it would be helpful to arrange the information, such as by drawing a diagram or making a table.

In these problems, the issue is not so much translating English into math as simply using your head. The problem may call for non-math skills, including the ability to organize and keep track of different possibilities, the ability to visualize something (for instance, the reverse side of a symmetrical shape), the ability to think of the exception that changes the answer to a problem, or the ability to deal with overlapping groups.

**Example:** If ! and ∫ are digits, and (! !)(∫ ∫) = 60∫, what is the value of ∫?

Since the symbols used each represent a digit from 0 to 9, you know that the product of the multiplication equals a value from 600 to 609. You know that each of the two quantities being multiplied consists of a two-digit integer in which both digits are the same. So, list the relevant two-digit integers (00, 11, 22, 33, 44, 55, 66, 77, 88, and 99) and see which two of them, when multiplied, have a product in the 600 to 609 range. Only (11)(55) satisfies this requirement, as $(11)(55) = 605$. The ∫ symbol equals 5.

## Tables, Graphs, and Charts

Some questions combine numbers and text with visual formats. Different formats are suitable for organizing different types of information. The formats that appear most frequently on GMAT math questions are tables, bar graphs, line graphs, and pie charts.

Questions involving tables, graphs, and charts may *look* different from other GMAT math questions, but the ideas and principles are the same. The problems are unusual only in the way that they present information, not in what they ask you to do with that information. Typically, they test your ability to work with percents and averages and your ability to solve for unknowns.

## Tables

The most basic way to organize information is to create a table. Tables are in some ways the most accurate graphic presentation format—the only way you can misunderstand a number is to read it from the wrong row or column—but they don't allow the reader to spot trends or extremes very readily.

Here's an example of a very simple table.

| John's Income: 2015–2019 | |
|---|---|
| YEAR | INCOME |
| 2015 | $20,000 |
| 2016 | $22,000 |
| 2017 | $18,000 |
| 2018 | $15,000 |
| 2019 | $28,000 |

An easy question might ask for John's income in a particular year or for the difference in his income between two years. To find the difference, you would simply look up the amount for both years and subtract the smaller income from the larger income. A harder question might ask for John's average annual income over the five-year period shown; to determine the average, you would have to find the sum of the five annual incomes and divide it by 5.

## Bar Graphs

Here's the same information about John's income. This time, it's presented as a bar graph.

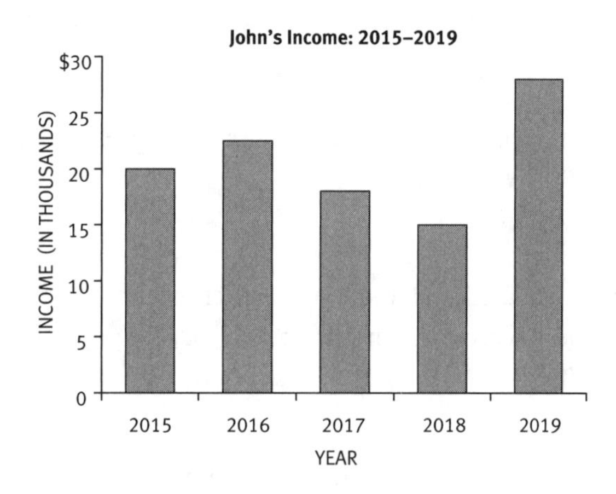


Bar graphs can be used to visually show information that would otherwise appear as numbers in a table. Bar graphs are somewhat less accurate than tables, but that's not necessarily a bad attribute, especially on the GMAT, where estimating often saves time on calculations.

What's handy about a bar graph is that you can see which values are larger or smaller without reading actual numbers. Just a glance at this graph shows that John's 2019 income was almost double his 2018 income. Numbers are represented on a bar graph by the heights or lengths of the bars. To find the height of a vertical bar, look for the point where a line drawn across the top of the bar parallel to the horizontal axis would intersect the vertical axis. To find the length of a horizontal bar, look for the point where a line drawn across the end of the bar parallel to the vertical axis would intersect the horizontal axis.

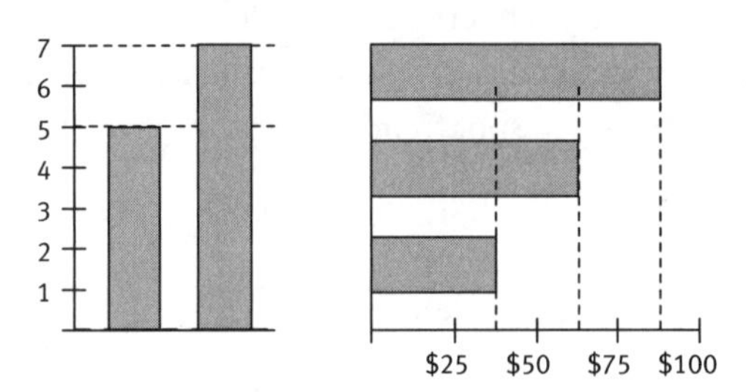


If the height or length of the bar falls in between two numbers on the axis, you will have to estimate.

## Line Graphs

Line graphs follow the same general principle as bar graphs, except that instead of using the lengths of bars to represent numbers, they use points connected by lines. The lines further emphasize the relative values of the numbers.

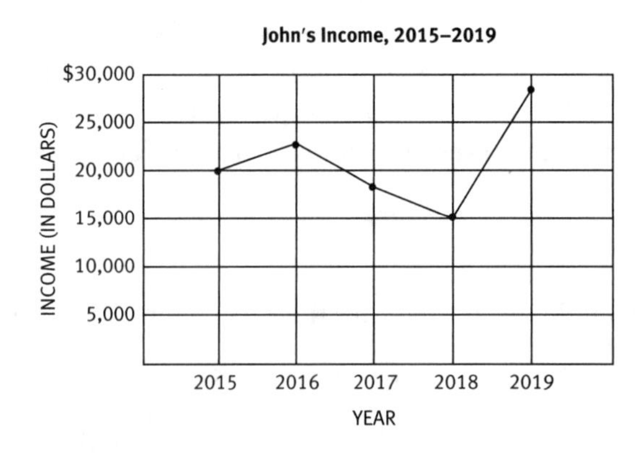


To read John's income for any particular year from this line graph, determine where a line drawn from the appropriate point would intersect the vertical axis.

## Pie Charts

Pie charts show how things are distributed: the fraction of a circle occupied by each piece of the "pie" indicates what fraction of the whole that piece represents. In most pie charts, the percentage of the pie occupied by each "slice" will be shown on the slice itself or, for very narrow slices, outside the circle with an arrow or a line pointing to the appropriate slice.

The total size of the whole pie is usually given at the top or bottom of the graph, either as "TOTAL = xxx" or as "100% = xxx." To find the approximate amount represented by a particular piece of the pie, just multiply the whole by the appropriate percent.

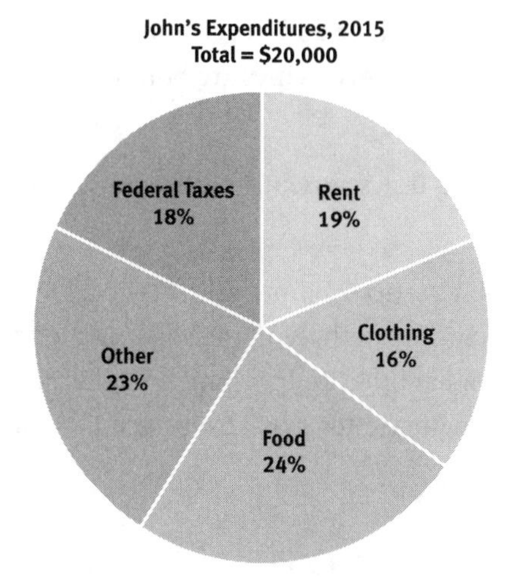


For instance, to find the total tax that John paid to the federal government in 2015, look at the slice of this chart labeled "Federal Taxes." It represents 18% of John's 2015 expenditures. Since his total 2015 expenditures were $20,000, he paid $0.18(\$20{,}000) = \$3{,}600$ in federal taxes in 2015.

One important note about pie charts: if you're not given the whole, and you don't know both the percentage and the actual number that at least one slice represents, you won't be able to find the whole. Pie charts are ideal for presenting the kind of information that ratio problems present in words.

# Geometry

## Lines and Angles

A **line** is a one-dimensional geometrical abstraction—infinitely long, with no width. A straight line is the shortest distance between any two points. There is exactly one straight line that passes through any two points.

A B C D

**Example:** In the figure above, $AC = 9$, $BD = 11$, and $AD = 15$. What is the length of $BC$?

When points are in a line and the order is known, you can add or subtract lengths. Since $AC = 9$ and $AD = 15$, $CD = AD - AC = 15 - 9 = 6$. Now, since $BD = 11$ and $CD = 6$, $BC = BD - CD = 11 - 6 = 5$.

A **line segment** is a section of a straight line of finite length with two endpoints. A line segment is named by its endpoints, as in segment $AB$.

6
A M B

**Example:** In the figure above, $A$ and $B$ are the endpoints of the line segment $AB$, and $M$ is the midpoint ($AM = MB$). What is the length of $AB$?

Since $AM$ is 6, $MB$ is also 6, and so $AB$ is $6 + 6$, or 12.

Two lines are **parallel** if they lie in the same plane and never intersect regardless of how far they are extended. If line $\ell_1$ is parallel to line $\ell_2$, we write $\ell_1 \parallel \ell_2$. If two lines are both parallel to a third line, then they are parallel to each other as well.

A **vertex** is the point at which two lines or line segments intersect to form an **angle**. Angles are measured in **degrees** (°).

Angles may be named according to their vertices. Sometimes, especially when two or more angles share a common vertex, an angle is named according to three points: a point along one of the lines or line segments that form the angle, the vertex point, and another point along the other line or line segment. A diagram will sometimes show a letter inside the angle; this letter may also be used to name the angle.

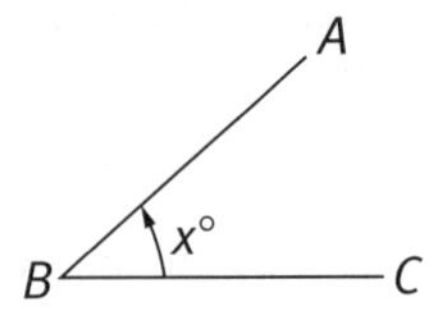


The angle shown in the diagram above could be called $\angle x$, $\angle ABC$, or $\angle B$.

### Sum of Angles Around a Point

The sum of the measures of the angles around a point is 360°.

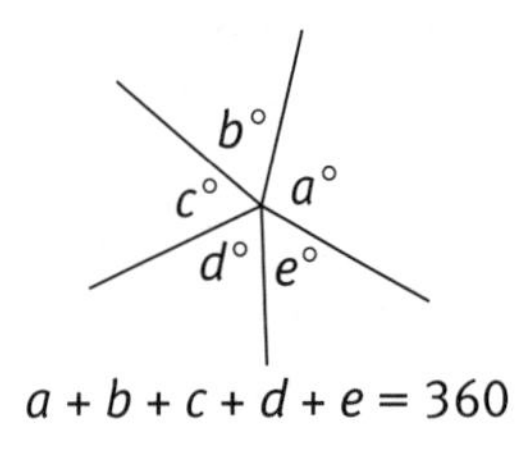


$$a + b + c + d + e = 360$$

### Sum of Angles Along a Straight Line

The sum of the measures of the angles on one side of a straight line is 180°. Two angles are *supplementary* to each other if their measures sum to 180°.

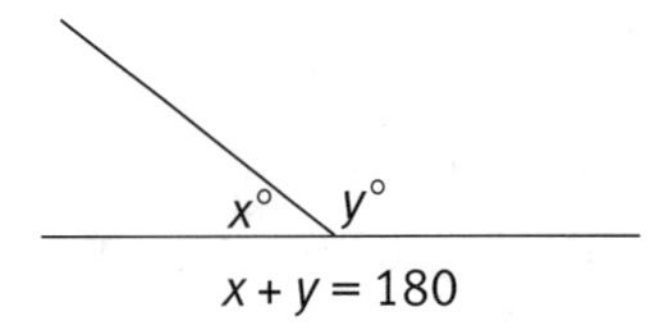


$$x + y = 180$$

### Perpendicularity and Right Angles

Two lines are perpendicular if they intersect at a 90° angle (a right angle). If line $\ell_1$ is perpendicular to line $\ell_2$, you write $\ell_1 \perp \ell_2$. If lines $\ell_1$, $\ell_2$, and $\ell_3$ all lie in the same plane, and $\ell_1 \perp \ell_2$ and $\ell_2 \perp \ell_3$, then $\ell_1 \parallel \ell_3$, as shown in the diagram below.

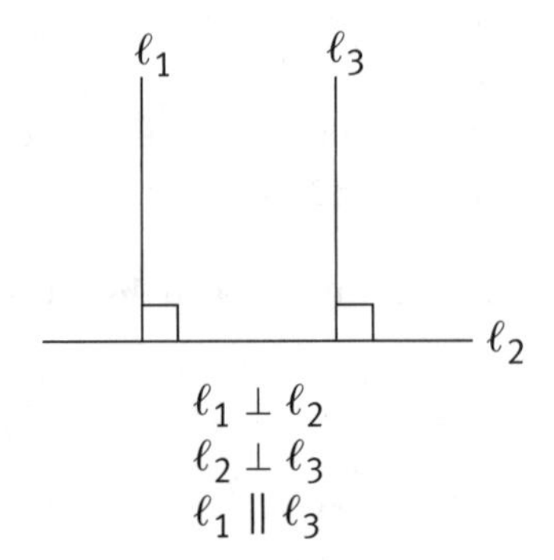

To find the shortest distance from a point to a line, draw a line segment from the point to the line such that the line segment is perpendicular to the line. Then, measure the length of that segment.

**Example:** $\angle A$ of triangle $ABC$ is a right angle. Is side $BC$ longer or shorter than side $AB$?

This question seems very abstract until you draw a diagram of a right triangle, labeling the vertex with the 90° angle as point $A$.

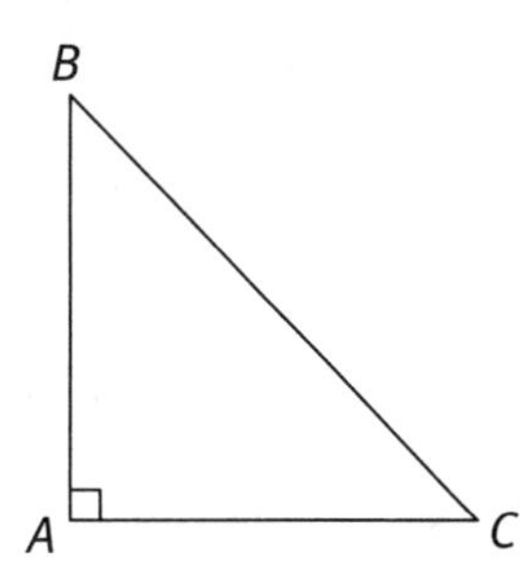


Line segment $AB$ has to be the shortest route between point $B$ and side $AC$, since side $AB$ is perpendicular to side $AC$. If $AB$ is the shortest line segment that can join point $B$ to side $AC$, $BC$ must be longer than $AB$. **Note:** The side opposite the 90° angle, called the *hypotenuse*, is always the longest side of a right triangle.

Two angles are *complementary* to each other if their measures sum to 90°. An *acute angle* measures less than 90°, and an *obtuse angle* measures between 90° and 180°. Two angles are *supplementary* if their measures sum to 180°.

## Angle Bisectors

A line or line segment bisects an angle if it splits the angle into two smaller, equal angles. Line segment $BD$ below bisects $\angle ABC$, and $\angle ABD$ has the same measure as $\angle DBC$. The two smaller angles are each half the size of $\angle ABC$.

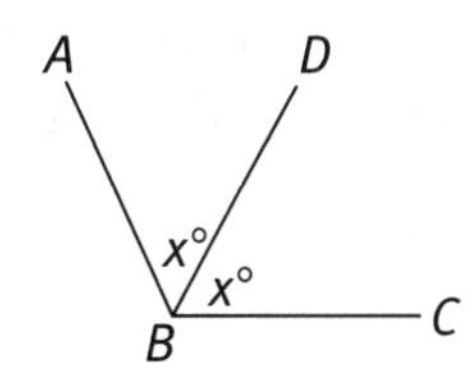


$BD$ bisects $\angle ABC$

$\angle ABD + \angle DBC = \angle ABC$

## Adjacent and Vertical Angles

Two intersecting lines form four angles. The angles that are adjacent (next) to each other are *supplementary* because they lie along a straight line. The two angles that are not adjacent to each other are *opposite*, or *vertical*. Opposite angles are equal in measure because each of them is supplementary to the same adjacent angle.

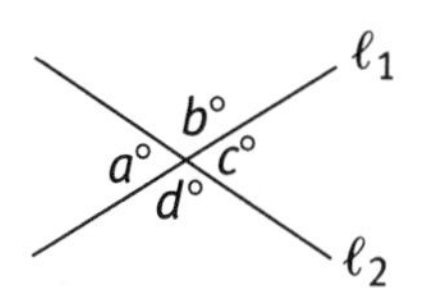

In the previous diagram, $\ell_1$ intersects $\ell_2$ to form angles *a*, *b*, *c*, and *d*. Angles *a* and *c* are opposite, as are angles *b* and *d*. So, the measures of angles *a* and *c* are equal to each other, the measures of angles *b* and *d* are equal to each other, and each angle is supplementary to each of its two adjacent angles.

### Angles Around Parallel Lines Intersected by a Transversal

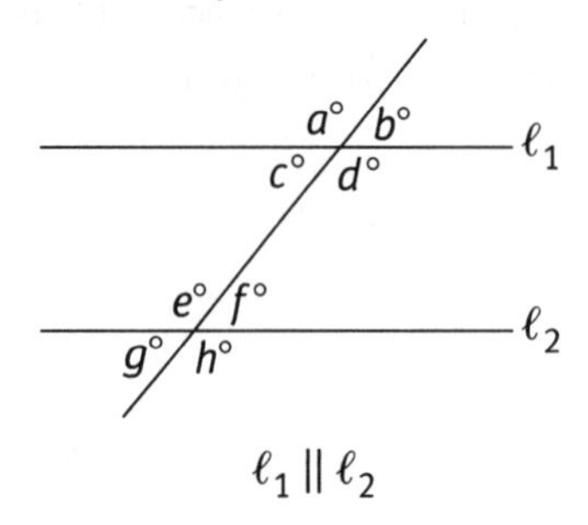


$\ell_1 \parallel \ell_2$

A line that intersects two parallel lines is called a *transversal.* Each of the parallel lines intersects the third line at the same angle. In the figure above, $a = e$. Since *a* and *e* are equal, and since $a = d$ and $e = h$ (because they are opposite angles), $a = d = e = h$. By similar reasoning, $b = c = f = g$.

In short, when two (or more) parallel lines are cut by a transversal, all acute angles formed are equal; all obtuse angles formed are equal; and any acute angle formed is supplementary to any obtuse angle formed.

**Example:**

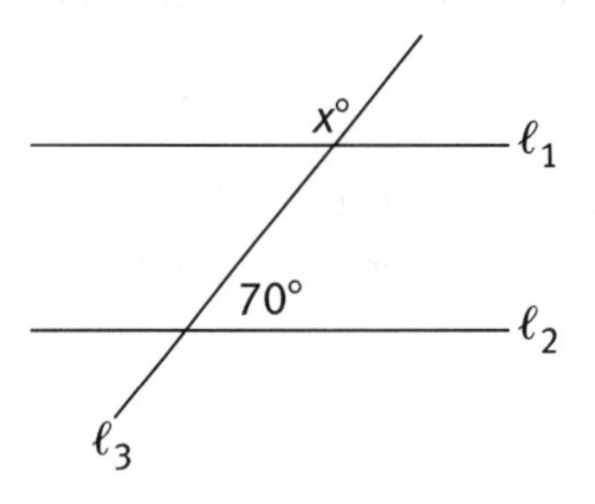


In the diagram above, line $\ell_1$ is parallel to line $\ell_2$. What is the value of *x*?

The angle marked $x°$ and the angle adjacent and to the left of the 70° angle on line $\ell_2$ are corresponding angles. Therefore, the angle marked $x°$ must be supplementary to the 70° angle. If $70° + x° = 180°$, *x* must equal 110.

## Polygons

### Important Terms

**Polygon:** A closed figure whose sides are straight line segments. Families or classes of polygons are named according to the number of sides. A triangle has three sides, a quadrilateral has four sides, a pentagon has five sides, and a hexagon has six sides. Triangles and quadrilaterals are by far the most important polygons on the GMAT; other polygons appear only occasionally.

**Perimeter:** The distance around a polygon; the sum of the lengths of its sides.

**Vertex of a polygon:** A point where two sides intersect; *pl.* vertices. Polygons are named by assigning each vertex a letter and listing them in order, as in pentagon $ABCDE$ below.

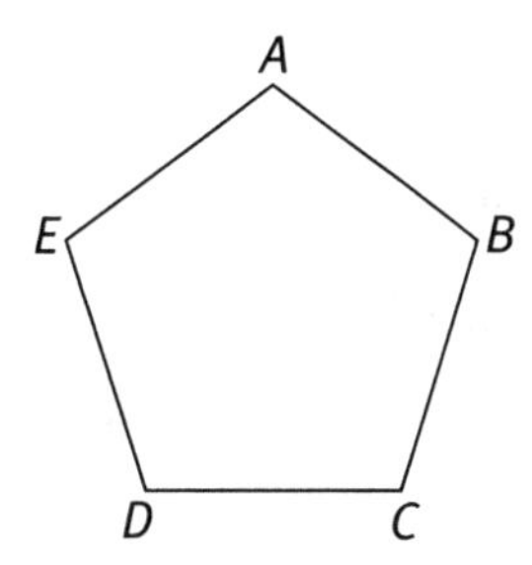


**Diagonal of a polygon:** A line segment connecting any two nonadjacent vertices.

**Regular polygon:** A polygon with sides of equal length and interior angles of equal measure.

Small slash marks can provide important information in diagrams of polygons. Sides with the same number of slash marks are equal in length, while angles with the same number of slash marks through circular arcs have the same measure. In the triangle below, for example, $a = b$, and angles $X$ and $Z$ are equal in measure.

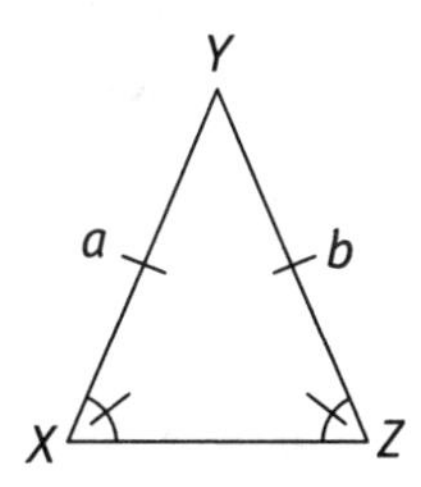


You can figure out the sum of the interior angles of a polygon by dividing the polygon into triangles. Draw diagonals from any vertex to all the nonadjacent vertices. Then, multiply the number of triangles by 180° to get the sum of the interior angles of the polygon. This works because the sum of the interior angles of any triangle is always 180°.

**Example:** What is the sum of the interior angles of a pentagon?

Draw a pentagon (a five-sided polygon) and divide it into triangles, as discussed above.

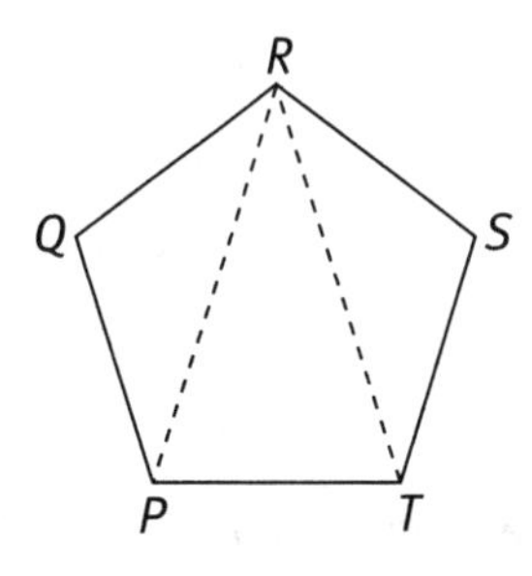


No matter how you've drawn the pentagon, you'll be able to form three triangles. Therefore, the sum of the interior angles of a pentagon is $3 \times 180° = 540°$.

## Triangles

### Important Terms

**Triangle:** A polygon with three straight sides and three interior angles.

**Right triangle:** A triangle with one interior angle of 90° (a right angle).

**Hypotenuse:** The longest side of a right triangle. The hypotenuse is always opposite the right angle.

**Isosceles triangle:** A triangle with two equal sides, which are opposite two equal angles. In the figure below, the sides opposite the two 70° angles are equal, so $x = 7$.

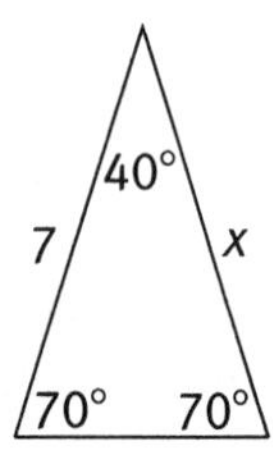


**Legs:** The two equal sides of an isosceles triangle, or the two shorter sides of a right triangle (the ones forming the right angle). **Note:** The third, unequal side of an isosceles triangle is called the *base*.

**Equilateral triangle:** A triangle whose three sides are all equal in length and whose three interior angles each measure 60°.

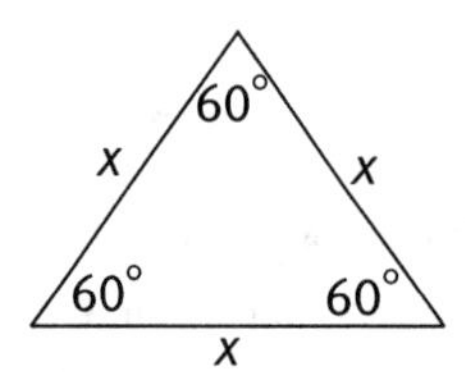


The **altitude**, or **height**, of a triangle is the perpendicular distance from a vertex to the side opposite the vertex. The altitude may fall inside or outside the triangle, or it may coincide with one of the sides.

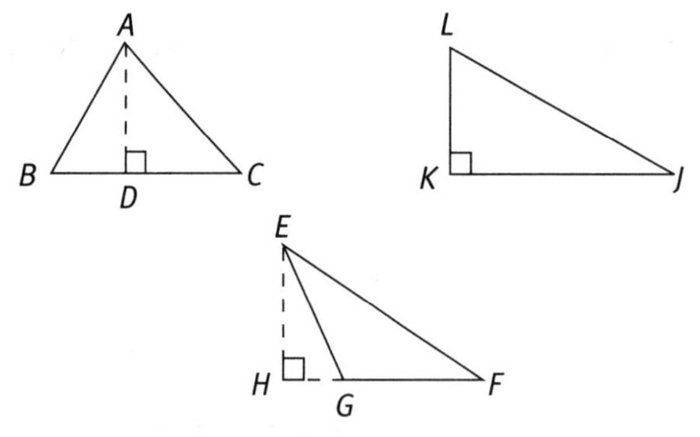


In the diagrams above, *AD*, *EH*, and *LK* are altitudes.

## Interior and Exterior Angles of a Triangle

The sum of the interior angles of any triangle is 180°. Therefore, in the figure below, $a + b + c = 180$.

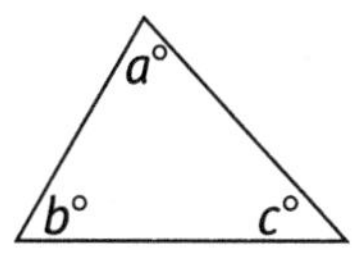


An *exterior angle of a triangle* is equal to the sum of the remote interior angles. In the figure below, the exterior angle labeled $x°$ is equal to the sum of the remote angles: $x = 50 + 100 = 150$.

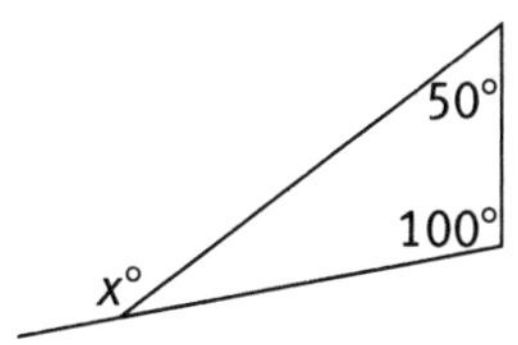


The three exterior angles of any triangle add up to 360°.

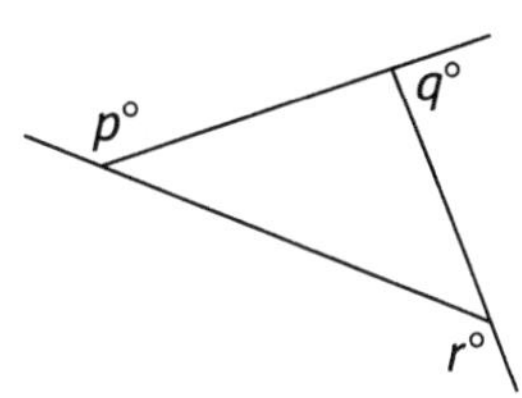


In the figure above, $p + q + r = 360$.

## Sides and Angles

The sum of the lengths of any two sides of a triangle is greater than the length of the third side. In the triangle below, $b + c > a$, $a + b > c$, and $a + c > b$.

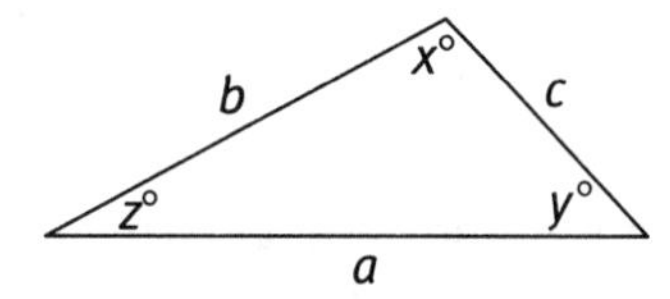


If the lengths of two sides of a triangle are unequal, the greater angle lies opposite the longer side, and vice versa. In the figure above, if $x > y > z$, then $a > b > c$.

Since the two legs of an isosceles triangle have the same length, the two angles opposite the legs must have the same measure. In the figure below, $PQ = PR$, and $\angle Q = \angle R$.

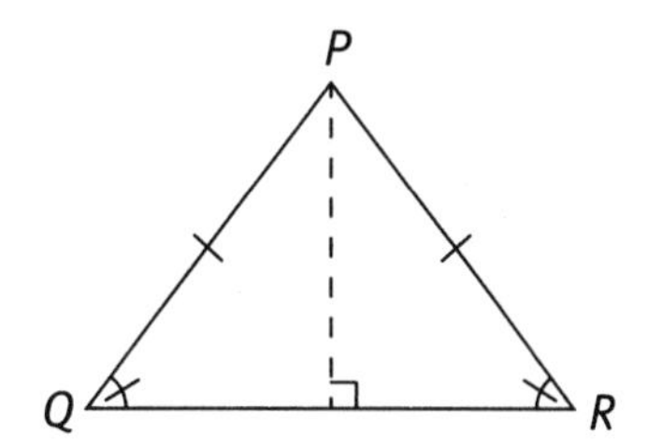

## Perimeter and Area of Triangles

There is no special formula for the perimeter of a triangle; it is just the sum of the lengths of the sides.

**Example:**

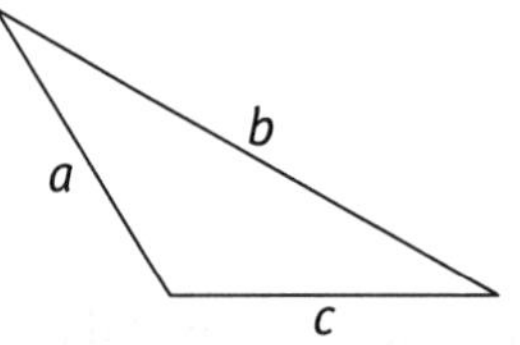


If $b = 2a$ and $c = \frac{b}{2}$, find the perimeter of the triangle above in terms of $a$.

Perimeter $= a + b + c = a + 2a + \frac{2a}{2} = 3a + \frac{2a}{2} = 3a + a = 4a$.

Incidentally, this is really an isosceles triangle, since $c = \frac{b}{2} = \frac{2a}{2} = a$.

The area of a triangle is $\left(\frac{1}{2}\right)$ (Base)(Height).

**Example:**

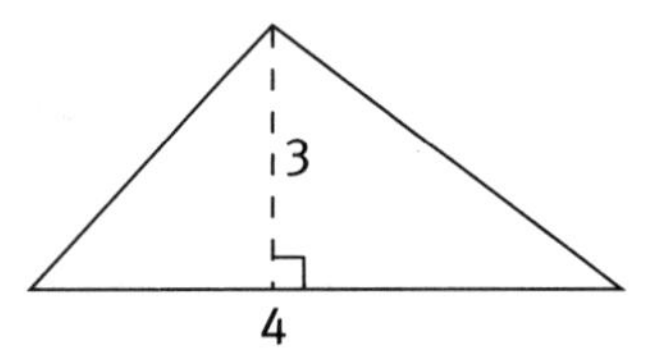


In the diagram above, the base has length 4 and the altitude has length 3. What is the area of the triangle?

$$\begin{aligned} \text{Area} &= \frac{1}{2}bh \\ &= \frac{bh}{2} \\ &= \frac{4 \times 3}{2} \\ &= 6 \end{aligned}$$

Since the lengths of the base and altitude were not given in specific units, such as centimeters or feet, the area of the triangle is simply said to be 6 square units.

The area of a right triangle is easy to find. Think of one leg as the base and the other as the height. The area is one-half the product of the legs, or $\frac{1}{2} \times \text{Leg}_1 \times \text{Leg}_2$.

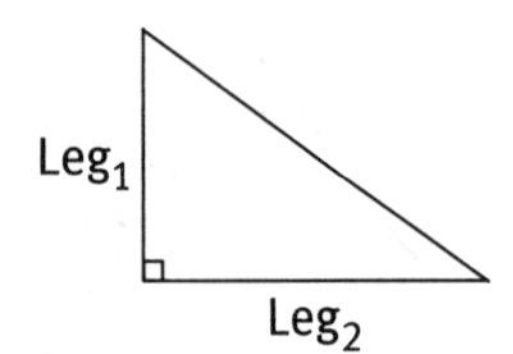

## Right Triangles

The right angle is always the largest angle in a right triangle; therefore, the hypotenuse, which lies opposite the right angle, is always the longest side.

### Pythagorean Theorem

The Pythagorean theorem, which holds for all right triangles and for no other triangles, states that the square of the hypotenuse is equal to the sum of the squares of the legs.

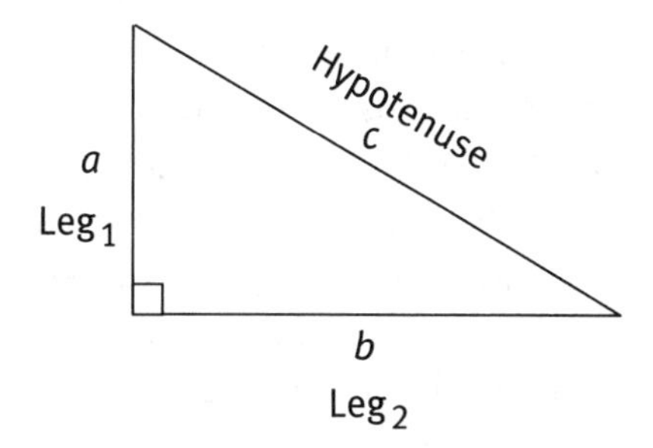


$$(\text{Leg}_1)^2 + (\text{Leg}_2)^2 = (\text{Hypotenuse})^2$$
$$\textbf{or } a^2 + b^2 = c^2$$

The Pythagorean theorem is very useful whenever you're given the lengths of any two sides of a right triangle; as long as you know whether the remaining side is a leg or the hypotenuse, you can find its length by using the Pythagorean theorem.

**Example:** What is the length of the hypotenuse of a right triangle with legs of lengths 9 and 10?

$$\begin{aligned}(\text{Hypotenuse})^2 &= (\text{Leg}_1)^2 + (\text{Leg}_2)^2 \\ &= 9^2 + 10^2 \\ &= 81 + 100 \\ &= 181\end{aligned}$$

If the square of the hypotenuse equals 181, then the hypotenuse itself must be the square root of 181, or $\sqrt{181}$.

### Pythagorean Triples

Certain ratios of integers always satisfy the Pythagorean theorem. You might like to think of them as "Pythagorean triples." One such ratio is 3, 4, and 5. A right triangle with legs of lengths 3 and 4 and hypotenuse of length 5 is probably the most common kind of right triangle on the GMAT. Whenever you see a right triangle with legs of 3 and 4, with a leg of 3 and a hypotenuse of 5, or with a leg of 4 and a hypotenuse of 5, you immediately know the length of the remaining side. In addition, any multiple of these lengths makes another Pythagorean triple; for instance, $6^2 + 8^2 = 10^2$, so a triangle with sides of lengths 6, 8, and 10 is also a right triangle.

The other triple that commonly appears on the GMAT is 5, 12, and 13.

## Special Right Triangles

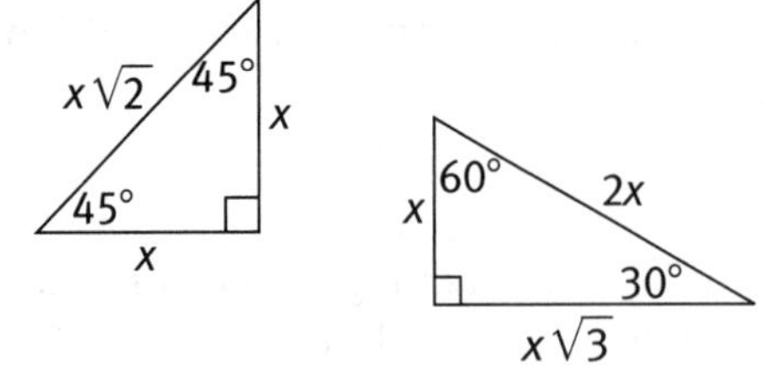


There are two more special kinds of right triangles for which you won't have to use the Pythagorean theorem to find the lengths of the sides. There are special ratios between the lengths of the sides in isosceles right triangles (45°/45°/90° right triangles) and 30°/60°/90° right triangles (right triangles with acute angles of 30° and 60°). As you can see in the first drawing above, the sides of an isosceles right triangle are in a ratio of $x{:}x{:}x\sqrt{2}$, with the $x\sqrt{2}$ in the ratio representing the hypotenuse. The sides of a 30°/60°/90° right triangle are in a ratio of $x{:}x\sqrt{3}{:}2x$, where $2x$ represents the hypotenuse and $x$ represents the side opposite the 30° angle. (Remember: The longest side has to be opposite the greatest angle.)

**Example:** What is the length of the hypotenuse of an isosceles right triangle with legs of length 4?

You can use the Pythagorean theorem to find the hypotenuse, but it's quicker to use the special right triangle ratios. In an isosceles right triangle, the ratio of a leg to the hypotenuse is $x{:}x\sqrt{2}$. Since the length of a leg is 4, the length of the hypotenuse must be $4\sqrt{2}$.

### Triangles and Data Sufficiency

In all Data Sufficiency questions, the approach is to focus on the information you need to answer the question. In geometry, that's often a matter of knowing the correct definition or formula (but not using it!). With triangles, keep in mind the following:

- If you know two angles, you know the third.
- To find the area, you need the base and the height.
- In a right triangle, if you have two sides, you can find the third. And if you have two sides, you can find the area.
- In isosceles right triangles and 30°/60°/90° triangles, if you know one side, you can find everything.

Be careful though! Be sure you know as much as you think you do.

**Example:** What is the area of right triangle *ABC*?

(1) $AB = 5$

(2) $BC = 4$

Clearly, neither statement alone is sufficient. You may think at first that both together are enough, since it looks like *ABC* is a 3:4:5 right triangle. Not so fast! You're given two sides, but you don't know which sides they are. If *AB* is the hypotenuse, then it is a 3:4:5 triangle, and the area is $\frac{1}{2}(3 \times 4) = 6$, but it's also possible that *AC*, the missing side, is the hypotenuse. In that case, the area would be $\frac{1}{2}(4 \times 5) = 10$. Together, then, the statements are still not sufficient. So the correct answer is **(E)**: neither statement by itself is sufficient, and the statements together are insufficient.

## Distances and Right Triangles in Coordinate Geometry

The distance between two points is equal to the length of the straight-line segment that has those two points as endpoints.

If a line segment is parallel to the *x*-axis, the *y*-coordinate of every point on the line segment will be the same. Similarly, if a line segment is parallel to the *y*-axis, the *x*-coordinate of every point on the line segment will be the same.

Therefore, to find the length of a line segment parallel to one of the axes, all you have to do is find the difference between the endpoint coordinates that do change. In the diagram below, the length of *AB* equals $x_2 - x_1$.

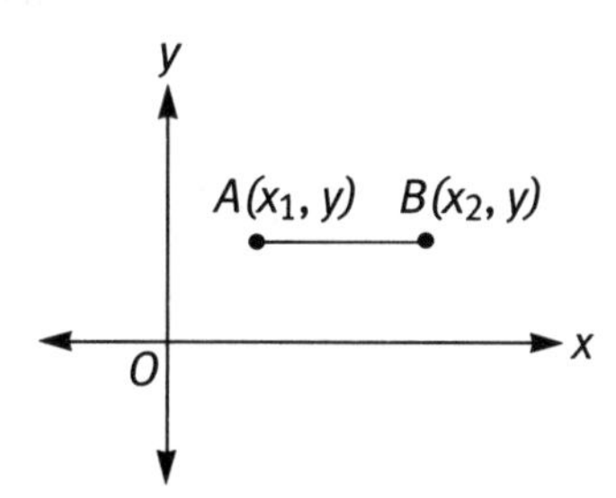


You can find the length of a line segment that is not parallel to one of the axes by treating the line segment as the hypotenuse of a right triangle. Simply draw in the legs of the triangle parallel to the two axes. The length of each leg will be the difference between the *x*- or *y*-coordinates of its endpoints. Once you've found the lengths of the legs, you can use the Pythagorean theorem to find the length of the hypotenuse (the original line segment).

In the diagram below, $(DE)^2 = (EF)^2 + (DF)^2$.

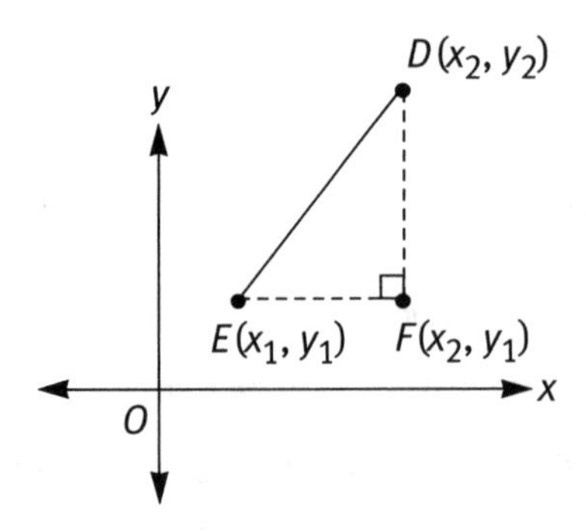


**Example:** If the coordinates of point $A$ are (3,4), and the coordinates of point $B$ are (6,8), what is the distance between points $A$ and $B$?

You don't have to draw a diagram to use the method just described, but drawing one may help you to visualize the problem. Plot points $A$ and $B$ and draw in line segment $AB$. The length of $AB$ is the distance between the two points. Now draw a right triangle, with $AB$ as its hypotenuse. The missing vertex will be the intersection of a line segment drawn through point $A$ parallel to the $x$-axis and a line segment drawn through point $B$ parallel to the $y$-axis. Label the point of intersection $C$. Since the $x$- and $y$-axes are perpendicular to each other, $AC$ and $BC$ will also be perpendicular to each other.

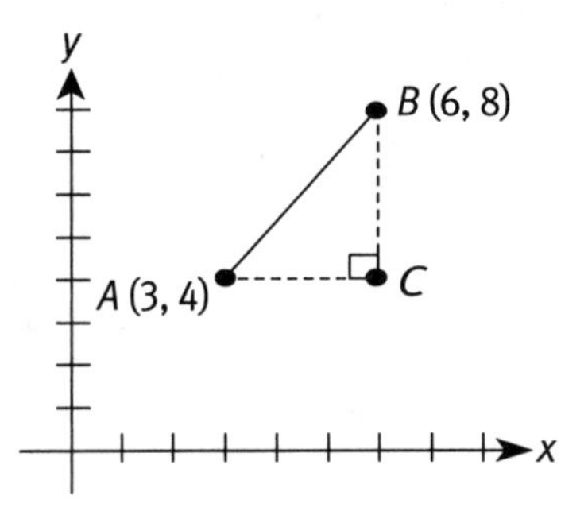


Point $C$ will have the same $x$-coordinate as point $B$ and the same $y$-coordinate as point $A$. That means that point $C$ has coordinates (6,4).

To use the Pythagorean theorem, you'll need the lengths of $AC$ and $BC$. The distance between points $A$ and $C$ is simply the difference between their $x$-coordinates, while the distance between points $B$ and $C$ is the difference between their $y$-coordinates. So, $AC = 6 - 3 = 3$ and $BC = 8 - 4 = 4$. If you recognize these as the legs of a 3:4:5 right triangle, you'll know immediately that the distance between points $A$ and $B$ must be 5. Otherwise, you'll have to use the Pythagorean theorem to come to the same conclusion.

## Quadrilaterals

A **quadrilateral** is a four-sided polygon. Regardless of a quadrilateral's shape, the four interior angles sum to 360°.

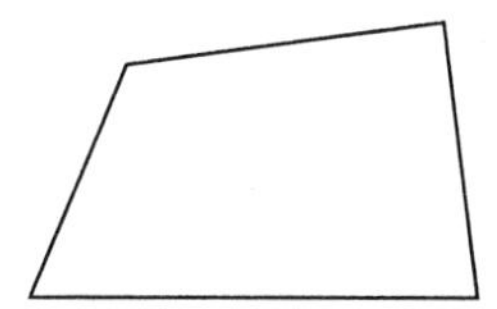

A **parallelogram** is a quadrilateral with two pairs of parallel sides. Opposite sides are equal in length; opposite angles are equal in measure; and angles that are not opposite are supplementary to each other (measure of $\angle A$ + measure of $\angle D = 180°$ in the figure below).

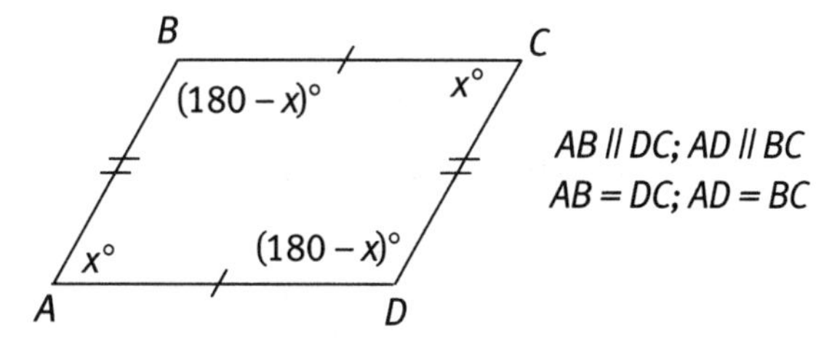


*measure of* $\angle A$ = *measure of* $\angle C$;
*measure of* $\angle B$ = *measure of* $\angle D$

A **rectangle** is a parallelogram with four right angles. Opposite sides are equal; diagonals are equal.

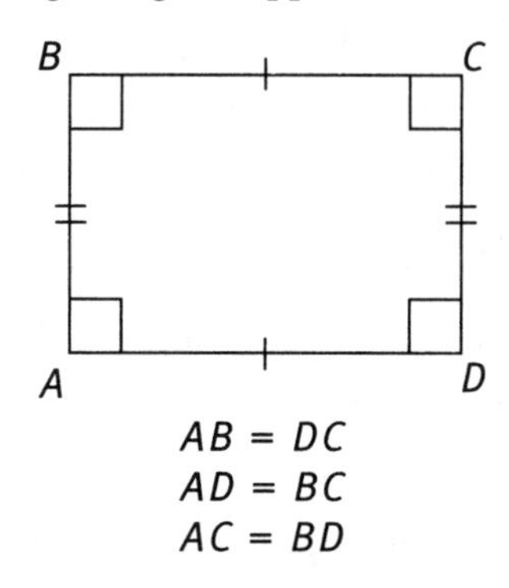


$AB = DC$
$AD = BC$
$AC = BD$

A **square** is a rectangle with equal sides.

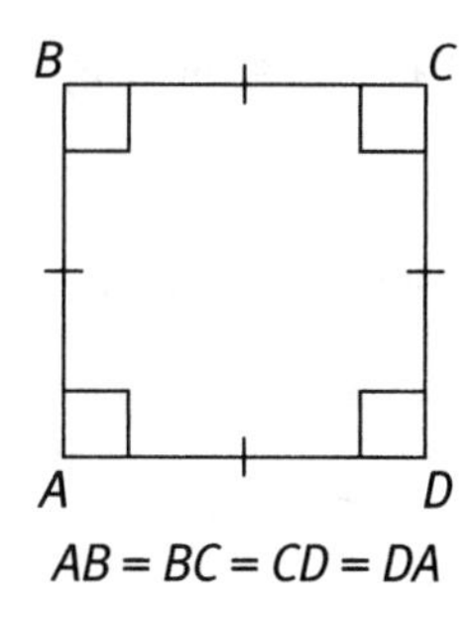


$AB = BC = CD = DA$

### Perimeters of Quadrilaterals

To find the perimeter of any polygon, you can simply add the lengths of its sides. However, the properties of rectangles and squares lead to simple formulas that may speed up your calculations.

Because the opposite sides are equal, the *perimeter of a rectangle* is twice the sum of the length and the width:

$$\text{Perimeter} = 2(\text{Length} + \text{Width})$$

The perimeter of a 5 by 2 rectangle is $2(5 + 2) = 14$.

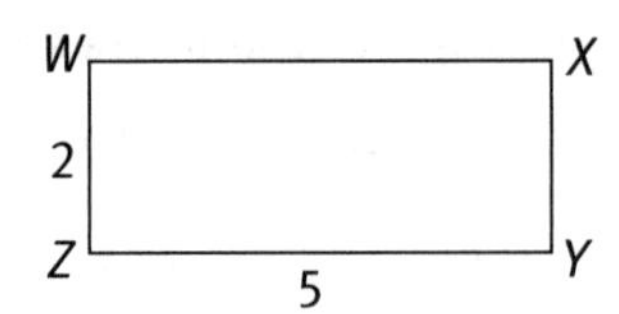


The *perimeter of a square* is equal to the sum of the lengths of the 4 sides. Because all 4 sides are the same length, Perimeter = 4(Side). If the length of one side of a square is 3, the perimeter is $4 \times 3 = 12$.

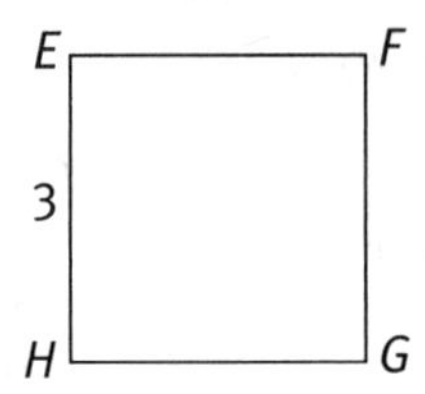


## Areas of Quadrilaterals

Area formulas always involve multiplication, and the results are always stated in "square" units. You can see why if you look at the drawing below:

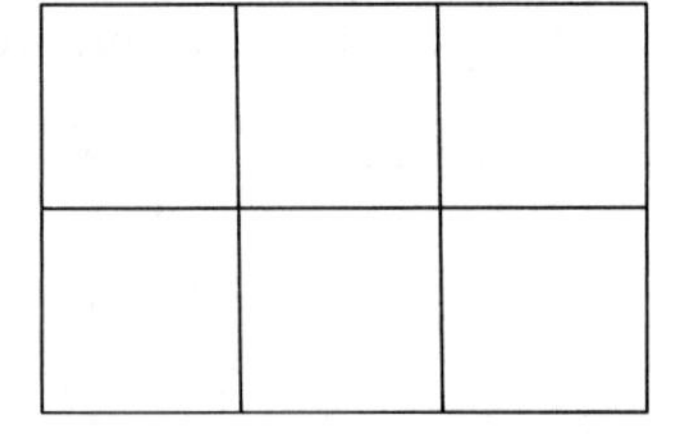

The rectangle is composed of six squares, all equal in size. Suppose the side of a single small square is 1 unit. Then, you would say that a single square measures "1 by 1." That translates into math as $1 \times 1$, or $1^2$—in other words, "one square unit."

As you can see from the drawing, there are 6 such square units in the rectangle. That's its area: 6 square units. But you could also find the area by multiplying the number of squares in a row by the number of squares in a column: $3 \times 2$, or 6. And since the length of the side of a square is 1 unit, that's also equivalent to multiplying the length of a horizontal side by the length of a vertical side: again, $3 \times 2 = 6$.

## Formulas for Area

To find the area of a rectangle, multiply the **length** by the **width**.

Area of rectangle = $lw$

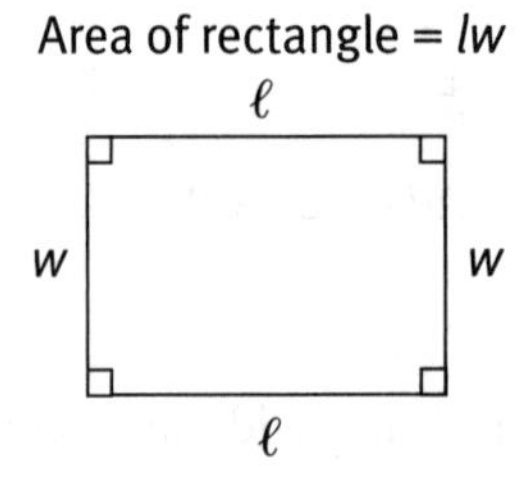

Since the length and width of a square are equal, the area formula for a square just uses the length of a **side**:

$$\text{Area of square} = (\text{Side})^2 = s^2$$

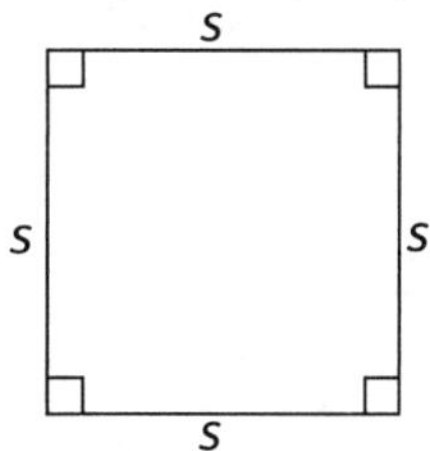


If you're working with a parallelogram, designate one side as the **base**. Then, draw a line segment from one of the vertices opposite the base down to the base so that it intersects the base at a right angle. That line segment will be called the **height**. To find the area of the parallelogram, multiply the length of the base by the length of the height:

$$\text{Area of parallelogram} = (\text{Base})(\text{Height}), \text{ or } A = bh$$

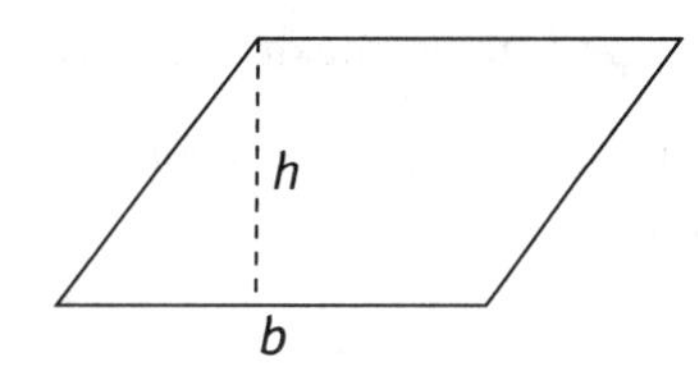


### Quadrilaterals and Data Sufficiency

Remember the following:

- In a parallelogram, if you know two adjacent sides, you know all of them; and if you know two adjacent angles, you know all of them.
- In a rectangle, if you know two adjacent sides, you know the area.
- In a square, if you're given virtually any measurement (area, length of a side, length of a diagonal), you can figure out the other measurements.

## Circles

### Important Terms

**Circle:** The set of all points in a plane at the same distance from a certain point. This point is called the center of the circle. A circle is labeled by its center point; circle *O* means the circle with center point *O*.

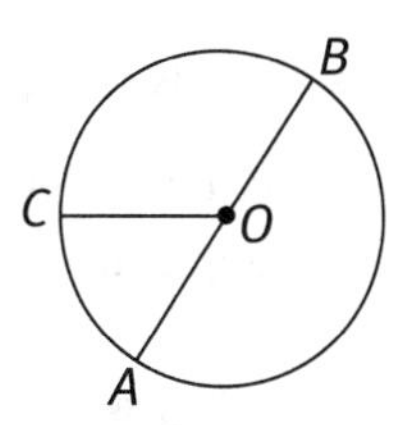


**Diameter:** A line segment that connects two points on the circle and passes through the center of the circle. *AB* is a diameter of circle *O* above.

**Radius:** A line segment that connects the center of the circle with any point on the circle; *pl.* radii. The radius of a circle is one-half the length of the diameter. In circle *O* above, *OA*, *OB*, and *OC* are radii.

**Central angle:** An angle formed by two radii. In circle $O$ above, $AOC$ is a central angle. $COB$ and $BOA$ are also central angles. (The measure of $BOA$ happens to be 180°.) The total degree measure of a circle is 360°.

**Chord:** A line segment that joins two points on the circle. The longest chord of a circle is its diameter. $AT$ is a chord of circle $P$ below.

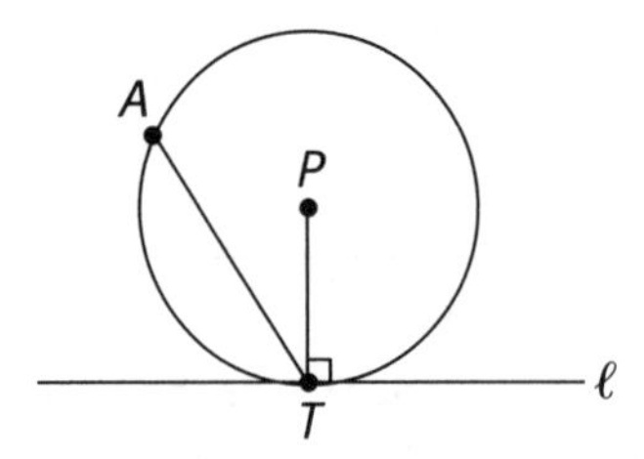


**Tangent:** A line that touches only one point on the circumference of a circle. A line drawn tangent to a circle is perpendicular to the radius at the point of tangency. In the diagram above, line $\ell$ is tangent to circle $P$ at point $T$.

## Circumference and Arc Length

The distance around a polygon is called its **perimeter**; the distance around a circle is called its **circumference**.

The ratio of the circumference of any circle to its diameter is a constant, called **pi** ($\pi$). For GMAT purposes, the value of $\pi$ is usually approximated as 3.14.

Since $\pi$ equals the ratio of the circumference, $C$, to the diameter, $d$, you can say that $\pi = \frac{\text{Circumference}}{\text{Diameter}} = \frac{C}{d}$.

The formula for the circumference of a circle is $C = \pi d$.

The circumference formula can also be stated in terms of the radius, $r$. Since the diameter is twice the length of the radius, that is, $d = 2r$, then $C = 2\pi r$.

An **arc** is a section of the circumference of a circle. Any arc can be thought of as the portion of a circle cut off by a particular central angle. For example, in circle $Q$, arc $ABC$ is the portion of the circle that is cut off by central angle $AQC$. Since arcs are associated with central angles, they can be measured in degrees. The degree measure of an arc is equal to that of the central angle that cuts it off. So, in circle $Q$, arc $ABC$ and central angle $AQC$ would have the same degree measure.

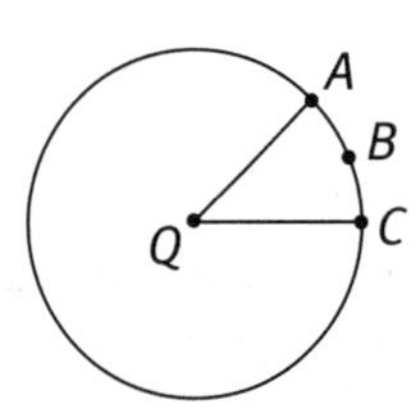


An arc that is exactly half the circumference of its circle is called a **semicircle**.

The length of an arc is the same fraction of a circle's circumference as its degree measure is of 360° (the degree measure of a whole circle). For an arc with a central angle measuring $n$°:

$$\begin{aligned}\text{Arc length} &= \frac{n}{360}(\text{Circumference}) \\ &= \frac{n}{360} \times 2\pi r\end{aligned}$$

**Example:**

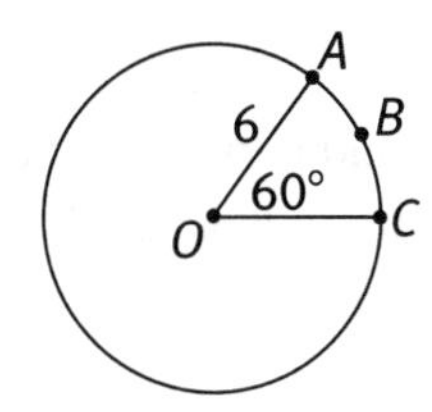


What is the length of arc *ABC* of circle *O* above?

$C = 2\pi r$; therefore, if $r = 6$, $C = 2 \times \pi \times 6 = 12\pi$. Since *AOC* measures 60°, arc *ABC* is $\frac{60}{360}$, or $\frac{1}{6}$, of the circumference. Thus, the length of arc *ABC* is $\frac{1}{6} \times 12\pi$, or $2\pi$.

### Area and Sector Area Formulas

The area of a circle is $\pi r^2$.

A sector is a portion of a circle's area that is bounded by two radii and an arc. The shaded area of circle *X* is sector *AXB*.

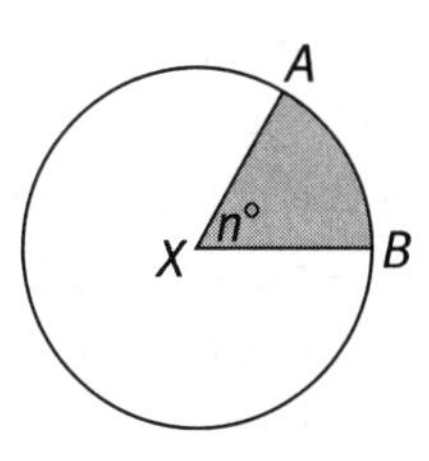


Like arcs, sectors are associated with central angles. And the process and formula used to find the area of a sector are similar to those used to determine arc length. First, find the degree measure of the sector's central angle and figure out what fraction that degree measure is of 360°. Then, multiply the area of the whole circle by that fraction. In a sector whose central angle measures $n°$:

$$\text{Area of sector} = \frac{n}{360}(\text{Area of circle})$$
$$= \frac{n}{360}\pi r^2$$

**Example:**

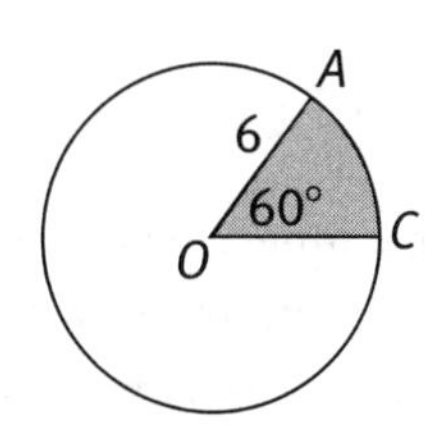


In circle *O* above, what is the area of sector *AOC*?

Since $\angle AOC$ measures 60°, a 60° "slice" of the circle is $\frac{60°}{360°}$, or $\frac{1}{6}$ of the total area of the circle. Therefore, the area of the sector is $\frac{1}{6}\pi r^2 = \frac{1}{6}(36\pi) = 6\pi$.

## Circles and Data Sufficiency

A circle is a regular shape whose area and perimeter can be determined through the use of formulas. If you're given virtually any measurement (radius, diameter, circumference, area), you can determine all the other measurements.

**Example:**

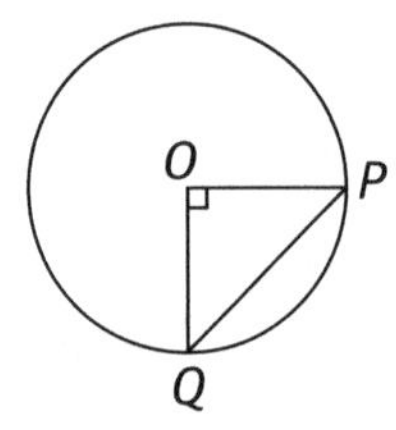


What is the circumference of the circle with center *O*?

(1) The length of chord $PQ = 4\sqrt{2}$.

(2) The area of sector *POQ* is $4\pi$.

To find the circumference, you need the radius, which is either *OP* or *OQ* in this circle. Statement (1) gives the length of *PQ*. *PQ* is a chord of the circle (it connects two points on the circle), but it's also the hypotenuse of right triangle *OPQ*. Do you know anything else about that triangle? Since *OP* and *OQ* are both radii of the circle, they must have the same length, so the triangle is an isosceles right triangle. That means that knowing the hypotenuse tells you the length of each leg, which gives the radius, and is enough to allow calculation of the circumference. Statement (1) is sufficient.

Statement (2) gives you the area of the sector. Since the angle at *O* is a right angle, you know that the sector must be one-quarter of the whole circle. Therefore, knowing the area of the sector can allow calculation of the area of the whole circle, and from that you can find the radius and then the circumference. Because Statement (2) is also sufficient, the correct answer is **(D)**: either statement, by itself, is sufficient.

# Solids

## Important Terms

**Solid:** A three-dimensional figure. The dimensions are usually called length, width, and height ($\ell$, $w$, and $h$) or height, width, and depth ($h$, $w$, and $d$). There are only two types of solids that appear with any frequency on the GMAT: rectangular solids (including cubes) and cylinders.

**Uniform solid:** A solid that could be cut into congruent cross sections (parallel "slices" of equal size and shape) along a given axis. Solids you see on the GMAT will almost certainly be uniform solids.

**Face:** The surface of a solid that lies in a particular plane. Hexagon *ABCDEF* is one face of the solid pictured below.

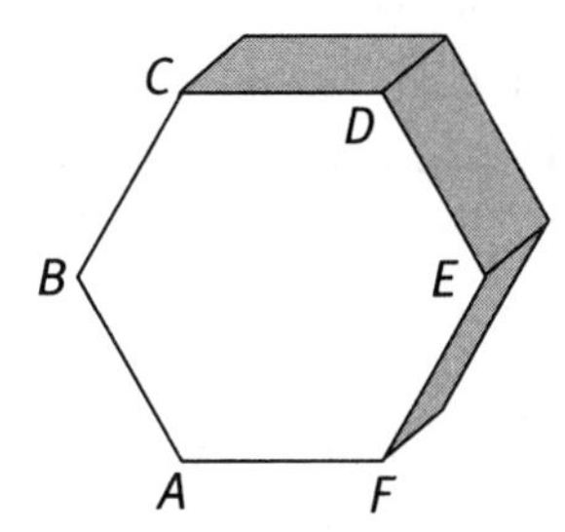


**Edge:** A line segment that connects adjacent faces of a solid. The sides of hexagon *ABCDEF* are also edges of the solid pictured above.

**Base:** The "bottom" face of a solid as oriented in any given diagram.

**Rectangular solid:** A solid with six rectangular faces. All edges meet at right angles. Examples of rectangular solids are cereal boxes, bricks, etc.

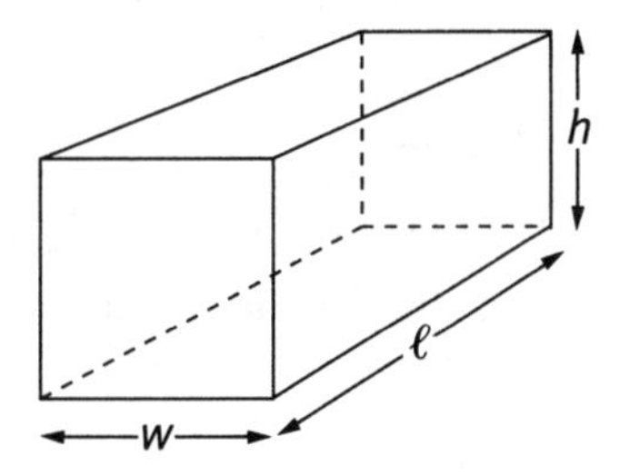


**Cube:** A special rectangular solid in which all edges are of equal length, *e*, and therefore all faces are squares. Sugar cubes and dice without rounded corners are examples of cubes.

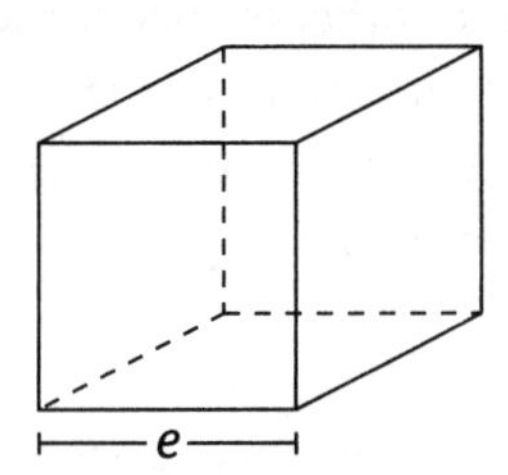


**Cylinder:** A uniform solid whose horizontal cross section is a circle—for example, a soup can or a pipe that is closed at both ends. A cylinder's measurements are generally given in terms of its radius, *r*, and its height, *h*.

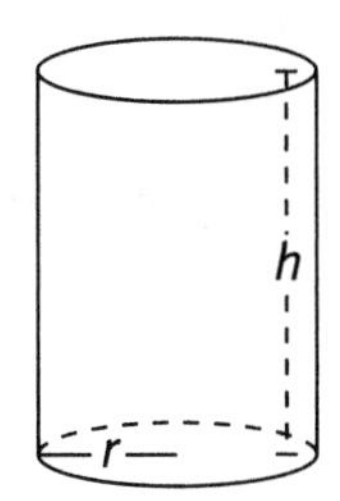

**Lateral surface of a cylinder:** The "pipe" surface, as opposed to the circular "ends." The lateral surface of a cylinder is unlike most other surfaces of solids that you'll see on the GMAT, first because it does not lie in a plane and second because it forms a closed loop. Think of it as the label around a soup can. If you could remove it from the can in one piece, you would have an open tube. If you then cut the label and unrolled it, it would form a rectangle with a length equal to the circumference of the circular base of the can and a height equal to that of the can.

### Formulas for Volume and Surface Area

Volume of a rectangular solid $=$ (Area of base)(Height) $=$ (Length $\times$ Width)(Height) $= lwh$

Surface area of a rectangular solid $=$ Sum of areas of faces $= 2lw + 2lh + 2hw$

Since a cube is a rectangular solid for which $l = w = h$, the formula for its volume can be stated in terms of any edge:

- Volume of a cube $= lwh =$ (Edge)(Edge)(Edge) $= e^3$
- Surface area of a cube $=$ Sum of areas of faces $= 6e^2$

To find the volume or surface area of a cylinder, you'll need two pieces of information: the height of the cylinder and the radius of the base.

- Volume of a cylinder $=$ (Area of base)(Height) $= \pi r^2 h$
- Lateral surface area of a cylinder $=$ (Circumference of base)(Height) $= 2\pi rh$
- Total surface area of a cylinder $=$ Areas of circular ends $+$ Lateral surface area $= 2\pi r^2 + 2\pi rh$

## Multiple Figures

Some GMAT geometry problems involve combinations of different types of figures. Besides the basic rules and formulas that you would use on normal geometry problems, you'll need an intuitive understanding of how various geometrical concepts relate to each other to answer these "multiple figures" questions correctly. For example, you may have to revisualize the side of a rectangle as the hypotenuse of a neighboring right triangle or as the diameter of a circumscribed circle. Keep looking for the relationships between the different figures until you find one that leads you to the answer.

### Area of Shaded Regions

A common multiple figures question involves a diagram of a geometrical figure that has been broken up into different, irregularly shaped areas, often with one region shaded. You'll usually be asked to find the area of the shaded (or unshaded) portion of the diagram. Your best bet will be to take one of the following two approaches:

1. Break the area into smaller pieces whose separate areas you can find; add those areas together.
2. Find the area of the whole figure; find the area of the region(s) that you're *not* looking for; subtract the latter from the former.

**Example:**

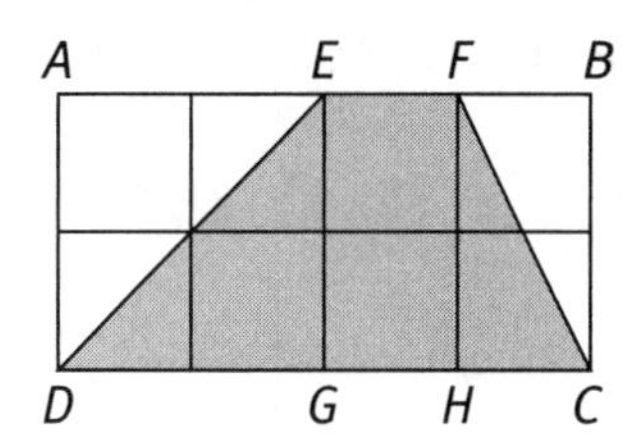


Rectangle *ABCD* above has an area of 72 and is composed of 8 equal squares. What is the area of the shaded region?

The first thing you have to realize is that, for the 8 equal squares to form a total area of 72, each square must have an area of 72 ÷ 8, or 9. Since the area of a square equals the square of the length of a side, each side of a square in the diagram must have a length of $\sqrt{9}$ or 3.

At this point, you choose your approach. Either one will work:

**Approach 1:**

Break up the shaded area into right triangle *DEG*, rectangle *EFHG*, and right triangle *FHC*. The area of triangle *DEG* is $\frac{1}{2}(6)(6) = 18$. The area of rectangle *EFHG* is (3)(6), or 18. The area of triangle *FHC* is $\frac{1}{2}(3)(6)$, or 9. The total shaded area is 18 + 18 + 9, or 45.

**Approach 2:**

The area of unshaded right triangle *AED* is $\frac{1}{2}(6)(6)$, or 18. The area of unshaded right triangle *FBC* is $\frac{1}{2}(3)(6)$, or 9. Therefore, the total unshaded area is 18 + 9 = 27. Subtract the total unshaded area from the total area of rectangle *ABCD*: 72 − 27 = 45.

## Inscribed/Circumscribed Figures

A polygon is inscribed in a circle if all the vertices of the polygon lie on the circle. A polygon is circumscribed about a circle if all the sides of the polygon are tangent to the circle.

Square *ABCD* is inscribed in circle *O*. You can also say that circle *O* is circumscribed about square *ABCD*.

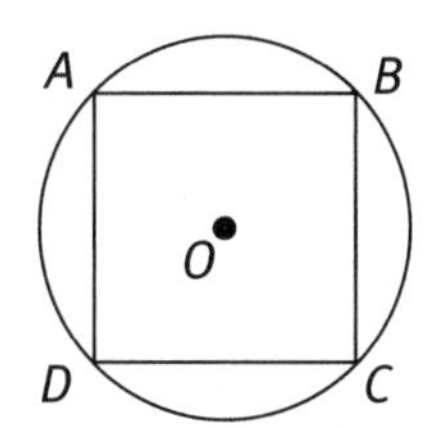

Square *PQRS* is circumscribed about circle *O*. You can also say that circle *O* is inscribed in square *PQRS*.

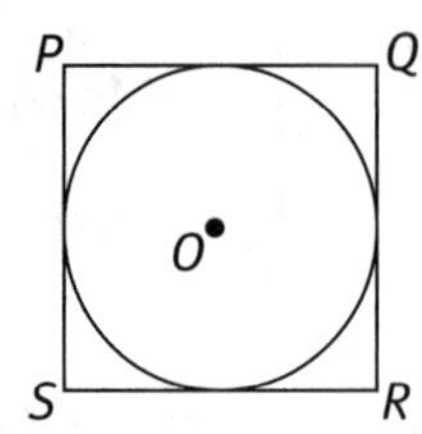


When a triangle is inscribed in a semicircle in such a way that one side of the triangle coincides with the diameter of the semicircle, the triangle is a right triangle.

**Example:**

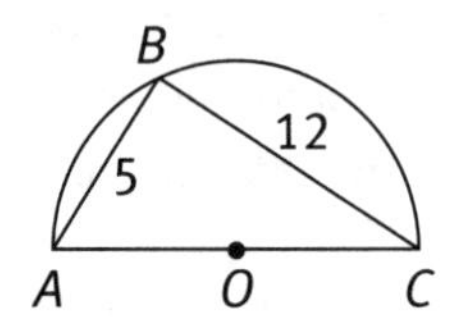


What is the diameter of semicircle *O* above?

*AC* is a diameter of semicircle *O*, because it passes through center point *O*. So, triangle *ABC* fits the description given above of a right triangle. Moreover, triangle *ABC* is a special 5:12:13 right triangle with a hypotenuse of 13. Therefore, the length of diameter *AC* is 13.